The United States and Russia

THE
UNITED STATES
AND

Russia

By

Vera Micheles Dean

With a **NEW PREFACE**
TO THE REPRINT EDITION

GREENWOOD PRESS, PUBLISHERS
WESTPORT, CONNECTICUT

MAPS PREPARED UNDER THE CARTOGRAPHIC
DIRECTION OF ARTHUR H. ROBINSON

CONTENTS

MAPS

INTRODUCTION

These introductory lines are written on the eve of the conference of the Foreign Ministers of the four major powers which has been summoned to meet at London in November, 1947. The reconstruction of the world is contingent upon the ability of the United States and of the Soviet Union still to find the means of ending the ever-increasing divergence in their national policies and to be able to coöperate in the establishment of a stable world order that can guarantee to all peoples freedom, economic security and a lasting peace.

At the same time, here on this side of the Atlantic, in New York City, the members of the Security Council are still trying to find the basis for an accord upon an effective system for the international control of atomic energy, and upon the measures which must be taken in order to bring about a progressive reduction in world armaments. The success of these endeavors again depends upon the possibility of attaining Russian-American agreement. Unless there is a successful conclusion of these negotiations, we will have scant reason for hope that the United Nations can eventually carry out the universal responsibilities envisaged in its Charter and thus fulfill the aspirations of humanity.

In the Far East China is still torn by civil war. Korea remains a land divided into two sealed compartments, one controlled by Russian armies and the other controlled by American armies. Whether or not the Japanese people can be transformed into peaceful and worthy members of inter-

national society is a problem which is still shrouded in un-
certainty. All of the Far East awaits uneasily, and with
increasing anxiety, some indication whether the future of
the hundreds of millions of human beings in that vast region
is to be a future of anarchy and of persistent impoverish-
ment, or whether it is to be a future of peaceful progress.
And the answer to that question also depends upon the
capacity of Washington and Moscow to coöperate.

The peoples of the Near East and of the Mediterranean
basin are increasingly fearful of what the years which lie
ahead may hold for them. There can be no surcease from
this fear until they are assured that there will be no clash
between the Soviet Union and the Western powers.

Above all individual aspects of the world problem such
as these looms the overshadowing question, "Is there to be
war or peace?" The assurance of future peace depends primarily upon the willingness of the American and Russian
peoples to collaborate in the task of world reconstruction,
and in the consolidation of that international order which
alone can provide the certainty of peace.

There is no subject today more immediate, more overwhelming, in its significance to every American citizen than
the question of the relations of the Soviet Union and the
United States.

I know of no book which throws more light on that all-
important problem than *The United States and Russia*, by
Vera Micheles Dean, now published by the Harvard University Press. Nor could the publication of this volume have
come at a more useful and a more opportune moment. Mrs.
Dean has for many years been one of our most authoritative
writers on foreign affairs. Her present book is written with
an exceptional knowledge of every aspect of her subject.
It is both comprehensive and constructive. It is impartial
and objective. It is filled with invaluable factual information.
It should help to end many misconceptions and do much

to counteract the results of much prejudiced and fanatical propaganda. But it will also serve to underscore many realities and to emphasize the gravity of many unsolved problems —ideological as well as material.

Chapter 12 of *The United States and Russia*, entitled "Is War Inevitable?" should be read, marked, learned, and inwardly digested by every fair-minded American who hopes and believes that the influence of his country can even yet be so intelligently and effectively exercised as to make it possible for the United States to lead mankind into the paths of peace.

Sumner Welles

PREFACE
TO THE REPRINT EDITION

In 1970, over half a century since the Communist revolution of 1917, the U.S.S.R. (Union of Soviet Socialist Republics) under Communist leader Leonid I. Brezhnev, despite its grueling experience in World War II, is more powerful and prosperous than Russia had ever been in its history, and is regarded as one of the two great powers of the world, second only to the United States. Yet, having reached this pinnacle, the U.S.S.R. stands at a crossroads, with many far-reaching decisions to make both at home and abroad.

The experience of the U.S.S.R. indicates that communism, like other forms of governance, has no secret formula to eradicate conflicts between peoples within a single state or between nations on the world stage. Moscow may continue to promote ideological expansion, in the hope of achieving worldwide Communist unity. But its experience with other Communist nations—notably with Yugoslavia under Marshal Tito and Rumania and China under Mao Tse-tung—indicates that among peoples of diverse histories and thus of diverse political, economic and social conditions, and of frequently clashing aspirations, Communist ideology cannot necessarily forge permanent links between peoples.

In Communist, as in non-Communist countries, the diversity of historical experiences, geographic locations, economic and social factors and political aspirations have wrought diverse conditions—notably between Communists of the U.S.S.R. and those of Communist China, between Moscow and Prague, and between Czechoslovakia and Yugoslavia, to give only a few examples. This diversity of national Communist interests between various countries, diverse also in their geographic and economic conditions, has made it increasingly difficult, with the passage of time, to forge a monolithic Communist group of nations—let alone a tight-knit Communist world. This had been strikingly revealed in 1970 by clashes between Moscow and Peking, to give the most important and dramatic example. China's Communist leader, Mao Tse-tung, was at no time dependent on Moscow, despised the Russians, and considered the Chinese as a people superior to all others.

Nor did the Communist leaders of the U.S.S.R. follow a policy toward neighboring countries notably different from that of the Tsars. Like the Tsars, who for centuries were concerned to maintain control over the Straits of the Dardanelles and thus commanded through the Black Sea access to the Mediterranean, the Communist leaders today insist on free entrances and exits in this geographically strategic area. As a result, the U.S.S.R. has expanded its role in this area with respect both to the United Arab Republic and to Israel. To give another example, the Soviet Commissars, like the Moscow Tsars, have used Moscow —not Leningrad, the capital Peter the Great had erected as St. Petersburg on the Neva River—as the center of its rule. In these, and many other instances, one may say that ideologies come and go, but geography remains a decisive factor.

As of 1970, the U.S.S.R., like the United States, finds itself in the paradoxical position of a country which had once been isolationist in sentiment but, in the twentieth century has assumed leadership in advocating international organization and cooperation—diverse as are the historical backgrounds, current goals, and future aspirations of these two greatest powers of the twentieth century.

Moscow's advocacy of cooperation between nations has taken two main forms: vertical cooperation between sovereign states, in traditional terms; and, in the past half-century, horizontal ideological cooperation which cuts across the territorial boundaries of nation-states. This was true not only in the past, when

Russia gave its support to Pan-Slavism before the advent of communism, but also more recently since the Communist revolution, all over the world, notably through Moscow's appeal to "the toiling masses" on a social, as well as political and economic base, in terms of international communism. Russian leaders have on some occasions alternated between these two forms of international relations, and on other occasions have made use of them simultaneously, depending on current circumstances and on the urgency of attaining specific goals. Both movements —Pan-Slavism and international communism—have appeared alien and, on occasion, peculiarly sinister to the non-Russian world. Both have had a comparable tendency to subordinate nationalism to ideology.

Yet nationalism has remained an important, and in recent years, an increasingly significant factor in the development of Communist countries, notably Hungary and Rumania (the Rumanian government, for example, has chided both Moscow and Peking, declaring that there should be no "superior" as contrasted with "inferior" countries in the Communist group). And Chinese Communists, for their part, have described Soviet leaders as "lackeys of imperialism," referring apparently to the increasingly closer communications (if not always official relations) between the ruling Communists of Moscow and leaders of non-Communist nations.

As the U.S.S.R. gradually recovered from the human and material losses of World War II, it sought to expand its trade with the industrial nations of the West. In the 1960's food headed the list of Moscow's exports to the West, followed by crude oil and petroleum sold primarily to Italy, West Germany, Finland, Japan and Sweden. Other exports of significance have been metal manufactures, forest products, and consumer goods. Meanwhile, among imports, grain, mainly wheat from Canada, dominated until 1966 while the U.S.S.R. economy was recovering from its wartime economic losses. At that time purchases of grain and other primary products required substantial sales of Soviet gold abroad. During this period imports of metals and machinery declined. But, as agricultural production has improved, Moscow has increased purchases of machinery and equipment, and in that period chemical and transportation equipment has made up two-thirds of total machinery imports.

An indication of Moscow's significant shift in imports from food and raw materials to industrial products was its 1966 agreement with the Fiat automobile company of Italy for the manufacture of transport equipment. In 1967 Moscow placed new machinery orders in the West for more than $600 million dollars. As of 1970 the Soviet government sought to obtain assistance for the production of automotive equipment from the Ford Motor Company following a visit to the U.S.S.R. by Henry Ford, but without success. Among the developing nations, India and the United Arab Republic have been the principal trade partners of the U.S.S.R. As of 1966, these two countries, together with Malaysia and Argentina, contributed 54 percent of all Soviet trade with the Third World.

In the 1970 midyear economic report published by the government newspaper *Izvestia,* the Soviet leadership stated that industry as a whole had shown a growth rate of 8.5 percent over the comparable period of 1969, when the Soviet economy had suffered a slowing of growth rate in virtually every sector, due largely to a severe winter. At the halfway point in 1969, industrial growth had been only 6.9 percent above the previous year.

In this report, other important indexes also showed significant improvement. Labor productivity which, according to *The New York Times* of July 22, 1970, is viewed by Soviet economists as crucial to real economic growth, was up by 7.5 percent, and profits, "a book-keeping index of an enterprise success, were up 15 percent. In 1969, the figures were 4.4 percent and 7 percent respectively." "These relatively high figures," *The New York Times* stated, "represent, in a sense, that the economy has returned to normal after the very poor showing of 1969." It argued, however, "that agriculture, the perennial sore point in the economy, and the subject of a recent report by the party leader, Leonid I. Brezhnev, to the Central Committee, was still lagging. Meat and milk production, the subject of special attention by the party and state, showed only slight increases. But poultry, reflecting an increase in 'chicken factories', was up 21 percent over the first half of 1969 and eggs by 18 percent. Apparently as the result of the better weather, there was a 28 percent increase in the sale of vegetables and a 50 percent rise in the sale of fruit. Fruit, vegetables and meat have become increasingly in demand in recent years as Soviet consumers have altered their traditional bread-and-potatoes diet."

On the same day, a government decree announced material incentives for farmers to grow and sell such vegetables and fruits as apples and lettuce, which are often hard to find in Soviet markets. This decree indicated the extent to which fruit, vegetables and meat have become more and more in demand, as the Soviet people have altered their traditional eating habits. A similar decree had been previously published aimed at increasing meat production.

It was expected by observers in Moscow that the 8.5 percent rise in productivity for the six months of 1970 would virtually guarantee, according to *The New York Times*, that, barring a national calamity, the U.S.S.R. would easily surpass the relatively low goal of a 6.3 percent growth rate announced in December 1969. Western diplomats, it was reported, "when they noted that the first quarter of this year was marked by an 8.6 percent rise," asserted that Soviet leaders had deliberately pegged their figures so that their industrial target would be reached by November 7, 1970, the anniversary of the Bolshevik Revolution, the date pledged by many enterprises to complete their five-year plans.

Thus, as of 1970, over half a century after the Communist revolution, the multinational, multilingual Union of Soviet Socialist Republics continued to carry out the difficult task of modernizing and expanding its economy through a government which retained and continued to wield dictatorial power within a society where universal education and the development of a modern industrial economy increasingly required a high level of study. This necessity, in turn, created an increasing interest in, and expansion of freedom of thought—not only in the fields of science of technology, but also eventually in the fields of economic and social ideas and practices, even though such freedom of thought in politics had not yet been achieved.

Predictions are always dangerous. But as the U.S.S.R. becomes more and more rapidly a modern industrial nation, ranking high among the small number of the world's great powers, its leaders may find it both necessary and desirable to adopt the practices, if not always the ideas, which have molded the democracies of the Western world—and increasingly to seek not only economic but also political cooperation with them in the world society of the twentieth century.

Vera Micheles Dean

New York
October 12, 1970

PREFACE

TO THIRD PRINTING, REVISED

Since the publication of this book in mid-November 1947 the tempo of the postwar struggle between the United States and Russia has been heightened to such a point that another World War was until recently regarded by many as just over the horizon. The events of this turbulent half year are briefly summed up in a new chapter, which also indicates new approaches toward possible adjustments opened up in the wake of the European Recovery Program.

But while the struggle has gained in bitterness and intensity, its over-all pattern remains unchanged. This pattern may be described in any one of several ways, depending on the observer. It may be viewed as an old-fashioned race for strategic positions based on estimates of respective geographic advantages and relative command of specific weapons of warfare. Or one may think of the "cold war" as competition between two superpowers for the vacuums left all over the globe by the defeat of wartime enemies and the decline of wartime allies, in an effort to strike a new balance of power. Or one may stress the clash of two ideologies, locked in combat to the death for possession of men's minds and souls. Whatever definition is preferred, this much is clear: the impact of this struggle is forcing all human beings to re-assess current concepts of political liberty and economic well-being, and to discover ways of harmonizing them for survival in the twentieth century.

With the whole world in a state of volcanic eruption, it would be frivolously naïve to expect that a settlement can be easily achieved in the near future. But it would be criminally irresponsible to assume that war alone offers a way out. As in all seedtimes of civilization, there is peculiar need today for steady nerves, clear heads, and courage to persevere in one's convictions. There should be no doubt today, as there has never been, that human beings can, if they so will, find answers to the problems of humanity. But, to use the words of Alan Paton in *Cry, The Beloved Country*, "when that dawn will come, of our emancipation, from the fear of bondage and the bondage of fear, why, that is a secret."

Vera Micheles Dean

New York
May 15, 1948

PREFACE

There can be few such soul-searching tasks as to attempt appraisal of a revolutionary epoch before the revolution has run its course—before its eddies, remote and near, have gradually disappeared, and the current of history runs smoothly again. Questions of fact, of personal integrity, of moral judgment rise to plague one so bold as to write of nations astir with revolution and stirring others to inquiry into accepted ideas and values.

Such questions become particularly harassing when relations between the United States and Russia are under discussion. To present Russia in too favorable a light is perhaps to lull the American people into a sense of security that events may prove to have been false. Yet to denounce Russia indiscriminately may be to mislead Americans into thinking that all movements for change in the world are Communist-inspired and therefore a threat to our institutions and way of life, and thus cause this country, the source in the past of so many bold and generous ideas, to become a bulwark of opposition to any alteration of the *status quo* abroad.

The best one can do under these trying circumstances is to take counsel of one's conscience, and to write about things as one sees them. Mistakes of fact or judgment can be dangerous. But far more dangerous is the temptation to interpret controversial events in such a way as to court this or that passing trend of public sentiment.

This is a time neither for fear nor complacency. Our

main problem is not whether we like Russia or dislike it, but whether, knowing what we do about it, we can find ways of living at peace with that country while continuing to adapt our own ideas and practices to the needs of a fast-changing age. Ralph Waldo Emerson described our task well when he wrote over a hundred years ago: "If there is any period one would desire to be born in, is it not the age of Revolution; when the old and the new stand side by side and admit of being compared; when the energies of all men are searched by fear and hope; when the historic glories of the old can be compensated by the rich possibilities of the new era? This time, like all times, is a very good one, if we but know what to do with it."

Vera Micheles Dean

New York
August 18, 1947

PART I

A GLANCE AT THE PAST

1. Russo-American Relations Before 1947

How far will Russia go? Can we trust the Russians? Why does this relatively backward people have such far-reaching influence even in advanced countries? Is the Russian system a menace to the American way of life? Can two such different ideologies as capitalism and communism coexist in one world without ultimate clash? If a conflict impends, how should we prepare for it? If it is to be avoided, what should we and the Russians do to arrive at a workable agreement?

These and many other questions about relations between the United States and Russia have come to dominate private conversations and public debates in this country to such an extent that, as a nation, we appear to be literally obsessed by Russia. In the opinion of some of us Russia is a grave threat both to our territorial security and to our accustomed pattern of existence—perhaps an even greater threat than Germany and Japan, whose peoples and systems, in the retrospect of victory, appear less alien than those of the U.S.S.R. Others among us feel that, while Russia undoubtedly challenges our accepted concepts, often using methods repugnant to our traditions, this challenge may ultimately serve a useful purpose, since it forces us to reassess many ideas and practices we had come to take for granted. Some believe that the Soviet leaders have made a genuine contribution to the development of the Russian people. Others regard them as ruthless and unscrupulous, but distinguish between Soviet leaders and the Russian people, whom many Americans have come to like and admire. Only a very few of us have become so angry or frightened as to insist that we should fight Russia now, while we enjoy the temporary advantage of possessing the secret of manufacturing the atomic bomb. The majority of Americans would probably agree, on the whole, with the policy hammered out by the Truman Administration in the heat and dust of post-war diplomatic clashes—a policy of attempting to find a basis for Russo-American agreement without abandoning the main objectives the United States wants to achieve all over the world, preferably through the machinery of the United Nations.

At the outbreak of the second World War in September 1939, hardly anyone could have foreseen that Russia would assume such paramount importance in the everyday calculations of the United States, both at home and abroad. Our concern about Russia's actions and the motives that inspire them—a concern reciprocated in Moscow—is a measure of the fundamental transformation in the world balance of power produced by the defeat of Germany and Japan, the economic and colonial difficulties experienced by Britain, and the decline of France's influence in Europe. When the United States and Russia first became aware of each other, at the end of the eighteenth century, the Americans were just emerging from a period of colonial tutelage, and the Russians from the shackles of feudalism. Both nations —one still in its infancy, the other of ancient historic lineage —lived on the fringes of the international community. Both were to be long divided between the desire for isolation, for playing a lone hand, and the urge to take an active part in shaping the destiny of the world. Out of World War II both have emerged as great powers, subject to the temptations, beset by the problems, and faced by the responsibilities that accompany possession of power. Neither is entirely certain how far it is prepared to go. Each is feeling out the other's strong and weak points. Accord between the Big Two would be the prelude to a long period of world stability, which is a prerequisite to world progress. Discord between them would be a portent of still more destructive war.

1. FRIENDSHIP AND MISTRUST

In trying to ascertain the future of Russo-American relations, what can we learn from the past? The record of nearly two centuries of contacts between the United States and Russia is on the whole a record of friendship based on mutual interests, but checkered again and again by distrust on the part of each concerning the internal system and external aspirations of the other.* In spite of this recurrent distrust, the two nations have at no time in the past come to the brink of war, nor have they found themselves until now in serious competition about territories, strategic bases, markets, or raw materials—the most common ingredients of friction between nations.

The Russians take satisfaction in recalling today that, when Francis Dana, first American envoy to Russia, went to St. Petersburg in 1781 charged with the task of obtaining recognition for the young republic born of revolution against Britain, he was not received by Empress Catherine the Great. Dana left the Russian capital empty-handed in 1783, and it was not until twenty-six years later that imperial Russia recognized the American government. The United States, say the Russians with some relish, was regarded two centuries ago as a dangerous revolutionary upstart, just as Russia is now regarded by the West—yet this country lived to become

* The author wishes to express appreciation to Foster Rhea Dulles for permission to draw on some of the material in his excellent book, *The Road to Teheran: The Story of Russia and America, 1781–1943* (Princeton: Princeton University Press, 1944).

highly respectable and, in the opinion of Soviet observers, even conservative.

In the early days of the nineteenth century the United States and Russia had a common interest in opposing Napoleon's Continental System, which sought to close European ports, including those of Russia, to overseas trade—for by that time American ships had begun to carry what Russians called "colonial wares" like tea, coffee, and pepper to Russia's Baltic ports. The American government looked to Czar Alexander I for protection against encroachments on maritime commerce by the two naval powers of that time, Britain and France. Thomas Jefferson commended the Czar for his interest in a "distant and infant nation." And in 1812 Secretary of State Monroe said that since 1780 "Russia had been the pivot on which all questions of neutral rights have essentially turned." When the United States became involved in war with Britain over these rights, the Czar offered to mediate, but the peace treaty of 1814 was eventually concluded without his intervention.

Following the defeat of Napoleon and the creation of the Holy Alliance, in which Alexander I played a decisive part, the United States began to fear Russia's intervention in this hemisphere at two main points: in the Pacific Northwest—California and Oregon—which had attracted the interest of Russian traders and fur hunters operating from the coast of Alaska; and in Latin America where, it was thought, the Holy Alliance might intervene for the purpose of preventing the establishment of republican institutions, as it had done in Spain and other nations of Europe. It was to Russia that President Monroe addressed one of the early statements of his doctrine when, in a note of July 1823 to the Russian Minister in Washington, he declared that "the American continents are no longer subjects for any new European colonial establishments."

While the United States looked with repugnance and

anxiety at the Holy Alliance, which symbolized the dark
forces of monarchist reaction inimical to the forces of liberalism and republicanism then flourishing in the Western
Hemisphere, landlocked Russia, aware of its weakness as a
naval power, feared an alliance between the two great maritime nations, Britain and America. A balance of interests,
however, was struck in an agreement of April 17, 1824—an
early example of division of spheres of influence which set
the southern boundary of Russian America at the parallel of
54° 40′ (the present boundary of Alaska), and provided for
complete freedom of the seas in the North Pacific. Forty-
three years later, in 1867, Russia abandoned its foothold in
the Americas by selling Alaska to the United States for
$7,200,000—a sum then regarded as so exorbitantly high by
Americans who had no desire for territorial expansion that
the transaction, negotiated by Secretary of State Seward,
was known as "Seward's Folly."

Meanwhile, the suspicion with which both the United
States and Russia regarded Britain continued to form a strong
bond between the two countries. When Russia fought off
a British-led attack on the Crimea (1854), public opinion in
this country was favorable to the Russians, and Secretary of
State Marcy, returning the compliment of 1812, offered to
mediate between the combatants. Less than ten years later
Russia showed its sympathy for the United States, then in
the grip of the Civil War, when it officially expressed the
hope that the Union would be maintained and refused to acquiesce in British proposals for recognition of the Confed-
eracy. Again Russia's policy was determined by its desire to
prevent an alliance between the United States and Britain
which might result in domination of the world by "the am-
bitious projects and political egotism of the Anglo-Saxon
race"—to quote a phrase used by the Russian Minister to
Washington during the Civil War. The United States, in
turn, in spite of pleas by England and France, refused to

intervene on behalf of the Poles during their 1863 rebellion against Russia, justifying its decision by its traditional policy of noninterference in European affairs.

2. CONFLICTING IDEOLOGIES AND IMPERIALISMS

The emancipation of the Russian serfs by Alexander II in 1861, which practically coincided with the emancipation of slaves in this country, was hailed here as a measure that advanced human progress and forged new understanding between the two nations. Wild enthusiasm greeted the arrival in San Francisco and New York of units of the Russian fleet which, it was thought, had come to demonstrate Russia's sympathy for the Union—although actually Russia had sent these vessels to American ports for safekeeping, fearing that its controversy with Britain and France over the Poles might lead to war. Public enthusiasm for Russia was at a high peak. An alliance with Russia against a potential Anglo-French combination was advocated by *Harper's Weekly*, which declared that "Russia, like the United States, is a nation of the future." This warm feeling for Russia carried over into the 1890's, when the American people contributed $77,000,000 in relief funds to famine-stricken Russia.

Common international interests, however, could not indefinitely conceal profound divergences in ideology between the autocracy of the Czars and the rapidly developing American democracy. The emancipation of the serfs had not led, as hoped here, to political liberalization of Russia. Czarism's repression of opposition groups, its failure to improve the welfare of the masses, and anti-Semitic outbursts like the Kishinev pogrom of 1903 shocked and alienated public opinion here. United States Ambassador Andrew D. White, describing Russia in the 1890's, gloomily came to the conclusion that it was impossible to have confidence in the Russian government.

To these ideological conflicts was soon added anxiety in this country that Russia, by extending its influence on the Asiatic mainland, would challenge the interests of the United States in that area. Inspired by strikingly similar ideas of "manifest destiny," both Russia and the United States were advancing from opposite directions to the Pacific—and sooner or later a collision was inevitable. This collision came in Manchuria where, the United States feared, Russia's influence would block further expansion of American trade. It was primarily to avert this danger that Secretary of State Hay sent to the great powers his notes of 1899 and 1900 proclaiming the American policy of the Open Door. The Czarist government declined to make any self-denying promises and, although it declared that it had no aggressive designs on China and would withdraw its troops from Manchuria, it retained control over this strategic region rich in raw materials. Hay said at that time that Russia's "vows are false as dicers' oaths when treachery is profitable." Theodore Roosevelt, who had succeeded McKinley as president in 1901, was "thoroughly aroused and irritated" by Russia's conduct in Manchuria. Czarist Russia was regarded in the United States as an imperialist power determined to build a universal empire and dominate the world.

It was not surprising, under the circumstances, that Japan's attack on Russia at Port Arthur in 1904 was welcomed by President Roosevelt who believed that Japan was "playing our game" and would uphold the Open Door. Public opinion agreed with this view, and an American magazine asserted that Russia stood for reaction and Japan for progress. The Russians, aroused by the hostility of the United States, in turn accused this country of imperialist designs in the Pacific, and of supporting Japan's attack on Russia. Japan's rapid victory over Russia, however, sharply altered the situation. The danger that a triumphant Japan might prove an even greater challenge to the United States than an expanding Russia caused this country to offer its services as mediator, in the hope of limiting Japan's territorial gains. Both combatants were at the point of exhaustion, and readily accepted President Roosevelt's mediation, which led to the conclusion of the peace treaty of 1905 at Portsmouth, New Hampshire—a treaty which, considering the magnitude of the defeat inflicted by Japan on Russia, was relatively favorable to the latter.

3. WAR HERITAGE OF MUTUAL SUSPICION

The effects of Japan's rise to power in Asia did not become fully apparent until the end of World War I when Russia plunged into revolution at the very time the United States joined the Allies against Germany and, incapable of defending itself in the Far East, found its Siberian mainland occupied by Japanese, as well as American and British troops. The avowed purpose of this Allied occupation, in which Japanese forces played a predominant part, was to recreate an eastern front against Germany and, also, to aid the evacuation of Czechoslovaks, former prisoners of war, who were on their famous "anabasis" across Russia and Siberia with the western front as their ultimate objective. Actually, however, the Allies hoped to checkmate the rise of the Soviet régime, whose leaders had seized power in the revolution of November 7, 1917. In urging intervention as early as January 1918, Japan had indicated its desire that the operation should be carried out entirely by its troops, and had objected to the use of American forces. President Wilson opposed intervention in Russia, although expressing regret at the "misfortune and unhappiness" which had "for the time" resulted from the Bolshevik revolution. American Ambassador Francis, however, was pressing for intervention, on the ground that the Allies should help the Russian people to overthrow the Soviet régime, whose actions were arousing widespread criticism in the United States.

President Wilson finally yielded to the pressure of the Supreme War Council of the Allies, which feared that failure to act in Russia against Germany would jeopardize the possibility of Allied victory, but, in an aide-mémoire of July 17, 1918 and in a State Department announcement of August 3, he insisted on the principle of noninterference in Russia's internal affairs. At the same time he indicated that the policy of the Allies was to give only such aid "as shall be acceptable to the Russian people in their endeavour to regain control of their own affairs, their own territory, and their own destiny." Thus, while continuing to oppose interference in the internal affairs of Russia, the United States acted on the assumption that the Russian people would welcome outside aid in overthrowing the Soviet régime.

From the point of view of the Soviet government Allied intervention constituted not only unwarranted interference in Russia's internal affairs but also a grave danger to its existence, and a threat to the territorial integrity of the country. This appeared to be particularly true as the Japanese increased their troops in Siberia to the peak figure of 70,000 and gave active support to anti-Bolshevik forces in that area, in direct defiance of the efforts of the American commander, General Graves, who sought in vain to prevent Allied intervention from developing into coöperation with Russian forces hostile to Bolshevism. Although Soviet Foreign Minister Chicherin admitted that the United States had given only formal consent to intervention, and did not denounce this country as harshly as Britain and France (which before the end of civil war in Russia had troops in the Baku oil fields and the Crimea respectively), the Soviet leaders felt growing resentment against the United States. A tragic vicious circle set in. Fearful of the consequences of foreign intervention, which had the sympathy of some Russian anti-Soviet groups, the Soviet régime instituted mass terror. This terror, in turn, increased anti-Bolshevik sentiment in Western countries.

With the defeat of Germany in November 1918 the Russians sought to bring Allied intervention to an end, and indicated their readiness to participate in a general peace conference. When the French refused to deal with the Bolsheviks in Paris, President Wilson suggested a separate conference between the Bolsheviks and other Russian political groups, and Prinkipo Island, in the Sea of Marmora, was selected for this purpose. The Soviet government promptly accepted, but White Russian emigré groups were adamant in refusing to attend a conference in which they would have to deal with the Bolsheviks. Russia was thus isolated from the Western world during the making of the peace in 1919. Nor were Britain and France ready to withdraw their troops from Russia, as proposed by President Wilson, who wanted to bring the whole episode to a close as rapidly as possible. On the contrary at that time Winston Churchill, who viewed the Soviet régime with profound apprehension, urged an increase of Allied intervention forces, and more active aid to Russian groups who opposed Bolshevism.

The final result of Allied negotiations about Russia was that the last of the occupying forces did not leave Russian territory until 1922. Yet the Allies never brought themselves to undertake a major operation against Russia. The American delegation to the Paris Peace Conference sent William C. Bullitt, subsequently first American Ambassador to Russia, as unofficial emissary to Moscow to discuss the possibility of a direct settlement between the United States and Russia. While Bullitt brought back a favorable report about conditions in Russia, and was convinced of the stability of the Soviet régime, no action was taken on his report. When the Allies finally did withdraw from Russia, they left in their wake the wreckage of a civil war which had been greatly embittered by the presence of foreign troops, and a deep-seated conviction on the part of Soviet leaders that the "capitalist" world was determined to "encircle" Russia and to crush the "dictatorship of the proletariat."

4. "AN ECONOMIC VACUUM"

The period 1919–1933, which opened with a sharp reaction in this country against further involvement in Europe and a strong urge to "return to normalcy," was marked by violent hostility toward the Soviet government which the United States did not recognize until 1933–a decade after recognition by Britain, France, and Italy. This hostility was due to four main reasons: revulsion against acts of repression by the Soviet government which, ruthless as they were in themselves, were further inflated by anti-Soviet propaganda here; dread that the abolition of capitalism in Russia would spell the end of private property in other countries; fear, which often reached the proportions of hysteria, that the Third (Communist) International established in Moscow in 1919 was seeking, through the American Communist party, to overthrow existing institutions in this country; and a feeling of shock at the measures taken by the Soviet régime against religion. There was much talk that this country was at "war with Bolshevism," although the American people were no more enthusiastic after World War I than after World War II to become engaged in another major conflict.

So violent was this Red Scare that it led, for a time, to attacks on liberal movements as well as on communism. The official attitude of the United States was expressed in a note addressed by Secretary of State Colby on August 10, 1920 to the Italian Ambassador in Washington, who had made an inquiry concerning American policy toward Russia. This note, after reiterating the sympathy of the United States for the Russian people, and our interest in preservation of Russia's territorial integrity, stated that the Soviet régime in no sense represented the Russian people, had come to power through force and cunning, and was maintaining itself in office only through savage oppression. Mr. Colby pointed out that the Soviet leaders had repudiated Russia's pre-revolutionary international obligations, were promoting revolutionary movements in other countries, using diplomatic agencies as channels of subversive propaganda, and supporting and subsidizing the Third International. He concluded with the following words, which governed the policy of the United States until the 1930's: "There can be no mutual confidence or trust, no respect even, if pledges are to be given and agreements made with cynical repudiation of the obligations already in the minds of one of the parties. We cannot recognize, hold official relations with, or give friendly reception to the agents of a Government which is determined and bound to conspire against our institutions; whose diplomats will be the agitators of dangerous revolt; whose spokesmen say that they sign agreements with no intention of keeping them." The Soviet government repudiated the charges made by Mr. Colby, and asserted that normal relations between the United States and Russia were possible in spite of fundamental differences in the internal systems of the two countries. The United States, however, found it impossible to reconcile itself to the ideology and practices of Soviet Russia, which seemed more alien, and more hostile to democracy, than the ideology and practices of the Czars.

Feelers for a settlement put out by Soviet leaders in the 1920's were rejected by the United States, and Secretary of Commerce Hoover described Russia as "a gigantic economic vacuum." In 1921 Secretary of State Hughes said that no proper basis for considering trade relations between the two countries existed until Russia had consummated fundamental changes "involving due regard for the protection of persons and property and the establishment of conditions essential to the maintenance of commerce." Russia was thus excluded from the American market, where it had hoped to obtain machinery and tools, essential for reconstruction. Nor was it invited to take part in the Washington Conference of 1921–22, which discussed settlement of political questions in the Far East and limitation of armaments in the Pacific. At the same time the United States held fast to its policy of preserving Russia's territorial integrity both in Europe and Asia. In view of contemporary controversies, it is interesting to recall that President Wilson had opposed recognition of the independence of Estonia, Latvia, and Lithuania, and had privately expressed the opinion that these countries would eventually be reincorporated into Russian territory. At the Washington Conference Secretary of State Hughes insisted on complete withdrawal of Japanese troops from the Siberian mainland, and declared that protection of Russian interests "must devolve as a moral trusteeship on the whole conference." In this respect Russia is indebted to the United States for assistance in recovering its Pacific coast, and in stemming Japan's plans for territorial gains at its expense. The United States further aided Russia during the 1921–1923 famine, when extensive relief was given through the American Relief Administration headed by Hoover—although Soviet leaders later contended that the relief program had not been free of anti-Bolshevik implications.

Political and economic relations between the two countries, however, remained at a standstill. The embargo on trade with Russia had been lifted in 1920, and Russia found it possible to obtain short-term credits here from private industry. But when the other Allies discussed future economic relations with Russia at the conferences of Genoa (1922) and The Hague (1923), the United States was not present. President Coolidge, on coming to office in 1923 upon the death of

Harding, said that Russia would have to fulfill three main
conditions before there could be resumption of official relations: it would have to compensate American citizens who
had been deprived of their property through the confisca-
tory decrees of the Soviet government; it would have to
recognize the debts contracted here by the Kerenski government; and it would have to demonstrate that it was not
seeking actively to undermine American institutions. When
the Soviet government, however, indicated willingness to
open negotiations on the basis of these three conditions,
Mr. Hughes replied that "there would seem at this time no
reason for negotiations." The nonrecognition policy was
reiterated by his successors, Mr. Kellogg and Mr. Stimson, in
spite of the fact that the United States participated in the
Disarmament Conference in Geneva (1928–1932) at which
Russia was present, and that Russia was permitted to sign the
Kellogg-Briand pact of 1928 for outlawry of war. But when
Mr. Stimson, in 1929, contended that Russia had violated
this pact by engaging in armed conflict with China over the
Chinese Eastern Railway, Soviet Foreign Commissar Litvinov
expressed surprise that the United States "deemed it possible to give advice and counsel to a government with which
it maintained no official relations."

Although the majority of Americans continued to oppose
recognition of the Soviet government, groups which felt
that the United States was unrealistic in refusing to recognize
a government that appeared to be firmly established brought
increasing pressure on the State Department in favor of
recognition. American exporters, who saw in Russia a vast
market for their products which might be captured by
Britain and Germany were particularly vigorous in urging
the resumption of trade, as well as diplomatic relations. The
Soviet government had already sent representatives of state
trading agencies to this country for purchases of tools and
machinery, and had established the Amtorg Trading Cor-

poration in New York as general agent for its export and import organs. In 1927 the State Department, yielding to the demands of business and industry, declared that it would not oppose long-term credits to Soviet purchasing agencies. The following year the International General Electric Company announced that it had concluded a contract with the Soviet government, providing for settlement of its claims for confiscation of its property, and for Russian purchases of electrical equipment at from $21,000,000 to $26,000,000. During the five-year period 1921–1925 Russo-American trade averaged $37,000,000 a year. The Soviet government, however, continued to encounter serious difficulties in financing its growing purchases in this country. Yet when it tried to sell Russian products abroad so as to obtain foreign currency for imports, it was accused of dumping goods, and for a time the Red Trade Menace became even more threatening than the Red Scare about communism. An embargo was imposed by the Treasury on the importation of Russian goods, on the ground that they were produced by convict labor. In spite of these difficulties the Soviet government continued to place orders here for machinery and automotive equipment, and to seek the aid of American technicians in the rebuilding of Russia's economy —among them Hugh L. Cooper, whose engineering firm built the Dnieprostroy dam.

5. RECOGNITION WITHOUT RECONCILIATION

It was not until President Roosevelt took office, however, that an official move was made to reëstablish relations with Russia. In a note of October 10, 1933 to President Kalinin of the U.S.S.R., Mr. Roosevelt said that he had "contemplated the desirability of an effort to end the abnormal relations between the one hundred and twenty-five million people of the United States and the one hundred and sixty million people of Russia." He added that he would be glad to receive any representative Kalinin might designate "to explore with me personally all questions outstanding between the two countries." This change in policy was due to a number of factors, among which the growing desire to expand trade with Russia, and renewed fear of Japan's aggressive aims in Asia as indicated by its invasion of Manchuria in 1931, played a decisive role in the United States. Russia, too, had reason to be alarmed by further Japanese encroachments along its Asiatic border. Meanwhile, Stalin since 1927 had been concentrating his policy on the "building of socialism in one country," and the activities of the Third International, although by no means terminated, had come to occupy a decidedly secondary place in Russia's relations with other countries. The Soviet government promptly and cordially accepted President Roosevelt's invitation, and sent as its representative to Washington Foreign Commissar Litvinov, its most internationally minded statesman.

A series of private conferences held at the White House November 8 to 16 resulted in an exchange of notes between the two countries which covered five main points. American nationals in Russia were to be assured the "free exercise of liberty of conscience and religious worship" as prescribed by existing laws and the conventions already concluded with other nations. They were also to enjoy legal protection on a basis no less favorable than that enjoyed in the U.S.S.R. by nationals of the most favored nation. The financial claims of the two countries against each other and outstanding debt obligations were to be considered together in subsequent negotiations. The Soviet government waived claims arising out of the military activities of American forces in Siberia. Litvinov, in conclusion, stated that it would be the fixed policy of his government "to respect scrupulously the undisputable right of the United States to order its own life . . . and to refrain from interfering in any manner in the internal affairs of the United States, its territories or possessions." Not only would it refrain from any revolutionary propaganda and restrain all persons under its control from such activity, but it also undertook "not to permit the formation or residence on its territory" of any organization whose aim was the overthrow of the political or social order of the United States. William C. Bullitt—whose earlier enthusiasm for the 1917 revolution was to turn into bitter disillusionment—was appointed American Ambassador to Moscow, and Alexander Troyanovsky became first Soviet Ambassador to Washington.

Negotiations for a settlement of debts and claims initiated by Mr. Bullitt in Moscow, however, ended in a stalemate, principally because the Soviet government made any debt agreement conditional on further loans by the United States which would have facilitated its purchases here. The United States was willing to extend long-term credits through the Export-Import Bank at current interest rates, but pointed out that the Johnson Act, which prohibited any further loans to governments that had defaulted on previous obligations, made any new loan impossible. From the point of view of the Soviet government, the principal difficulty was that it had already concluded compensatory arrangements with other countries, and did not want to accord more favorable treatment to the United States for fear other countries might demand similar treatment. Although debt negotiations broke down on February 1, 1935, a commercial treaty was signed by the two countries in Moscow in July 1935, by which the United States undertook to grant Russian products tariff concessions granted to similar imports from other countries under the terms of the reciprocal trade agreements, while the Soviet Union pledged itself to make purchases here over the next twelve months amounting to $30,000,000.

While trade was facilitated by this treaty, political relations between the two countries did not materially improve.

Fear of communism was revived when, in the summer of 1935, the seventh congress of the Third International heard reports on the progress of Communist propaganda in the United States—reports which seemed to indicate a violation of Litvinov's pledge of noninterference in this country's internal affairs. The Soviet government, in accordance with its accepted practice, denied that it had any connection with the Third International, but apprehension persisted here as to the ultimate objectives of the U.S.S.R.

In the meantime both the United States and Russia had become preoccupied with the rise of Nazism and Fascism in Europe. When Germany and Italy intervened in Spain's civil war on the side of Franco, Russia extended aid to the Spanish Republicans, while the United States, following the lead of Britain and France, sought to maintain a policy of nonintervention, contradicted by the imposition of an embargo on arms to Spain which worked to the benefit of Franco, already armed by Hitler and Mussolini. In the League of Nations which Russia had joined in 1934, but from which the United States was still absent, Foreign Commissar Litvinov, insisting that peace was indivisible, pressed for sanctions when Italy invaded Ethiopia, but found that Britain and France were unprepared to adopt drastic measures. When Hitler reoccupied and remilitarized the Rhineland in 1936, in his opening move for reconstitution of Germany's military power, Britain and France did not oppose him. At the Brussels Conference called to consider Japan's attack on China, Russia advocated effective action to restore peace in Asia—but without obtaining support on the part of the United States, Britain, and France. The Western powers accepted the Munich settlement which yielded the Sudetenland to Hitler, and the United States gave no indication that it opposed extension of German domination toward the east. Nor did this country take any active steps to prevent the occupation by Germany of Austria and Czechoslovakia, or its invasion of Poland. Under these circumstances it would have been difficult for the Soviet government to persuade itself that it could rely on international organization to safeguard the security of the U.S.S.R., or rely on the United States for support in case of attack by either Germany or Japan.

The United States, for its part, felt no confidence in the aims of Russia. The belief persisted here that the Soviet government ultimately hoped to spread communism throughout the world, that war in Europe and Asia would facilitate its designs, and that the armaments it had been building for two decades were designed not merely for defense, as claimed in Moscow, but for offense at a propitious moment. Many Americans, moreover, took the view that the world would be better off if Germany did attack Russia, and hoped, in the words of William Henry Chamberlin, that the "two systems of streamlined neobarbarism" would destroy each other. At the eleventh hour Ambassador Joseph E. Davies, who later gave a realistic but on the whole favorable picture of Russia in his book, *Mission to Moscow*, tried to stem the tide of opinion that was running against Russia, and predicted that efforts to isolate the Soviet government in Europe would "drive Russia into an economic agreement and ideological truce with Hitler." * Yet when this happened in August 1939, many people in the United States denounced Russia for a move which they regarded as a betrayal of the Western world. Russia's invasion of Finland in 1939 served to deepen American hostility, although the United States, in spite of warm professions of sympathy for the Finns, made no move to aid the invaded country.

6. WAR'S UNANSWERED QUESTIONS

It was not until Russia, in turn, had been invaded by Germany on June 22, 1941, that sentiment here underwent a sharp change, and unbounded admiration for the heroism of

* See *Nazi-Soviet Relations, 1939–1941*, containing documents from the archives of the German Foreign Office (Department of State, Washington, D. C., Publication 3023).

the Russian people in their defense of Moscow and Stalingrad swept aside, for the time being, the fear and mistrust of the previous quarter of a century. The United States promptly extended lend-lease aid to Russia, and, at great risk to its vessels, menaced by German submarines, shipped large quantities of war material, trucks, and food at a total cost of over $11,000,000,000, which greatly enhanced Russia's capacity to withstand Germany's assault. Because of this country's belated entrance into the war, however, it proved technically impossible for the Allies to open a second front in Europe, urgently demanded by Stalin, until the spring of 1944, when Normandy was invaded. During the intervening three years Russia had to bear the brunt of Germany's armed might on land, suffering losses of armed forces and civilians estimated at between ten and twenty million.

While controversy about the second front raged back and forth across the Atlantic, Russia participated in conferences with the United States and Britain at Moscow (1942), Teheran (1943), and Yalta (1945), at which problems of military strategy and post-war international organization were discussed. Russia attended conferences summoned by the United States at Hot Springs on food, at Atlantic City on relief and rehabilitation, and at Bretton Woods on arrangements for the establishment of an International Bank and an International Monetary Fund, but abstained from attending the Chicago Civil Aviation Conference held in Chicago. Russia also participated, along with Britain and the United States, in the work of the European Advisory Commission in London which charted Allied plans for Germany, subsequently discussed at Potsdam.

Although highly controversial issues were discussed at all these conferences, the urgency of war caused the United States to postpone for future decision many fundamental issues on which it had proved difficult to reach an agreement with Russia. The death in April 1945 of President Roosevelt, who had won the confidence of Soviet leaders, proved a serious setback for Russo-American relations, although available evidence indicates that after Yalta the President had begun to feel the need of reconsidering American policy toward Russia. The "get-tough-with-Russia" policy advocated by some of President Truman's advisers aroused increasingly violent Russian newspaper attacks on the United States. When the pressure of war was somewhat relaxed after V–E Day, and especially after termination of the war with Japan, unsolved issues came up sharply at every turn as the Big Three wrestled with the manifold problems of peace-making in Europe and Asia. By 1947 it became apparent that, in spite of the warm feeling generated between the two countries by their joint participation in war against the Axis powers, they remain sharply divided by differences in their internal systems, by clashes at strategic key points of the world, by Russia's fear of the atomic bomb, and by our renewed fear of communism.

In contrast to the nineteenth century, the United States finds its interests frequently identified in Eastern Europe and the Balkans, in the Middle East and in Asia, with the interests of Britain, traditionally regarded by Russia as an opponent; and to an extent never before duplicated Russia, which for nearly two centuries had feared collaboration between the two great maritime nations, finds them acting in unison on a wide range of political and economic issues. Yet a community of views still persists between the United States and Russia on long-term problems like the necessity for termination of colonial rule, the advancement of dependent peoples, the improvement of human welfare by constructive use of modern industrial inventions, including atomic energy for peacetime purposes. What will be the future course of relations between the Big Two? Is Russia strong or weak? In what respects is its strength to be feared, in what respects is it to be welcomed? Is Russia's policy in world affairs the product of Communist machinations, or does it represent just another stage in the development of trends deeply rooted in the country's history? Before attempting to answer these questions, it is necessary to look at Russia as it is at the end of World War II—the land, the people, the political and economic system, which are the components of any nation's foreign policy.

Russia's territorial advance toward the west has not been steady or uninterrupted. The map opposite attempts to show schematically the sum of its westward gains to date without indicating the complications of temporary territorial changes. The following summary lists the more important interruptions of Russia's westward advance, and the general regions concerned:

I. *Finland* acquired in 1809; achieved independence after World War I. Rybachi peninsula (A), a section of northern Karelia (B), part of southern Karelia (C), and a section of Finland's Arctic coast including the warm-water port of Petsamo (D) regained by Russia in 1940 after first Russo-Finnish war. At that time Finland leased to Russia the Hangoe peninsula for thirty years at an annual charge of 8 million marks, this peninsula to become a Russian naval and military base.

II. *Baltic states*—Estonia (E), Latvia (F), and Lithuania (G)—controlled by Russia since the eighteenth century, achieved independence after World War I. Reincorporated into Russia in 1940.

III. Russian acquisitions of Polish territory (H) began with the first partition of 1772 culminating in the creation of the Grand Duchy of Warsaw (I) in the Russian empire in 1815. Russian section of Polish territory lost after World War I upon recreation of an independent Polish state. Eastern Poland occupied by Russia in 1939. The same year Polish White Russia was incorporated into the Byelorussian SSR, and Polish Ukraine into the Ukrainian SSR. Russo-Polish frontier established approximately at the Curzon Line (J) by the Yalta Conference of 1945.

RUSSIA'S TERRITORIAL GAINS
IN THE WEST

To 1725

1725 to 1775

1775 to 1800

1800 to 1815

1815 to 1914

1914 to 1947

Lost since World War I

IV. *Bessarabia* (K) acquired from Turkey in 1812; occupied by Romania in 1918; regained by Russia in 1940. At the same time Russia obtained from Romania the province of Northern Bukovina, which had been a part of the Austro-Hungarian empire before 1918, when it was taken over by Romania, and had never belonged to the Russian empire.

After World War II Russia, for the first time in its history, acquired a section of eastern Germany bordering on the Baltic, including the port of Koenigsberg (now Kaliningrad) at the Potsdam Conference of 1945; and Ruthenia (Carpatho-Ukraine), a former province of the Austro-Hungarian empire incorporated after World War I into the new state of Czechoslovakia, from Czechoslovakia under an agreement of June 29, 1945.

PART II

RUSSIA AFTER WORLD WAR II

2. The Land

No country exists in a vacuum. National existence is being constantly molded and remolded by climate, the character and skills of the population, available economic resources, and geographic proximity to other nations. If there is one thing that can be learned from history, it is that political systems and ideologies come and go, but geography remains. Nor has the immutability of geography as a determinant of international relations been to any marked extent affected by modern technological inventions. The airplane, the submarine, the V–1 and V–2 weapons, the atomic bomb may have shrunk the globe to "one world," but even the industrial nations most capable of producing these weapons wrestled, at Teheran, Cairo, Yalta, Potsdam, and Moscow, with the very same geographic problems of security that preoccupied statesmen at the conclaves of Westphalia, Vienna, Berlin, Portsmouth, and Paris.

1. A CONTINENTAL EMPIRE

Yet, while the influence of geography on politics has gradually come to be recognized in studies of the foreign policy of the Western powers, and of Germany and Japan, there is still a tendency to appraise the foreign policy of Russia as if it were the product of mental lucubrations unrelated to geographic considerations. Russia's critics dogmatically assume that every move it makes in world affairs is inspired by a sinister determination to destroy private enterprise, religion, and democracy. Its admirers, equally dogmatic, insist that Russia is actuated solely by selfless concern for the oppressed of all nations and especially for the peoples of colonial areas. Few in either group pause to ask themselves whether the foreign policy of the Soviet government, however important its ideological preconceptions, may not be affected by factors inherent in the country's geographic location, the nature of its economy, and the character of its people which any other régime would have to take into consideration.

One glance at the end-map in this book suffices to recall some of these factors. The Union of Soviet Socialist Republics is continental in expanse. It is a world in itself, with a wide range of climate, vegetation, and population characteristics, from Arctic wastes to subtropical deserts, from dense forests to flat rolling steppes, from the conifers of the north to the palms and orange groves of the Crimea. This vast and varied country spans two continents, Europe and Asia and, without having ever been an integral part of the historical development of either, partakes of the civilization of both, blending them into a combination properly described as Eurasia. Within the confines of the U.S.S.R., inheritor of the vast territorial empire gradually "gathered together," to use a familiar Russian phrase, by successive Muscovy princes and Russian Czars, live some 180 national groups, which differ from each other as Leningrad and Moscow with their westernized culture differ from legendary Samarkand and the primitive settlements of Mongolian tribes. It is as if all the peoples of the British Empire had come to dwell side by side, the English, Scotch, and Welsh with their industrial skills and ancient traditions of political liberty inextricably mixed with Hindus and Moslems, with natives of Nigeria and British Guiana.

This comparison may perhaps convey something of the

infinite variety of a country which far exceeds our accepted concept of a nation. This land mass that spans two continents can best be understood if we think of it as an empire, an empire which—unlike that of the British Isles, scattered all over the globe and held together by ties of loyalty, common economic interests, and Britain's "life line" of naval power and merchant marine—is organically linked to the original core of Russia in spite of persisting transportation difficulties; an empire which can be reached by overland routes less vulnerable to enemy attack than the sea lanes on which Britain is peculiarly dependent. This empire, moreover, is economically self-sufficient to a degree exceeded only by the United States. The U.S.S.R. produces most of the goods and raw materials needed for modern industry and warfare. Like this country, it lacks rubber and tin, which it must import, as well as "colonial wares" such as tea, coffee, and cocoa.

2. A WEALTH OF RESOURCES *

The U.S.S.R. ranks second to the United States as a potential producer of coal, having reserves estimated at one and two-thirds trillion tons, largely bituminous of good quality. Before 1939 the U.S.S.R. occupied third place in Europe as a producer of coal, next to Britain and Germany. Prior to 1914 nearly nine-tenths of Russia's coal came from the Ukraine, primarily from the Donets coal basin (Donbas) north of the Black Sea, nearly half of whose coal is anthracite. Since 1919, however, many other new coal fields have been developed, principally in the Ural region, where the Kuznetsk basin (Kuzbas) has become the nucleus of a vast center of industrial production. During World War II, when the Ukraine was occupied by the Germans who sys-

* Figures on Russia's resources are drawn from George B. Cressey, *The Basis of Soviet Strength* (New York, Whittlesey House, 1945).

tematically damaged the area's coal mines, the output of coal east of Moscow was vastly expanded to meet the country's wartime needs. It is expected that in the future the Kuznetsk basin, and the recently surveyed Karaganda coal fields, will play an increasingly important part in the national economy, especially because they are far less vulnerable to enemy attack than the Ukraine. The opening up of new coal fields in central and eastern regions is in accordance with the Soviet government's long-range plans for geographic decentralization of industry, which is favored not only on grounds of security but also because it reduces the strain on the country's inadequate transportation system, which remains one of the principal bottlenecks in its economic development.

While Russia's production of oil has lagged far behind that of the United States, its reserves, "proved and prospected" as well as "visible," are estimated at 230,700,000 tons, as compared with 1,765,000,000 tons for these two categories in the United States. The center of oil production has been the area of Baku in the Azerbaijan Republic. A second important producing area is along the northern slopes of the Caucasus in the vicinity of Grozny and Maikop. No oil reserves have so far been discovered in most of Siberia and Middle Asia. The chief producing area in the Far East is the island of Sakhalin, whose fields in 1936 yielded 470,000 tons, one-third of which was obtained by Japanese concessionaires under an arrangement terminated in 1943. In modern times several foreign powers have shown interest in Russia's Baku oil fields, where production was first started in 1869. Germany had hoped to obtain oil from that region during both world wars, and under a secret agreement concluded by Britain and France in 1918 Britain was to have acquired the Baku area while France acquired the Crimea. The Baku fields, whose output is carried by two pipe lines to the port of Batum on the Black Sea, lie only about three hundred miles by air from Teheran, capital of Iran, and are highly vulnerable to combined air and naval attack from the Black Sea. This strategic location of Russia's principal source of oil explains in part Moscow's concern about the security of the Black Sea, as well as its post-war interest in obtaining the establishment of a "friendly" régime in the neighboring province of Iranian Azerbaijan. Some oil experts, however, believe that Russia's own oil production was so damaged by the Germans during the war that, all considerations of strategy and security apart, Moscow may have genuine need for the additional oil supplies it has been seeking to obtain in northern Iran under a 51–49 per cent concession patterned on that held in southern Iran by the British-controlled Anglo-Iranian Company, which in 1946 announced it was to share its output with the American Standard Oil Company.

Russia also has at its disposal considerable potential resources of water power, estimated at 280,690,000 kilowatts. The electrification program initiated by Lenin in 1920 and since then greatly expanded calls for a series of hydroelectric installations along some of the country's principal rivers – the Volga, the Dnieper, and the Yenisei, especially on the Angara near Lake Baikal. While many of these plans are still in the exploratory stage, the largest hydroelectric installation in Europe and, when built, the largest in the world, was the Dnieprostroy dam, constructed with the assistance of American engineers, notably the late Hugh L. Cooper, which had an installed capacity of 900,000 kilowatts in 1941 when it was destroyed by the Russians during World War II as part of "scorched earth" policy. The total hydroelectric capacity of the U.S.S.R. in 1940 was estimated at 2,500,000 kilowatts.

The U.S.S.R. is rich in most of the metals necessary for modern industrial production. In 1933 its reserves of iron were estimated at 16,447,000,000 metric tons, actual reserves amounting to 9,238,000,000 tons. The principal center of iron ore production is the Krivoi Rog area in the Ukraine. The conjunction of Krivoi Rog iron, Donbas coal, the water power of the Dnieper River, and the wheatlands of southern Russia, has long marked out the Ukraine as one of Russia's main industrial regions. But its proximity to the Black Sea and to Russia's western border, crossed by invading Germans twice in a quarter of a century, has caused the Soviet leaders to accelerate the development of other potential industrial regions farther removed from possible invasion. As a result, the iron ore deposits of the Urals, which became known in 1701, have been energetically developed since 1931, especially in the area of Magnitogorsk. The conjunction of Magnitogorsk iron and Kuzbas coal promises the creation in the Ural region of an industrial center comparable to that of the Ukraine. The country's total iron ore production in 1938 amounted to 26,529,700 metric tons, of which 16,069,-700 came from the Ukraine and 7,729,000 came from the Urals.

In resources of manganese, an essential component of steel, the U.S.S.R. ranks first in the world, its reserves being estimated at 700,000,000 tons in 1936, with annual production exceeding 4,000,000 tons. The principal deposit of manganese is that of Nikopol, also in the vulnerable area of southern Ukraine, with another deposit at Chiatury in Georgia, mined chiefly for export. The U.S.S.R. has copper, but for the most part of poor quality, the principal deposits being situated in the Urals and in Kazakhstan. Russia's lead reserves represent 11 per cent of the world total, and its zinc reserves 19 per cent of the world total. As a producer of bauxite Russia ranked third in 1940, with an output of 54,900 tons, largely from deposits in the Urals. Russia is classed as a poor third in world output of nickel, following Canada and New Caledonia, with a production of 3,000 metric tons in 1938, chiefly from the Urals and the Kola Peninsula. This output was barely sufficient for domestic needs. Under its peace treaty of 1940 with Finland Russia obtained the nickel mines of Petsamo, formerly developed by the Canadian-controlled International Nickel Company, Ltd., which received $20,-000,000 in compensation from the Soviet government.

The U.S.S.R. is rich also in precious metals. No production figures on gold are published by the Soviet government, but conservative foreign estimates place the 1939 output at 4,500,000 ounces, as compared with 5,173,000 in 1936. Russia ranks second to the Union of South Africa in production of gold, obtained principally from areas along the Aldan and Kolyma rivers in Yakutia. Russia's platinum production, which provides over a third of the world's supply, is situated near Nizhni Tagil in the Urals. In production of chrome ores Russia ranks first, ahead of Turkey and South Africa, with an annual output of 200,000 metric tons. No information is available as to possible resources of uranium and thorium, principal components of the atomic bomb, but it is reported that the Russians are exploiting deposits of pitchblende, a source of uranium, in Saxony.

Russia leads the world in the production of apatite, a source of phosphate, which is urgently needed for its agricultural expansion, and of potash, outranking Germany, previously the world's leading potash producer. It ranks second to Canada in output of asbestos, with an annual yield of 100,000 tons, and is first in production of magnesite, exporting a considerable part of its annual output of 800,000 tons to western Europe.

The list of Russia's resources of strategic raw materials is impressive but, as Dr. George B. Cressey has pointed out, it must be borne in mind that some of the country's deposits, notably copper and bauxite, are low-grade ores whose development might not have been considered economical by private investors. Estimated reserves as well as actual production must also be weighed in terms of the industrial output required to provide a population of 200 million, which before 1941 was growing at the rate of 3 million a year, with a standard of living comparable to that achieved in Western

industrial nations. Russia's ultimate goal for 1960, as proclaimed by Stalin in 1946, is an annual production of 60
million tons of steel, 500 million tons of coal, and 60 million
tons of oil. But, as Professor Abram Bergson of Columbia
University has pointed out, even when this far-off goal has
been achieved, the Russians will be producing 80 per cent as
much steel, about as much coal, and less than one-third as
much oil as the United States, with a considerably smaller
population, produced in 1941.

3. LACK OF ACCESS TO OPEN SEAS

Moreover, this vast rich empire suffers from a grave
fundamental weakness. In contrast to the British Isles, and
to the United States which fronts on two oceans, the U.S.S.R.
is a landlocked continent, with practically no direct access
to ice-free waters. For centuries Russia has sought to overcome this weakness, and its history bears the deep imprint of
a three-pronged drive for outlets to open seas. In the north
the Russians fought the Teutonic knights, the Poles, the
Swedes, and, in our own times again the Germans, Poles, and
Finns, to establish themselves on the Gulf of Finland—to
open, as Peter the Great said, "a window on Europe." Russia
did succeed, by the nineteenth century, in obtaining control
of Finland, part of Poland, and the territories of Estonia,
Latvia, and Lithuania, but lost all these gains after World
War I. In the course of World War II the U.S.S.R. recovered the Baltic states, a portion of Poland, and strategic
areas of Finland, as well as the province of Bessarabia. And
at the close of World War II Russia, under the Potsdam
agreement of 1945, for the first time in its history obtained
a part of eastern Germany, including the port of Koenigsberg on the Baltic, renamed Kaliningrad; as well as the territory of Ruthenia from Czechoslovakia under a Russo-
Czech agreement.

But even with bases on the Gulf of Finland and on the Baltic Sea, Russian vessels still have to travel a long and devious route through the straits of Skagerrak and Kattegat before reaching the North Sea, and from the North Sea must pass through the English Channel or north of the British Isles to arrive ultimately in the Atlantic Ocean. At any point along the route a hostile Germany or Britain—especially if aided by one or more of the Scandinavian countries—might challenge a Russian fleet. The precariousness of this sea connection with the Atlantic explains Russia's interest in the strategic Danish island of Bornholm, which it occupied toward the end of World War II but evacuated in 1946, and in the possibility of developing a line of overland communication across northern Finland and northern Norway terminating on the Norwegian shore of the North Sea.

Similarly, in the South, the Russians for centuries fought Tartars and Turks to obtain a strategic position on the Black Sea, and an outlet through the Turkish-controlled Straits of the Dardanelles into the Eastern Mediterranean. In the tenth century Russian soldiers were battering at the gates of Constantinople, long coveted by the Russian Czars. On behalf of its Slav "brethren" living under the yoke of the Ottoman Empire Russia struggled in the nineteenth century to eject the Turks from Europe, but found itself opposed by France and Britain, the two naval powers of that time, and was later dispossessed of its territorial gains at the Berlin Congress of 1878 arranged by Bismarck.

But even though Russia had bases on the Black Sea, its vessels must pass through the Dardanelles and then, having crossed the Mediterranean, regarded by Britain as its "life line," through the Straits of Gibraltar, controlled by the British, before they reach the southern Atlantic. Along this southern route a Russian fleet could easily be checked by hostile forces based on the shores of Europe or Africa. The precariousness of this sea lane explains Russia's opposition to the presence of British troops in Greece and Egypt; its proposal for demilitarization of the Dodecanese Islands which, under the 1947 peace treaty, Italy must return to Greece; its demand in 1945, subsequently shelved, for trusteeship over one of Italy's African colonies; its insistence upon dominant control over navigation of the Danube, which flows into the Black Sea; its demand for bases on Turkish territory at the Dardanelles; and its desire to recover the strategic areas of Kars and Ardahan, ceded to Turkey under the Brest-Litovsk treaty of 1918. As will be pointed out in Part III, Russia appears to be less concerned in assuring itself an unchallenged exit through the Turkish Straits than in preventing the entrance of hostile fleets in time of war into the Black Sea, which it regards as a "closed sea."

Aside from Moscow's apprehension about the vulnerability of its Black Sea coast to air and naval attack, World War II amply demonstrated the wartime importance of the Mediterranean route for Russia. Even after the United States and Britain had defeated German and Italian forces in North Africa, they were unable to send essential war materials to Russia through the Dardanelles, closed by Turkey as a war measure and, instead, had to use the long and difficult route through the Persian Gulf and across the territory of Iran. This alternative route remains of interest to Russia, which is seeking to consolidate in Iran the influence it had gained there during the nineteenth century, when it clashed over spheres of influence with Britain, and Moscow has been reported eager to obtain an outlet on the Persian Gulf as well as, possibly, a base on the Indian Ocean.

The third prong of Russia's drive to the sea has reached out across Europe and Asia to the Pacific Ocean. The Russians opened up the unexplored regions east of the Ural Mountains in a vast movement of populations comparable to the surge of American pioneers pushing the frontier farther and farther west in this country until they, too, reached the shore of the Pacific. In their drive to the Pacific Ocean the Russians, except for occasional skirmishes with the Chinese along the Amur River and with some local tribes, encountered little resistance until the end of the nineteenth century, when they clashed with Japan for possession of China's Liaotung Peninsula, and for influence in Korea, where the Russians hoped to obtain an ice-free port. Russia's defeat in the Russo-Japanese war of 1904–05 temporarily checked its attempts to obtain adequate outlets on the Pacific. When the United States and Britain, however, pressed Russia in 1945 to enter the war against Japan, Stalin at the Yalta conference asked, as the price of participation, restoration of the rights and privileges Russia had enjoyed in China before 1904–05, including a share in control of the ports of Dairen and Port Arthur. President Roosevelt and Prime Minister Churchill acquiesced in these terms, which were subsequently embodied in a Russo-Chinese treaty signed on August 14, 1945. As a result of World War II, Russia also reoccupied the southern half of Sakhalin, held since 1905 by Japan; acquired the Japanese-controlled Kurile islands, which constitute a barrier between Japan and the Siberian mainland; and obtained a share, with the United States, in the administration of Korea, to which the Western powers and China at the Cairo conference of 1944 had promised independence "in due course." Russia's foothold in northern Korea, although intended to be temporary, gives it access to the Korea Sea, whose waters are free of ice all the year around.

4. POLAR FRONTIERS AND THE ATOMIC BOMB

In the opening up of Siberia, as in the opening up of our western frontier, hunters, fur traders, prospectors for gold and other precious metals, law-breakers, adventurers of all kinds, were followed by farmers, merchants, and administrators. Frontier conditions there, as here, nurtured similar qualities of daring, initiative, and creative imagination. Nor is the frontier yet closed for either country. The diversion of industrial development from European Russia to the region of the Urals, inaugurated in the 1930's and greatly accelerated by World War II, has brought about a vast shift of population, with many of the peasants and workers who had been transferred from west to east at the time of the German invasion now permanently settled in the factories and on the farms of Siberia and the Russian Far East. Diligent search is being made for new sources of raw materials throughout the area east of the Urals, which with time is destined to become the main industrial area of the U.S.S.R., relatively safe from most known weapons, even the atomic bomb. The double-tracking of the Trans-Siberian railroad permits easier access to Siberia's resources. Active efforts are being made, with the aid of icebreakers and scouting planes, to develop the Northern Sea Route linking Murmansk on the Arctic Ocean with Vladivostok on the Pacific. In the Russian Arctic, explorers, scientists, and hardy settlers are still opening up hitherto unexplored territories. The United States, too, has shown its keen interest in the regions of the far north by participating in Canada's Arctic area maneuvers in 1946, and by experimenting with fighting equipment in Alaska and the Aleutian Islands.

The interest of both the United States and Russia in the Polar regions is due not only to the realization that air routes over "the top of the world" would materially shorten communications around the globe, but also to strategic considerations. When we study maps that show the world not flat, but in the round, we can readily see that, in case of war, the United States would be in a better strategic position to strike at Russia by air from the north than to attempt an overland invasion across that country's western border, which proved the nemesis of Napoleon, the Kaiser, and

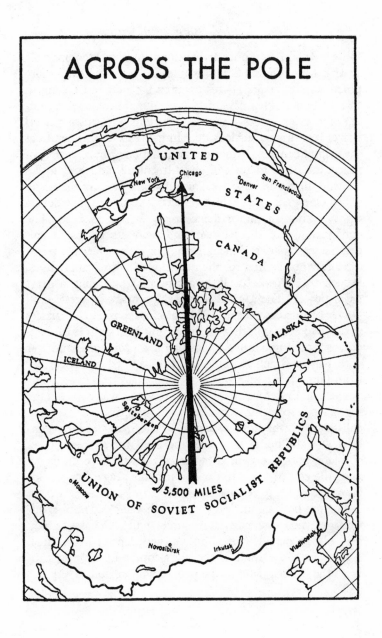

Hitler. Russia, too, once it develops air power comparable to that of the United States, would find it strategically more practicable to strike at this country by air from the north than to undertake a naval attack on our shores, or the landing of invasion forces—operations for which its existing naval power is at present inadequate. Mutual fears of air operations give significance to American negotiations for retention of peacetime bases in Iceland and Greenland, and to Russia's demand, first made in 1945, for a military base on the island of Spitsbergen, over which Norway has exercised sovereignty under an international treaty signed in 1920. The configuration of the Russian land, with its extensive vulnerable sea-frontiers which, because of lack of ice-free ports, offer few possibilities for the development of naval facilities, is such that Russia has little prospect of becoming a great naval power. The United States, the world's greatest naval power of our day, succeeded in placing considerable armies in the field during both world wars, but its resources of manpower would not prove sufficient for a prolonged land war with Russia which might have to be waged much farther from home bases than our two wars against Germany. Air power will therefore be the key to peace or war between the Big Two, especially now that its destructiveness has been enhanced by the atomic bomb. While many experts contend that the bomb has made the need for strategic bases obsolete, both the United States and Russia have displayed since the end of World War II what some regard as an old-fashioned desire to retain existing bases and acquire new ones.

The use both countries will make of their geographic advantages, their raw material resources, and such bases as they may obtain outside their borders, will depend in the final analysis on the attitude of the two peoples. Let us now turn from the Russian land to the people who inhabit it.

3. The People

All too often we tend to think of other peoples, to use Walter Lippmann's phrase, in terms of "stereotypes." Of few peoples has this been so true as of the Russians, who were little known to the Western world until the Bolshevik revolution, by one of the paradoxes characteristic of Russian history, catapulted Russia into Europe and, at the same time, deepened the chasm separating it from the civilization of the West. Before 1917 the stereotypes by which Westerners identified Russia ranged from Jewish pogroms to the saturnalias associated with the sinister name of Rasputin, from bewhiskered anarchists with sticks of dynamite in their fists to exquisite ballerinas like Pavlova in *The Swan*. Few foreigners, even those who spent many years in Russia and were captivated by the spell it has always cast over non-Russians, were aware of the dark, deep-rooted forces of revolt that were gathering below the shimmering surface of Czarism, of the ardent faith in human progress that inspired many of the reformers, of the gay yet poignant quality of the Russian spirit, compounded of vital hope for humanity and sorrow over its failings and sufferings.

1. STEREOTYPES OF RUSSIANS

Nor did foreigners find a guide to understanding of Russia in the few examples of Russian literature available in translation. From a perusal of Tolstoi, Turgenev, Dostoevski, and

Chekhov they gleaned a composite picture of Russians as vacillating and frustrated people, with no clear purpose in life, who either philosophized grimly as they lay on top of stoves, or wondered helplessly what to do next, as in *The Cherry Orchard*. The more energetic, according to this literary reconstruction of the Russian character, might suddenly commit baffling murders, like the hero of *Crime and Punishment*, or indulge in frenzied but hopeless love affairs, only to expiate their guilt, real or assumed, by being exiled to Siberia as in Tolstoi's *Resurrection*, or "going to the people," like Turgenev's Nezhdanov in *The Virgin Land*.

This glimpse of Russian life left Westerners in ignorance of the politically mature poetry of Pushkin, who also contributed beautifully molded lyrics to world literature; the Byronic torments of Lermontov; the poetry of Nekrasov, imbued with deep sympathy for the sorrows of the peasants and eloquent support of the country's revolutionary aspirations; the penetrating critical essays of such contrasting philosophers and critics as the pro-Westerner Herzen and the Slavophil Khomyakov, the haunting humor of Gogol, who bequeathed to Russia the phrase so descriptive of his own works—"it would all be very funny if it were not so sad"; the tender poetry of Bunin, redolent of the fragrance of the damp black earth of Russia in springtime; the uncompromising realism of Gorky, unsparing painter of the evils of Russia's early Industrial Revolution well expressed by the title of his play, *Lower Depths;* the melancholy poetry of Anna Akhmatova, who sang of love like a Russian Elizabeth Barrett Browning and is still quoted by Russian youth; the somber lyrics of Alexander Block, who wrote amid the ominous snowstorms of the revolutionary winter of 1917. Nor do these authors merely belong to a golden era of creative literature in Russia's past. The Soviet government did not indulge in "book-burning." On the contrary, huge editions of Russia's classics are made available to a reading public constantly expanded with the spread of literacy, which is estimated to have reached between 80 and 90 per cent by 1947, as compared with about 60 in 1917. A recent survey of readers' interests by Robert Magidoff, veteran American correspondent in Moscow, indicated that the most widely read Russian classical writers are Pushkin, Gogol, Tolstoi, Dostoevski, and Gorky, with Dostoevski perhaps in the lead. Among individual works the most popular are the poetry of Pushkin and Lermontov, Gogol's *Dead Souls*, Tolstoi's *War and Peace*, and Dostoevski's *Brothers Karamazov*. If foreigners want clues to what the Russians feel and think today, they should seek them not in statistical material or official reports, but in current novels and poems which, although sometimes crude and usually affected by political considerations, especially during the years of party purges, give an extraordinarily faithful reflection of the evolution of Russian attitudes during this turbulent quarter of a century. The most popular Soviet authors are Nikolai Ostrovski (*How Steel Was Tempered*—a remarkable autobiography), Mikhail Sholokhov (whose *And Quiet Flows the Don* is known in this country), Alexander Fadyev (whose *Young Guard*, the story of the struggle of an underground organization of youngsters against the Germans is being put on the stage as well as filmed), and Mayakovski, the futurist poet, whose work aroused the admiration of Stalin. Common misconceptions to the contrary, the Russians know how to laugh at themselves, and great popularity is enjoyed by *The Little Golden Calf*, a Soviet satire by Ilf and Petrov.

2. A MULTINATIONAL EMPIRE

Glib generalization about the "Russian people" is particularly difficult because of the varied ethnic composition of the approximately 200 million citizens of the U.S.S.R. The most recent surveys estimate that there are in the Soviet Union some 180 national groups speaking 125 different languages or dialects and practicing 40 different religions.* Sixty of these national groups, in accordance with the Soviet policy of encouraging national autonomy, have special autonomous territories of one kind or another. This does not mean that they enjoy political or economic autonomy, for control over the entire country is centralized in the hands of the Soviet government in Moscow which, in turn, is strictly controlled by the Communist party. But the national groups are represented in the Soviet Congress through the Council of Nationalities; and they are assured a large measure of cultural autonomy, being not only permitted but strongly urged to use and develop their own languages or dialects and to cultivate their own literature, music, and art. Moscow's policy toward national minorities, which offers a sharp contrast to the rigid policy of "Russification" followed by the Czarist régime, is generally recognized as one of the most constructive achievements of the Soviet government.

This conscious attempt to foster various cultures is all the more significant because, in actuality, the principal single ethnic division in the U.S.S.R. is the Slav group, which numbers 154,000,000 or more than three-fourths of the entire population, and might have succeeded in forcing smaller groups to accept its cultural pattern. Within the Slav category the numerically largest element are the Great Russians, or Russians proper, who number about 105,000,000 or over one-half of the population of the Soviet Union and, because of their more advanced education and experience, occupy a position of commanding importance in the political and economic life of the country. The two other main Slav

* For detailed study, see Frank Lorimer, *The Population of the Soviet Union: History and Prospects* (League of Nations, Geneva, 1946). A useful brief summary is found in Corliss Lamont, *The Peoples of the Soviet Union* (New York: Harcourt, Brace, 1946).

groups are the Ukrainians, estimated at 37,000,000, who live in the industrial and agricultural areas of southern Russia bordering on the Black Sea and the Sea of Azov, and the White Russians or, as they are now known, the Byelo-russians, who number 8,600,000 and live in the western zone of the U.S.S.R. The Great Russians, Byelorussians, and Ukrainians have the same alphabet and speak closely related languages. To the Slav category must be added about 4,000,000 Poles, inhabitants of Eastern Poland which was incorporated into the U.S.S.R. in 1940, who are divided between the Ukrainian and Byelorussian republics, and approximately 270,000 Bulgarians and 30,000 Czechoslovaks, chiefly in the Ukraine. The Slavs have for centuries been predominantly members of the Orthodox Eastern Church, commonly known as the Greek Orthodox Church, which split off from the Roman Catholic Church in the schism of 1054 and except for brief periods has not been reconciled with the Vatican. Some of the inhabitants of Eastern Poland belong to the Uniate Church, formed in 1596 by Orthodox believers who, while retaining their rites and liturgy, accepted the Papacy—and have been subjected to repressive measures by the Soviet government.

Second in numbers to the Slavs are the Turco-Tatars, estimated at 21,000,000. The Turco-Tatar peoples, Asiatic in appearance, are chiefly mixed descendants of the Mongolian, Tatar, and Turkic warriors who invaded Russia in feudal times. Among them can be distinguished the Crimean and Kazan Tatars, the Bashkirs and Chuvash of the Volga River basin, the Azers of the Transcaucasus, the Uzbeks and Turkmenians, the Kazakhs and Kirgiz of Central Asia, and various peoples in remote areas of Siberia such as the Yakuts. The Turco-Tatars are chiefly Moslems.

The third important ethnic group is that of the Japhetic peoples of the Caucasus and Transcaucasus, including the Armenians, Abhazians, Georgians (the most famous of whom is Joseph Zhugashvili, better known as Stalin), Kurds, and others, totaling 7,000,000. Some of the Japhetic groups are Moslems, others belong to the Russian Orthodox faith, and the Armenians have their own form of Christianity.

The fourth important group is the Jews, who in 1939 numbered 3,000,000, located mainly in the western zones of the U.S.S.R., where in the days of the Czars Jews had been forced to live in a ghetto region known as "the pale," and in the Asiatic province of Birobidzhan. As a result of German executions during the period of occupation, the number of Jews in the occupied area, estimated in 1939 at 2,500,-000, was reduced to 500,000. With the addition of Jews in Eastern Poland, and others who fled to Russia during the war from neighboring countries, the number of Jews in the U.S.S.R. was estimated early in 1947 at approximately 2,000,000.

To these four main groups must be added Finno-Ugrians, totaling 5,000,000, settled in the northwest part of the U.S.S.R., who are related racially to the Hungarians; Latvians, Estonians, and Lithuanians, who together number about 5,000,000; Germans, for the most part Lutherans, who had been settled on the Volga by Catherine the Great, but had been transferred eastward at the time of the German invasion in 1941; Iranians and Mongols, and others.

3. CURIOSITY AND SUSPICIOUSNESS

When we look at this federation composed of so many races, nationalities, cultures, and religions, what can we say are the significant characteristics of those whom, for want of a more accurate term, we call "the Russians"? How do they differ from the stereotypes we have come to use about ourselves and about other Western peoples? To begin with, it is fair to say that, while many Russians, before the 1917 revolution, and many more after it, acquired the techniques of the Western world, they appear to outsiders as more primitive than the peoples of Western Europe and the United States, less sophisticated. This explains, in part, their unvarnished bluntness of expression, which often startles and even shocks Westerners. Sir Bernard Pares quotes Paul Milyukov, famous pre-revolutionary political leader, as having said: "We Russians are without the cement of hypocrisy." Being forthright themselves, the Russians are skeptical of moralizing statements by the British and the Americans, especially if unsupported by concrete action.

The Russians, as seen from the outside world, present a peculiar combination of intense curiosity about the way other people live, and equally intense suspicion of all foreigners, who in olden days were called by the generic name of "nemtzi" (Germans), because foreigners of German origin occupied prominent positions at the Russian court and in many branches of Russian administration. The Russians have little arrogance in their relations with other peoples. They are eager to benefit from the experience of more advanced nations, and have no false pride in this respect, although they sometimes make up for their admitted lack of experience by overconfidence bordering on bumptiousness. Peter the Great, Russia's most famous anti-isolationist, was not too proud to visit incognito the shipyards of Holland, where he studied naval construction; and the Soviet government spared no expense before the war in sending engineers abroad to acquire technical knowledge in Western countries, especially the United States, and in bringing American and other foreign engineers to Russia.

At the same time, Russians suffer from recurrent attacks of acute xenophobia. Czar Ivan the Terrible, who allowed English merchants to enter Russia through Archangel, feared that his Florentine architect might betray his secrets abroad, and ordered him to be blinded. Nicholas I, frightened by the revolutionary movements of 1830 and 1848 in Europe, strove to prevent Russians from becoming acquainted with "dangerous ideas." Slavophilism, which in the nineteenth century captured the imagination of creative minds like that of Dostoevski, was itself a powerful revulsion against foreign, in this case Western thought, preaching the superiority of Slav culture and the Orthodox faith, as opposed to Western civilization. After the Crimean war, the Slavophil movement inspired the movement for Pan-Slavism, a form of Russian nationalism calling for the liberation of all Slavs and their union against their actual or potential enemies— the Germans, the Turks, the Austro-Hungarian Empire. The Soviet government, during the great purges of the middle 1930's, pursued with particular relentlessness Russians accused of having had contacts with representatives of foreign powers, and it continues to oppose anything but the most formal relations between its representatives abroad and the peoples to whom they are accredited.

Yet it would be false to think of Russia as inherently isolationist in temper. Peter the Great fought stubbornly, as we have already noted, to open "a window on Europe." Alexander I, with what amounted to religious fervor, pressed for acceptance by other nations of his concept of the Holy Alliance, which contained the germ of a League of Nations. In the reign of Nicholas II the Russian government took the lead in summoning the Hague Conference of 1898, which formulated procedures of international arbitration. The main criticism directed against Lenin and Trotsky in the early years of the Soviet régime was their advocacy of world revolution and their support of the Third International, established in Moscow in 1919. Yet many Westerners have also criticized Stalin, who has placed greater emphasis on "building socialism in one country" than on "permanent revolution," for not giving Russia's foreign policy a sufficiently international character.

Nor can it be said that the Russians, isolated though they

were from the Western world during most of their history, remained unaffected by Western ideas. Byzantine liturgy, saints' lives, and rhetoric left a deep imprint on Russian life and literature. Struggles with the Tatar invaders from the east and the Teutonic Knights in the west colored Russian folklore. Peter the Great studied the administrative practices of the advanced nations of Europe before undertaking some of his most important reforms. Catherine the Great, herself German-born, was profoundly influenced by Voltaire and the ideas of the French Enlightenment, especially with respect to the administration of justice—although she did not put many of her ideas into practice. The army officers who staged the Decembrist coup of 1825, first in a series of Russian revolutions, derived their inspiration from the concepts of political liberty they had learned in France during the Napoleonic wars. Nowhere else in the world did the theories of Marx and Engels have such far-reaching repercussions and receive such determined application as in Russia. Today the Russians, although described as living behind an "iron curtain," are voracious readers of foreign authors. According to Robert Magidoff, the most popular European writers in Russia are Shakespeare, Schiller, Hugo, Zola, and Dickens among the classics, and Romain Rolland, Anatole France, H. G. Wells, Galsworthy, and Priestley among the moderns—all writers whose ideas of liberty might well be regarded as "dangerous" by a dictatorial government. The most widely read American authors are James Fenimore Cooper, Harriet Beecher Stowe, Edgar Allan Poe, and Walt Whitman and, among recent writers, Jack London, O. Henry, Upton Sinclair, John Steinbeck, and, above all, Ernest Hemingway, particularly popular with Russian intellectuals.

That the Russians are primitive and, in Western terms, still backward, does not mean that they are not capable of being trained in the use of modern techniques. On the contrary, the

Russians have shown marked aptitude for learning to operate modern machinery. During the past quarter of a century masses of illiterate peasants have been transformed into industrial workers, many of them highly skilled and able to run vast and complex industrial enterprises. This should not surprise us when we remember that in industrial centers of the United States, for example Pittsburgh and Cleveland, a large proportion of the workers is composed of people of Slav origin (Czechs, Slovaks, Serbs, and Croats), many of whom were no better prepared for industrial civilization when they first came to this country than the Russians were in 1917—although, of course, they had the advantage of American training and leadership.

But the fact that the Russians still feel new to the industrial environment into which they have been suddenly projected often gives them a feeling of inferiority in their relations with technically more advanced peoples. The official slogan is that Russia "must catch up with and surpass" advanced industrial nations like the United States and Britain. And, like Americans at the height of this country's boom development in the last century, the Russians are boisterously and even annoyingly boastful about their achievements, proclaiming them in tones of inflated pride reminiscent of Paul Bunyan's "tall tales," or of American *Innocents Abroad* who used to assure anyone ready to listen to them that America was "the greatest country in the world." Many of the Soviet leaders, however, realize that they still have a long hard road to travel before they can begin to satisfy their people's long-postponed demands for consumer goods. Unlike some of their uncritical Western admirers, who do Russia the great disservice of representing it as a faultless Utopia, Soviet officials are acutely aware of the country's weaknesses and shortcomings. They want foreigners to see Russia only at its best—hence the officially conducted tours which remind one of the efforts of an eighteenth-century minister to impress Catherine the Great with his administrative achievements by building along her route impeccable artificial villages which became known as "Potemkin villages."

4. RESPECT FOR OTHER PEOPLES

From the grueling experience of World War II, which cost the U.S.S.R. the loss of 10 to 20 million lives, both soldiers and civilians who died of starvation, or were executed by the Germans, or perished in guerrilla warfare, the Russians have emerged with a proud consciousness of having inflicted an unparalleled defeat on Germany (for which many of them believe they are solely, or at least primarily, responsible), and an urgent desire to improve their lot, which had been hard for the past twenty-five years but became infinitely harder during the war. The Soviet leaders are by no means sure that the Russian people have been made immune, by prolonged indoctrination, against the temptations of the outside world. John Foster Dulles gave an accurate description of this attitude when he said in 1945: "It often seems as though the Soviet leaders do not want to expose their system or their people to outside contacts until the system has been strengthened internally and that, therefore, they keep up barriers of a kind which normally are used only against an unfriendly and dangerous outer world." Yet through force of circumstances some two and a half million Russian soldiers fought their way across Eastern Europe into Germany and many of them remained quartered for as long as a year in Poland, Hungary, Rumania, and Bulgaria, as well as Russia's zones of Germany and Austria. Their relations with native populations have been a mixture of primitive ruthlessness and tolerant consideration for practices different from those with which they are familiar in Russia. Even when the Russians, by Western standards, have been brutal, they have shown little of the sheer enjoyment of other people's sufferings, the *Schadenfreude* characteristic of the behavior of the Germans in conquered countries. The Russians themselves noted this difference when they had to live under German rule. Harsh treatment they had expected from the invader. But one of the recurring surprises of the Russians was the way the Germans spared no effort to insult human dignity. As one peasant woman testified to war crimes investigators: "They spit upon our souls."

The attitude of the Germans seemed all the more alien because Russia itself has offered an example of how it thinks relationships between advanced and backward peoples can be developed by its policy toward national minorities, including the Germans. This policy has proved of value both in accelerating the advancement of backward peoples within the U.S.S.R., and in cementing the unity of a nation whose stability might have been gravely imperiled by perpetuation of too great economic and cultural inequalities among the various component groups. In his speech of February 9, 1945 on the eve of the first national elections held in the U.S.S.R. since 1938, Stalin, himself a member of a national minority, said that this multinational state might have disintegrated under the impact of war, as the Austro-Hungarian Empire had done in 1918. But, in spite of many strains and stresses, notably in the Ukraine where a movement for national independence has long been in existence, the U.S.S.R. withstood the test of war, and the demonstration it has given of how people differing widely in racial origins, language, historic traditions, and economic and cultural development could work together in a common cause has not passed unnoticed in Asia and other regions confronted by comparable problems.

Not that Russia itself has escaped the effects of nationalist agitation. The full story of what happened within the country during the war is not yet available. It is known, however, that the Chechen Ingush and other peoples in the Caspian area staged a rebellion, as a result of which many of them were exiled and some of their autonomous republics were abolished. There are also indications that the national aspirations of some of the most advanced groups, notably the Ukrainians, were sufficiently strong to call for repressive action by the Soviet government, as well as for concessions on its part. When Stalin, at Yalta, asked for admission of the Ukrainian and Byelorussian republics into the United Nations Organization as charter members, he was conceivably seeking to match votes with the British Dominions, each of which has a seat and a vote in the UN. But he also told Roosevelt he was anxious to satisfy nationalist desires on the part of these two republics, both of which had been enlarged in 1940 by the incorporation of adjoining Polish territories. Centrifugal forces exist even under the strong dictatorship exercised by the Soviet government. The federal structure of the U.S.S.R., however, has the advantage of providing for unlimited territorial expansion should other peoples ever want to become associated with the Union, while at the same time offering national groups included in it the promise of wide cultural autonomy. When the name Union of Soviet Socialist Republics was adopted in 1923, it was purposely kept free of national connotations which might have overemphasized the predominance of the Great Russians, or the Slavs, and the possibility was left open that soviet socialist republics, wherever and whenever formed, might eventually join the U.S.S.R. At that time it seemed that revolutions modeled on that of the Russian Bolsheviks might come to fruition in Bavaria, Hungary, China, and some other countries. This prospect did not materialize. But the incorporation of Estonia, Latvia, and Lithuania as component republics in 1940, as well as of Polish White Russia into the Byelorussian republic and of Polish Ukraine into the Ukrainian republic, offers precedents that might be followed at some future time if nations now independent, or peoples now dependent on advanced Western nations, should be brought into the federation of the U.S.S.R. At this stage of history, when Western nations are weighing the advantages of various forms of federation linking backward colonial areas with the mother countries—in French Indo-China, the Dutch East Indies, Burma, Puerto Rico—the particular pattern evolved by the Russians deserves study.

Primitive as the Russians may appear to more sophisticated foreigners, they are for the most part free from one of the most grievous sicknesses of Western civilization—racial prejudice. It is true that the *agents-provocateurs* of the Czarist government found it relatively easy to incite anti-Semitic disturbances among the poor and ignorant peasants of the western provinces where Jews were segregated in the "pale." But even then the passions of the peasants were inflamed not so much by racial or religious considerations as by the practical fact that Jews, barred from ownership of land and the exercise of most professions, tended to monopolize the calling of moneylending, which was hardly popular among the always-hard-pressed village folk. It is also true that, since the war, a trend toward anti-Semitism has been reported from Russia, in spite of drastic government measures against racial discrimination.

5. PITY FOR HUMAN SUFFERING

By and large, however, the widely varying inhabitants of Russia have little sense of racial superiority, and are not only tolerant of each other's differences—tolerance after all is negative—but actively interested in the art, literature, and music of other national groups in the Union. Nor have the Russians shown bitterness toward the Germans as a people, in spite of the sufferings the Germans inflicted on Russia. Soviet leaders have consistently emphasized that their quarrel was with the Nazis and the militarists, industrialists, and Junkers who supported them, not with the common man and woman in Germany, and have repeatedly stressed their admiration for the achievements of German pre-Nazi culture. Even when the Soviet government adopted harsh measures against the peoples of other lands, as when it sent thousands of Poles from Eastern Poland into exile in Siberia, a tragic hegira most recently described by a Polish writer in *The Other Side of the Moon*, the Russian people showed kindness toward individual Poles and, as Eve Curie relates in *Journey Among Warriors*, were ready to share their last crust of bread with Poles released from prison. Side by side with primitive cruelty, an infinite pity for the downtrodden, the oppressed, the miserable of the entire world has been a dominant theme of Russian life, vividly reflected in Russian literature. Because of their own pity for the sufferings of others, the Russians think that Americans, who have suffered so little in World War II, are callous to the hardships experienced by Russia.

The feeling of pity which embraces the universe has given rise to what might be described as a missionary zeal on the part of many Russians to improve the lot of suffering mankind — a spirit which is readily understandable to Americans who have devoted themselves to missionary activities. Both Pan-Slavism, which limited its scope to the oppressed Slavs, and what might be called Pan-Communism, which has embraced the oppressed "toilers" of the whole world, typify the sense of mission, of Messianic destiny, which is a notable characteristic of the Russians. The feeling of pity expressed by the Russians often bears the hallmarks of a religious dedication, even though, paradoxically, Russian leaders of the past century who have been most ardent in preaching and practicing service to mankind have at the same time been agnostics or nihilists, with little respect for traditional religion. This is not surprising, since the dominant Russian Orthodox Church, following Byzantine practice, was sub-

servient to the Czars and, far from opposing or questioning
the absolutism of the civil authorities, abetted them in their
obscurantist policies, notably in the field of education. Both
Czars and priests feared, with justification, that the spread of
education would lead to a demand for fundamental political
reforms, a demand identified with dreaded "revolution."

6. REVIVAL OF RELIGION

The attitude of the Church's ruling hierarchy inevitably
drove those members of the Russian intelligentsia who believed in the need for reforms, and were ready to sacrifice
their personal interests and even their liberty or life to service
of the people, into revolt against church organization and
church dogmas. Men and women who, as university students,
had tasted heady draughts of freedom of thought, and
learned the joys of untrammeled scientific inquiry, were repelled by the Church's perpetuation of pagan-inspired superstitions among the illiterate peasantry. They could not but
know that information about crop rotations and a supply of
modern agricultural implements would be far more effica-
cious in improving harvests than ritual blessings of the fields
by village priests; or that diseases might be cured and the
chances of healthy childbirth improved by adequate medical facilities rather than by the priest-encouraged custom of
kissing the relics of long-dead saints. Their intellectual revolt
against superstition and obscurantism was unfortunately distorted into the mockery of all religion instituted by the
Soviet government, which brutally tore off the veil of some
church mysteries by exposing them to the rude laughter of
the masses in anti-religious museums. The growing feeling
of many Russians during the nineteenth century that Czarism was using religion to dope the people into submission
was bluntly voiced by Lenin when he reiterated Marx's
dictum that "religion is the opium of the people."

It would be a mistake, however, to assume that Russian intellectuals were opposed to religious beliefs as distinguished from the superstitions the Church had allowed to become attached to faith like barnacles to the bottom of a ship. On the contrary, Russians have a deep-seated religious sentiment to which, in the case of the more sophisticated, was added an aesthetic appreciation of the impressiveness of Church ritual and the beauty of liturgic music. But Russians in all strata of society, long before the Bolshevik revolution, shared a longing to translate their religious beliefs into concrete good works, to help the poor and neglected ones of the world, as Christ had urged his followers to do. This concern for human welfare led many Russians of great talent and high ideals to work in the *zemstvo* (local government) institutions created at the end of the nineteenth century, and the *zemstvos* did yeoman work in bringing medical, educational, and recreational facilities to Russia's "dark villages."

The Soviet government's extensive program of reforms in all fields of human endeavor, although often carried out with ruthless disregard for the feelings and interests of individuals, opened up innumerable new outlets for this spirit of service which is characteristic of the Russians—in contrast, for example, to the French, whose emphasis on individualism has prevented the development of community concern for human welfare, or the Germans, who since Bismarck have looked to the state, not to themselves, for social reform. Today the Russians have a better opportunity than in the nineteenth century to implement their desire for improvement of the lot of mankind through use of the tools placed at their disposal by industrial civilization. Like Americans, the Russians have great faith in the efficacy of the machine—in fact, their faith is greater than ours, since they are still intent on achieving the industrialization we now take for granted. Like us, the Russians believe that industrial progress is important not in itself, but because of the contribution it can make to improvement of human existence. To the Russians who, unlike the British and Americans, had had little experience with political liberty or private property, and for the most part had known a standard of living much lower than that of the Western world, the opportunity to improve their material existence was of greater immediate importance than freedom to vote, freedom of the press, or freedom of religion. It is with this consideration in mind that Westerners must pass judgment on Russia's political and economic system as it exists at the end of World War II.

4. The Political System

The fundamental problem any government faces in modern Russia, with a territory of eight million square miles inhabited by approximately 200 million people or one-tenth of the world's population, is how to achieve some form of unified control over a vast empire whose inhabitants vary so widely in political and economic development. At no time in Russian history has such control been achieved by what Westerners would consider as democratic methods. A highly centralized autocracy or dictatorship, whichever term is preferred, has so far been the traditional form of administration in Russia. It is conceivable that the Russian princes who, after two centuries of bitter struggles recorded in Russian song and legend, had finally succeeded in freeing their lands from the yoke of Tartar khans by 1500 might then have turned upon each other, as feudal lords did in Western Europe and created independent princedoms. At that decisive moment, however, the rulers of Muscovy, strategically situated on the Moscow River in what was then the center of Russian lands, emerged as the dominant element in a still inchoate society. Ivan the Terrible (1533–1584) was the very prototype of the absolute sovereign who brooked no opposition, even from his son, whom he did not hesitate to kill when he suspected him of hostility. Ivan was relentless in whittling down the powers claimed by the boyars, or nobles, and many of his measures, much as they were resented by

the boyars, won him the respect and even affection of the
people, who saw in him a protector against the oppression
of the nobles.

1. TRADITION OF ABSOLUTISM

So deeply had the concept of centralized absolutism become implanted in the lands over which Moscow held sway
that even the internecine and foreign clashes of the Troubled
Times (1604–1618) when Russians and Poles struggled for
possession of the Kremlin, and three false Dimitris, claiming
to be the son and heir of Ivan, perplexed men's minds by
their appearance, failed to break up Muscovy. Out of this
turmoil, finally ended by a popular revolt against Polish
usurpers of the throne commemorated in Glinka's opera *A
Life for the Czar*, emerged the new dynasty of the Ro-
manovs, lower gentry in origin, but clothed at the outset with
all the pomp and circumstance of monarchy as instituted by
the earlier Czars with the aid of the Russian Orthodox
Church, itself inspired by Byzantine traditions of absolutism.

The autocratic character of the government became fully
apparent by the end of the seventeenth century when Peter
the Great (1682–1725) made Russia, in the words of Pushkin,
rear up like a mastered horse on its hind legs and do his
bidding. Like Ivan the Terrible, Peter was brutal and ruthless in carrying out the reforms he deemed essential, from
the building of a fleet to the shaving of his nobles' beards to
make them look like Westerners, from thoroughgoing
changes in the administrative system to the erection of his
dream-city of St. Petersburg, the "window on Europe," on
unhealthy swamps at the mouth of the Gulf of Finland. Like
Ivan, too, Peter did not flinch at killing his own son who, he
thought, had joined the ranks of his opponents. But, and this
is a notable feature of many Russian autocrats, whether
high-born princes or commoners raised to power by revo-

lution, Peter was driven not merely by personal ambition or thirst of glory, but by a deep-seated conviction that he was working for the good of his people.

His campaign for administrative reform was continued by Catherine the Great, who was interested in the most advanced ideas of her period made popular by the writers of the French Enlightenment, and sought to humanize various aspects of the autocracy, especially in the administration of law. Alexander I (1801–1825), regarded in his day as a great idealist and mystic, continued the reformist tradition, and carried it into the field of international relations by his activities at the Congress of Vienna and in the Concert of Europe. He granted to "Congress" Poland, incorporated into Russia in 1815, the most liberal constitution hitherto known to the Russian realm, and instructed his adviser, the great administrative expert Speranski, to work on reforms for the empire as a whole. The Decembrist coup of 1825 immediately following his death, however, brought a halt to this progressive trend. Alexander's brother, Nicholas I (1825–1855), a military martinet and not a visionary, was frightened by the revolutions of 1830 and 1848 in Europe. He aided other monarchs in quelling rebellions, canceled the constitution Alexander had given the Poles and, instead, subjected them to a stern policy of Russification, tightening the reins over his Russian subjects, especially in matters of censorship and education.

2. MOUNTING TIDE OF REVOLT

Russia's defeat in the Crimean war in 1856, when it had to yield at Sevastopol to the combined forces of Britain, France, Turkey and Piedmont, opened the floodgates of rebellion, as military disasters were to do again in 1905 and 1917. A far-reaching and immediate result of demands for internal changes that would strengthen the country was the

emancipation of the serfs in 1861 by Alexander II, the Eman-
cipator—at practically the same time when another emancipation was being effected in the United States through civil
war. With the freeing of the serfs, most of whom were unable to purchase land and therefore had to hire themselves
out as laborers either on the estates of landowners or in the
cities, came the emergence of landless, land-hungry peasants
and of an urban proletariat who suffered all the indignities
and cruelties of the early stages of industrial revolution. In
this atmosphere of unrest and frustration revolutionary
movements flourished, and, in the absence of opportunities
for orderly reforms through parliamentary institutions, ter-
rorism became a short cut to removal of hated officials. The
climax of this period was the assassination of Alexander II in
1881. His son, Alexander III (1881–1894), fearful of the ultimate consequences of growing revolutionary agitation, inaugurated a policy of repression in which he was aided by
his minister, Pobedonostsev, whose name became a symbol of
extreme obscurantism. Pobedonostsev worked in intimate
coöperation with leaders of the Russian Orthodox Church,
who shared his belief that, by suppressing freedom of
thought and learning, the government could kill the seeds
of revolution.

The opposition, driven underground or into exile, carried on its activities by conspiratorial methods which left a
lasting imprint on the work of the Russian Bolsheviks and,
after the rise to power of Lenin and his associates, also on
the work of Communists in other countries. In the prisons
of Siberia and in shabby quarters in Zurich, London, or Paris,
men like Kropotkin and Plekhanov, Lenin and Trotsky, continued to write articles and books which stirred the minds
of the young generation of their times, and opened new
vistas of what Russia could become once the autocracy of
the Czars had been curtailed or abolished. The theories of
Marx and Engels, as well as the experience of the short-

lived Paris Commune of 1871, had a profound formative influence on the thinking of Russian revolutionary leaders. But even the most abstract theorists among them were thinking about actual conditions in Russia first, and only then of how these conditions could be altered by the application of Marxist principles.

The gradual industrialization of Russia at the end of the nineteenth century, the building of railways and oil refineries, of textile mills and power plants, mostly with foreign capital furnished by France, Belgium, Britain, and the United States, aided the cause of the revolutionaries. For industrialization fostered the growth of the urban proletariat and enhanced the influence of the small group of intellectuals who were to become its leaders. At the turn of the century emerged two parties which were to play a historic role in the revolution of 1917—the Social Revolutionaries, one of whose leaders was Alexander Kerenski, and the Social Democrats, who at the London Congress of 1903 split into two groups: the extremist Bolsheviks (who happened to have a small majority on this occasion) and the more moderate Mensheviks.

It was not until Russia had been defeated by Japan in the war of 1904–05 that the revolutionary groups could function with any degree of freedom on a national scale. At that time Nicholas II (1894–1917), alarmed by the popular unrest generated by the war, agreed to the creation of the first representative assembly in Russian history, the Duma. This assembly, given a period of peace and stability, might have succeeded in directing the rising demand for reform into orderly parliamentary channels. The moment the ill effects of military defeat showed signs of abating, however, Nicholas retreated from his promises, and his Minister of the Interior, Stolypin, curtailed the power of the Duma, whose membership was drastically restricted by property qualifications. The Czar retained autocratic powers over the administration of the country. The ideals of moderate reformers, who hoped to establish in Russia a constitutional monarchy modeled on that of Britain, were just as far from realization as ever when Russia entered World War II.

The first result of the war was to unify the country behind the Czar in a strong upsurge of patriotism. But as the Russian armies, poorly armed and ill prepared to repel German forces, suffered successive defeats, and the transportation system, strained beyond endurance, proved inadequate to the task of bringing supplies both to the front and to the population of the cities, who, by 1917, faced growing food shortages, disillusionment and unrest swept the country. The Social Revolutionaries and the Social Democrats took advantage of this atmosphere favorable to change, and by March 1917 public clamor had reached a point where Nicholas II was persuaded, for the good of the country, to resign the throne in favor first of his son and then, when that proved unacceptable, of his brother the Grand Duke Michael. The administration was taken over by a moderate Provisional Government headed by Prince Lvov, chairman of the Council of Zemstvos which had made a major contribution to the defense of the country by their unceasing efforts with respect to supply, Red Cross work, and social welfare.

Had the Provisional Government come to power under peacetime conditions it, too, might have helped to steer the country toward progressive reform without resort to revolution. But the country was seething with revolt and the urge to end the war. In June Alexander Kerenski, Minister of Justice in the Lvov government, became Prime Minister. In spite of his great eloquence, which held crowds spellbound, Kerenski was unable to stem the tide of defeatism, and after a last spurt in June the Russian troops laid down their arms, encouraged to do so by the Bolsheviks, who were preaching a threefold slogan of "bread, land and peace." Lenin had returned in April from his exile in Switzerland to St. Petersburg, renamed Petrograd in 1914. The Germans, hoping that Lenin might undermine Russia's resistance, had allowed him to cross German territory in a sealed railway car. While Lenin remained in the background, Soviets (Councils) of workers and peasants guided by the fiery and inexhaustible Trotsky assumed rapidly growing importance, and finally challenged the authority of the Provisional Government, which by autumn was losing its hold on the country. By a *coup d'état* on November 7, 1917, the Bolsheviks ousted the Provisional Government and set up in its place a Soviet régime headed by Lenin. This régime, with many internal transformations in the course of a quarter of a century, still maintains strongly centralized authoritarian control over the erstwhile empire of the Czars, which in the course of World War II it not only restored to the territorial limits of 1914 but also expanded in several directions.

3. COULD RUSSIA HAVE BECOME A DEMOCRACY?

It is always difficult to determine, in any period of crisis, whether revolutions are precipitated by the propaganda and organized activities of revolutionaries, or whether revolutionaries merely take advantage of existing dissatisfaction and unrest to carry out their plans. In the case of Russia, the ingredients for an explosion had been accumulating for at least a century, and little had been done to alleviate growing internal tensions. The past century had been vibrant with aspirations for freedom and reform. There is no reason to assume that, given time and wise leadership, Russia might not have developed democratic forms of government by peaceful means—although it is by no means a foregone conclusion that a Russian democracy would have been patterned on that of Britain and the United States, whose historical background differs profoundly from that of Russia.

On the eve of World War I, however, Russia lacked many

of the prerequisites for democracy, such as basic voluntary agreement on the form of the state, respect for the rights of political opposition and of national minorities, a strong middle class capable of defending human liberties against extremists of both Right and Left, a tradition of individual liberty, and a stable and prosperous economy. Yet in March 1917 many Western observers who had only a superficial knowledge of Russia jumped to the conclusion, unwarranted by the existing situation, that the downfall of Czarism would usher in a democratic régime similar to that of Britain and the United States. When the Provisional Government, whose leaders, despite their personal integrity and intelligence, lacked both political experience and popular support, proved unable to remain in power, Westerners blamed the Soviet régime for destroying "democracy."

It was unrealistic, however, to expect that a vast and backward country like Russia would overnight, in the midst of a disastrous war, effect the transition from absolutism to democracy which in Western lands had been under way for centuries, and even there has not in all respects been completed. What happened—and this should have been anticipated by anyone familiar with Russian history—was that Russia passed from one form of autocracy to another.

It would be misleading to minimize the influence of Marxist ideas on the political structure and methods of the Soviet state. But until Marxism has been tried in a country which, unlike Russia, has been nurtured in traditions of political liberty, it would be premature to assert that Marxism is necessarily synonymous with totalitarianism and political dictatorship. Marx and Engels had looked, perhaps mistakenly, toward the gradual "withering away of the state" and the emergence of a classless society which, presumably, would govern itself through voluntarily accepted controls. At the present time the Soviet system bears little resemblance to that ultimately envisaged by Marx and Engels. It embodies many of the features of administration made familiar by the Czarist régime, sometimes in altered, and often in more ruthless, form—among them lack of separation of executive, legislative, and judicial power in government organs; censorship of the written and spoken word; restrictions on political opposition; government control of education; and use of secret police, with all the attendant evils of spying, stool pigeons, denunciations, exile, forced labor, and execution of opposition elements. This perpetuation by the Soviet government of the worst excesses of the Czars profoundly disillusioned those among Russians and foreigners who had seen in the Bolshevik revolution the dawn of a new day of greater liberties and privileges for toiling peoples everywhere. The "ten days that shook the world" had inspired high hopes in men like Trotsky and John Reed, Max Eastman and Arthur Koestler. Many of them, upon discovering that reality fell far short of the dream, turned bitterly against both Communism and Russia. Initial misunderstanding of the conditions that existed in Russia at the time of the Bolshevik *coup d'état* has led to a violent and often confused world debate on the issue whether or not Russia is a democracy—a debate which was temporarily suspended during World War II, but has since then been renewed with fresh vigor and contentiousness.

4. "DICTATORSHIP OF THE PROLETARIAT"

The Soviet leaders themselves bluntly described their government in 1917 as "the dictatorship of the proletariat," that is the workers and peasants or "toiling masses." The initial object of this dictatorship was to overthrow the rulers of the country—the "capitalists," landowners, and Church hierarchy. During the period described as "transition from capitalism to socialism," between 1918 and 1936, the vote was regarded as a privilege reserved for the "toiling masses." Persons who lived on unearned income or hired labor for profit —private merchants and *kulaks* or rich peasants—as well as members of the former aristocracy, bourgeoisie, and priesthood and their children, were disfranchised. Industrial workers enjoyed voting advantages over the peasants on the ground that, during the transitional period, the "politically educated" workers had to assume leadership over the backward peasant masses.

By 1935 the completion of collectivization, which tended to equalize working conditions on farms and in factories, and the gradual disappearance, through death or exile, of individuals subject to disfranchisement, opened the way to changes in political attitudes. Stalin, in introducing the new constitution of 1936, declared that "the first phase of communism, socialism" has "in the main" been achieved in the Soviet Union. The "exploiting" classes, he declared, had been "liquidated." Only two classes remained, workers and peasants, plus the group of the intelligentsia, now called "toiling intelligentsia." Under the circumstances, Stalin said, economic differences between social groups were being gradually obliterated, basic class antagonisms were disappearing; and the Soviet Union, having achieved a socialist economy, was moving in the direction of "socialist democracy" and a classless society. Since that time Soviet spokesmen have made little reference to "dictatorship of the proletariat," and have increasingly used the phrase Soviet or socialist "democracy" to describe the political system of the U.S.S.R.—especially during and after World War II.

5. WHAT IS SOVIET "DEMOCRACY"?

Definition of what we and the Russians mean by "democracy" has become one of the most controversial questions between Russia and the United States. Any definition of this term is bound to arouse differences of opinion. One thing, however, can be said with certainty. If by democracy we mean the political institutions familiar to the English-speaking peoples and to a few European nations, then democracy does not exist in Russia today. Political power is in the hands of a small group of men, all members of the Communist party, who hold key positions both in the government of the U.S.S.R. and in the *Politbureau*, the party's steering committee. Marshal Stalin combines the functions of Premier— and actual chief of state—and also Secretary-General of the Communist party. The 1936 constitution gives citizens the right to be united in various organizations—trade unions, coöperative associations, youth, sport and defense organizations, cultural and scientific societies—which may nominate candidates for election to soviets or councils. But it does not permit the formation of political groups other than the Communist party, which it describes as "the vanguard of the working people in their struggle to strengthen and develop the socialist order." The Soviet state is thus a one-party state and this, in fact, means a one-party dictatorship.

The membership of the Communist party, estimated in 1939 at 2,500,000 out of a total population of 170,000,000, increased during the war to 5,500,000 out of a total population of approximately 200 million. The relatively small size of the membership is due in part to the rigid conditions required of candidates for admission, in part to the searching control exercised over members by party officials through periodic investigations known as "purges." At the same time it must be borne in mind that millions of young men and women under 18 are enrolled in *Komsomol*, youth organization of the party, and millions of boys and girls in the still younger organization of *Pioneers*. The party's *Politbureau*, composed since the war of fifteen members, formulates all laws and policies, which are then carried into effect by the administrative officials. Vyacheslav M. Molotov, Andrei A. Zhdanov, and Georgi M. Malenkov, all mentioned as Stalin's successors, are members of the *Politbureau.*

The elective bodies of the U.S.S.R. do not initiate laws or policies, as is done by legislative bodies in democratic countries, but they do hold discussions. While elections are now held by secret ballot and not, as earlier, by show of hands, members of the Communist party dominate all elected organs, from town and collective farm councils to the Supreme Council of the U.S.S.R. composed of two chambers, the Council of the Union, and the Council of Nationalities. Of the deputies elected to both chambers in the February 10, 1946 elections, 81 per cent were party members, as compared with 76.2 per cent in the last preceding elections of 1937. The experience of the war, during which many communities, cut off for long periods of time from direct contact with Moscow, had to resort to local initiative in their defense against the Germans, has so far brought no appreciable change in the centralized authority exercised by the government of the U.S.S.R. Yet the federal character of the government structure holds out promise of possible flexibility in administration. When a proposal was made in 1936 to abolish the Council of Nationalities, which represents the national groups of the U.S.S.R., and to establish a single-chamber parliament, it was rejected by Stalin on the ground that the Soviet Union is not a national, but a multinational state, and that the special interests of national minorities should be represented in the Supreme Council. In 1945 the Soviet government, while retaining overall control of the foreign relations and military preparedness of the U.S.S.R., granted to each of the sixteen republics the right to conduct relations with foreign states and to maintain its own military forces. This right was accorded apparently to meet the growing nationalist aspirations of the Ukrainians, as well as to facilitate the appearance of independence for the Ukraine and Byelorussia prior to their admission as members of the United Nations Organization. In practice, however, both foreign policy and defense are controlled by the Soviet government in Moscow.

There has been no relaxation, since the war, of government restrictions on freedoms which in Western countries are considered an integral part of democracy—freedom of speech, of the press, and of political opposition. On the contrary, Communist party leaders, apparently alarmed by the letdown that followed the war, have redoubled their efforts to keep literature and the arts strictly within the limits traced by the "party line" and to eradicate all taint of "bourgeois mentality." As a direct result of the war, however, the government has modified its restrictions on freedom of religion, and has granted facilities for the exercise of religious activities to the Russian Orthodox Church, as well as to other religious organizations. This decision was caused by several factors. Among them were the loyalty displayed during the war by the Church hierarchy; recognition among Soviet leaders of the strength of religious sentiment among the people, which became particularly apparent under the strain of war; the fact that the Church, separated since 1917 from the state, is no longer regarded as a threat to the Soviet system; and the intention to use the Church in world affairs both as a rallying-point for other nations which adhere to the Greek Orthodox faith, and as a weapon against the Vatican.

We can thus see that there is no democracy in Russia in the Western sense of the word. But if the term democracy includes active participation by citizens in the economic and social development of the community—subject to drastic limitations on political activities—then it could be said without disingenuousness that democracy in that sense exists in Russia. The Soviet leaders themselves do not deny the absence in Russia of freedom as we understand it. They contend, however, that during the past quarter of a century Russia has been in a state of mobilization for an anticipated war against "capitalist encirclement." Under these emergency conditions, they argue, individual wishes and liberties had to be subordinated to the needs of the state as defined by the Communist party. But they point out that the Russian people have considerable scope for initiative and criticism in the economic sphere. It is true that, while the Soviet press never questions the government's political decisions, always recording them with approval, it carries daily comments, frequently couched in terms of vigorous denunciation, on inadequacy of coal production, shortcomings in collective farm administration, delays in the manufacture of electric bulbs, and a thousand and one other items affecting the country's development. Such comments are not only permitted but encouraged under the name of "self-criticism," and have done much to focus the attention of the Russian people on economic and social conditions in their own country, both good and bad, both the successes and the failures. Workers in factories and peasants on collective farms are also urged to criticize their own administration of factories and farms, to submit suggestions for improvements, and to exchange ideas regarding the state of the world as described in the Soviet press and in special "wall-papers" prepared by each unit of production. The Russians are not free, however, to discuss the possibility of abandoning the Soviet economic system and of replacing it, for example, with unrestricted private enterprise. But within the limitations imposed by prohibition of political opposition and of basic changes in the economic system the Russians, who in 1917 were 60 per cent illiterate, are receiving through the process of discussion a considerable measure of education concerning matters that directly affect their daily life and work.

To us who are accustomed to discussion of all political

and economic questions of interest at a given moment, these limitations may appear so drastic as to nullify the value of "self-criticism." Two points, however, must be borne in mind in this connection. First, the Russian people before 1917 had had little experience with freedoms familiar to Western peoples. This does not mean that they do not want these freedoms, or that they could not effectively use them if achieved, but that they may be less disturbed by the Soviet government's restrictions than we would be if we were in their place. It is entirely possible that, with the spread of literacy and improvement in material conditions, the Russians will come to feel an increasingly urgent need for political self-expression and for self-government, and that then, either through gradual evolution or through a revolt against the Soviet rulers, they may attempt to establish another form of government. For the time being, however, distressing as this may seem to the democratic nations of the West, considerations of bare subsistence have had precedence over considerations of political liberty. Whether an autocracy can of its own accord evolve toward some degree of liberalism must, for the time being, remain an open question. It is important to note, however, that by encouraging, in fact enforcing, literacy among the various peoples of the U.S.S.R., the Soviet government has taken the risk—which the Czarist government refused to take—of placing in their hands a weapon that might some day be used to achieve political liberty.

The second point we must bear in mind is that the Soviet leaders genuinely do not understand our concept of tolerance of political opposition. From the point of view of men like Stalin and his associates, who had to wage a life and death struggle first to gain power, then to maintain it, any kind of opposition represents a threat to their authority and even to their existence. Only after opposing elements have been removed by death or neutralized by imprisonment or exile is it possible, in their opinion, to permit a measure of popular discussion within the framework set by the government. The Russian Communists would not be troubled by our scruples about permitting the free expression of political views inimical to our own system. Following this same reasoning, the Russians do not understand why the United States and Britain tolerate the continued existence and even open activities of Nazi and Fascist elements in Germany, or of groups they regard as Fascist in liberated countries or in the Axis satellites.

6. "SOCIALIST" RIGHTS AND DUTIES

The fundamental difference between the Western and the Russian view of democracy lies in our concept of the relationship of the individual and the state. Those of us who are nurtured in the Western tradition have learned to respect the dignity and worth of the individual, and to believe that the individual has certain rights which the state must not infringe except in times of dire emergency, and even then only through voluntary consent and for limited periods of time. The Russians, nurtured in a tradition of absolutism, both political and religious, take the view that the state is paramount, and that since the Soviet state, as they see it, represents the collective interests of all the citizens, the individual must bow to the will of the state. This does not mean that the individual has no formal rights, but that such rights as he has are enjoyed through the permission of the state, to which, in turn, the individual owes duties.

This Soviet concept is reflected in the 1936 constitution, which contains a comprehensive and elaborate list of basic "socialist" rights, such as the right to guaranteed employment, material security in sickness, accident and old age, education, rest and leisure activities, and so on. These rights, in the opinion of Soviet spokesmen, are more important in modern industrial society than political rights. Although not all the rights have become a reality in the U.S.S.R., the list itself has had a powerful influence on the aspirations of other peoples, similar provisions, for example, having been included in the French constitution of 1946. Emphasis is also placed by the 1936 document on equal rights for women, and on equal enjoyment of rights by all citizens, irrespective of nationality or race—two issues which were the subject of lively debates during the second part of the first session of the 1946 United Nations General Assembly. Direct or indirect restriction of rights or establishment of privileges for citizens on account of race or nationality, as well as propagation of racial or national hatred or contempt, are punishable by law. In accordance with the Soviet concept of intolerance of political opposition, however, the constitution does not bar propagation of hatred and contempt on political grounds.

The same view of the relationship of the individual to the state marks the definition in the 1936 constitution of the duties of the citizen. The Soviet citizen is obliged to fulfill the laws, maintain labor discipline, respect the rules of socialist society, and safeguard socialist property "as the sacred and inviolable foundation of the Soviet system." The constitution prescribes that "persons attempting to infringe upon public socialist property" shall be regarded as "enemies of the people." In accordance with this concept a man who commits murder because of a personal grudge or in a fit of "passion" receives a lighter punishment than one who steals state property, no matter how insignificant the theft. Treason against the state—"violation of the oath, desertion to the side of the enemy, impairing the military power of the state, espionage"—are to be punished "with the full severity of the law as the gravest crime." It was on the charge of committing acts of treason that leaders among the Old Bolsheviks—Zinoviev, Radek, Pyatakov, and others —were brought to trial during the great purges of 1936–

1938. The severity of punishment meted out for treason, a term subject to elastic interpretation, explains the reluctance of Russians to have contacts with foreigners, especially in Russia. This concept of the relationship of the individual and the state explains the unwillingness of many Russians in displaced persons camps in Europe to return to their homeland, as well as the unswerving determination of the Soviet government to effect their return by force if necessary—an attitude deeply shocking to Western negotiators.

The natural question often asked by Westerners is whether the Russians can possibly be happy under a political system like that established by the Soviet leaders. This is a difficult question to answer. Many foreigners, and some Russians who have repudiated the Soviet government, among them Kravchenko, author of *I Chose Freedom*, contend that the Russians are enslaved by the régime, suffer from the limitations placed upon their personal freedom, and long for a new political order. Others, similarly familiar with conditions in Russia during the past quarter of a century, while recognizing the ruthlessness of the Soviet police state, contend that the young generation, who now occupy positions of command in all sectors of the nation's life, are impressed with the opportunities for advancement offered them by the Soviet régime, and feel exhilarated by the prospect of future progress in a country which is still on the threshold of modern industrialization. The truth, probably, lies somewhere in between. It is difficult, at best, to define happiness, especially when speaking of a whole nation. There is no question that most Westerners would not be happy if they had to live permanently under the Soviet régime. But the lassitude, doubt, disillusionment, and frustration which darkened life in many of the countries of the West during the inter-war years of growing international and internal insecurity force one to pause before asserting dogmatically that the democracies alone have discovered the secret of human happiness. And there is little doubt, even among critics of the Soviet system, that most Russians have a profound attachment to their country, whatever may be the hardships they personally experience. The ultimate test will be twofold. Which of the two systems, Western or Russian, can assure the highest measure of material well-being to the largest number of people? And which can give the individual the fullest measure of personal satisfaction in living? These questions require consideration of the character and achievements of the Soviet economic system.

5. The Economic System

Probably no aspect of the U.S.S.R. has so alarmed and perplexed the Western world as the Soviet government's attitude toward economic questions, especially toward private property and private enterprise. Many Westerners have feared that the example set by Russia would find followers in other countries, and that the economic system we call capitalism would be gradually undermined and ultimately destroyed, with disastrous consequences not only for economic progress but also for political liberty. This fear was based on several assumptions: that, at the time when the Bolsheviks seized power in 1917, Russia had reached a stage of economic and social development comparable in character, if not in actual performance, to the development of leading Western industrial countries; that Russia had a capitalist system, which the Bolsheviks abolished root and branch; and that the West cannot effectively coöperate with Russia in matters of trade and finance until the Soviet government restores capitalism.

These basic assumptions were historically incorrect. In 1917 Russia was still in the early stages of industrialization, and was comparable to the United States of the 1850's, not of the 1920's. Capitalism was still in its initial stages, and much of the capital and equipment for industry came from foreign sources. Any Russian government today would be hard put to it to restore a system which had existed only in fetal form. Moreover, Russian political thinkers of the nineteenth century were repelled by Western capitalism. As Berdyaev has pointed out, "what the socialists desired more than anything was that Russia should avoid the Western path of development, that whatever happened it might escape the capitalist stage."

1. RUSSIA NEVER A CAPITALIST COUNTRY

It is true that in the first decade of the twentieth century, as some Soviet sympathizers neglect to mention, Russia was already being industrialized. Railway building was in full swing, although the transportation system proved inadequate to the wartime needs of the far-flung empire in the Russo-Japanese war and in World War I. Oil wells were being drilled; streetcars, power plants, and factories producing consumer goods, especially textiles, were in operation. Fundamentally, however, Russia was still at what Lenin called the "colonial" stage—a stage once familiar to Americans, and known today to many countries which are only beginning to develop their resources. Like Latin America, the Balkans, China, and India, Russia exported food, mostly wheat, and raw materials, mostly oil, and a wide range of precious stones and metals, importing in return the manufactured goods it was as yet not equipped to produce. Agriculture was still the keystone of the nation's economy. Industrial development was financed in large part by foreign capital—British, French, Belgian, and American. Such native capital as existed in Russia was in the hands of large landowners, who either put it back into the development of their estates, or spent part of it on visits to Paris, or Monte Carlo, or the watering-resorts of Germany and Austria. Native enterprises were restricted largely to the production of consumer goods, notably textiles. Many Russian landowners of the pre-1914 era, like Argentine landowners today, feared large-scale industrialization, believing that the growth of an urban working class and an urban intelligentsia would ultimately spell the end of their influence. Meanwhile, industrial workers, who in 1914 constituted only 3 per cent of the population, were subjected to sweatshop conditions made familiar in other countries by the early stages of the Industrial Revolution; and half a century after emancipation of the serfs, millions of land-poor peasants, the real proletariat of Russia, still did not possess adequate land. A majority of the Russian people thus had had no experience with either the concept or practice of private property. Both industrial workers and land-poor peasants literally had, in the words of the Communist Manifesto, "nothing to lose but their chains."

Under these circumstances, expropriation of private property proved far easier in Russia than would have been the case in any advanced industrial country, with wide distribution of private property among the population. The fact that most of the capital invested in infant industries had been furnished by foreign investors, moreover, gave the Bolshevik attack on private enterprise an anti-foreign, as well as anti-capitalist, character. It is conceivable that, had the Bolshevik revolution not occurred, Russia's economic development would have proceeded along the lines made familiar by that of the United States—from the stage of imports of capital and exports of food and raw materials to that of greatly reduced imports of capital and greatly expanded exports of manufactured goods, both capital equipment and consumer products. Lenin, however, took the view that Russia would never emerge from the status of a colony of the advanced Western industrial nations unless it developed its own heavy industry, capable of furnishing the country with the sinews both of wartime defense and peacetime progress. This task, he believed, could be accomplished only if Russia undertook a far-reaching program of electrification—one of his most cherished objectives—and if it modernized agricultural production in such a way that the peasants would supply adequate food for factory workers and raw materials for industry.

Lenin's economic program set the stage for the series of Five-Year Plans launched in 1928, four years after his death. As in the case of the Soviet political system, it would be a mistake to minimize the influence of the ideas of Karl Marx on the economic projects of the Soviet leaders. It should be borne in mind, however, that Marx, when he wrote *Das Kapital,* was thinking primarily of conditions that existed in England and Germany in the 1860's, and had not even imagined that his theories would be applied to a backward agrarian country like Russia. Both Lenin and Stalin, although unremitting in their references to Marx, actually displayed marked gifts of flexibility in adapting Marxist theories to the particular conditions of Russia in the 1920's and did not hesitate to retreat from advanced positions, or to revise their programs and time schedules, when confronted with practical difficulties. It is therefore not very illuminating to assay Russia's economic achievements by Marxist standards; nor is it useful to compare the economic situation in Russia during the past quarter of a century with that of the United States, Britain, or other industrial countries. If we are to judge Russia's economy in accurate perspective, we should approach it, as Edgar Snow has suggested, not from the West but from the East—from the vantage point of China, India, and the colonial territories of Western powers. Then, instead of being shocked or disheartened, as many Westerners are, by Russia's relative backwardness today, we may be impressed or astonished by what it has accomplished in a quarter of a century, compared to some of its Asiatic neighbors who now face many of the same problems Russia faced in 1917, and for that very reason have a direct interest in the methods by which the Soviet government has carried out its economic program.

Nor is it particularly rewarding to speculate, as some writers have done, on whether Russia might not have accomplished just as much, and even more, with far less expenditure of human lives and efforts and less wastage of materials if the Bolshevik revolution had never taken place and the economic evolution from agrarian economy to modern industrialization begun in 1890 had been allowed to continue undisturbed by political explosions. This is one of the fascinating "iffy" questions of history. As has been pointed out in the preceding chapter, Russia was not given adequate opportunity during the first decade of our century to effect those internal reforms which might have averted revolution or at least cushioned its shock. It can also be argued that Russia would have advanced more rapidly toward the goals set by Lenin if, instead of repudiating the nation's external debts and antagonizing foreign investors, it had sought loans abroad for the development of its resources. This, however, the Soviet leaders were determined to avoid, fearing rightly or wrongly that foreign loans would be accompanied by attempts on the part of lending countries to intervene in Russia's internal affairs through what backward peoples call "exploitation" of their resources. Determined to avoid all need for dependence on the capitalist world, which was regarded in Moscow as hostile to the Soviet system, the Bolsheviks forced Russia to pull itself up by its own bootstraps, with a zeal, a ruthlessness, and a persistence reminiscent of Peter the Great, who later became one of the most honored heroes of the U.S.S.R. When China, whose political and economic conditions resemble, in many respects, those of Russia in 1917, weighed during World War II possible methods of speeding its postwar industrialization, Chinese economic experts, after examining Russia's experience, advised their government to seek foreign loans provided they could be obtained on terms involving no political intervention, rather than subject the Chinese people to the hardships and sacrifices imposed on the Russians.

Among these hardships was the imposition, practically overnight, of the techniques of industrial production on a predominantly peasant population, which had had little experience with any machinery more complicated than the old-fashioned plow. Most of the initial damage inflicted on expensive equipment imported from abroad, often blamed on treasonable sabotage, was actually caused by the inexperience and carelessness of peasants suddenly transferred from their farms to workmen's benches in modern factories. These production problems were further complicated by a shortage of managerial talent and of trained engineers, which was only gradually remedied by the use of foreign technicians and the intensive training—resumed since the war—of engineering students at home and, in some instances, also abroad.

2. A "SOCIALIST ECONOMY"

Today, after grueling internal struggle, the U.S.S.R., according to the terms of the 1936 constitution, has a "socialist economy," and the state controls all means of production, which are described as "socialist property." The state has assumed the functions of banker, industrialist, and landowner, and is the sole employer of labor. All Russians are either employees of the state in government offices, banks, factories, and other enterprises, or members of collective farms and coöperatives. Russia has jumped from the stage of primitive agriculture, tempered by the beginnings of industrialization, to large-scale development of all its resources under the direction of the state. It has by-passed the period of individual enterprise financed by private capital at private risk for private gain, which characterized the transition of Western Europe and the New World from agricultural to industrial economy. Within the span of twenty-five years Russia has telescoped many of the revolutions which in other countries were spread over several centuries. It has seen the downfall of monarchy and aristocracy; the breaking up of the remnants of feudalism; and the advanced stages of the Industrial Revolution. This breath-taking tempo of change in a country which, rightly or wrongly, considered itself menaced by hostile "capitalist encirclement," explains much that to Westerners seems chaotic, cruel, and enigmatic in Russia.

The two main features of Soviet economy that are particularly striking to Americans are the absence of private capitalist enterprise, and state planning of the nation's economic development. Since the state controls all of the country's resources, there is no room for private capitalism. What we usually mean by capitalism is the opportunity for private individuals to accumulate money, or capital, and to invest this capital—in an enterprise controlled either by an individual or by a group formed into a corporation—at private risk and for private gain. It also means the opportunity for the individual to create his own private business and sell his products on a competitive basis for whatever the current market will bring. These kinds of opportunity do not exist in the U.S.S.R.

But again we must remember that, before 1917, only a very small minority of the population owned anything—land, or industrial resources, or cash—that could be invested in private enterprises. The suppression of capitalism by the Soviet government in 1917 therefore did not constitute the fundamental change in the country's economic system that a similar change would involve in the United States, where property is widely distributed through the ownership of bonds, shares, insurance, and so on. The relatively small group of the aristocracy and the rising middle class were deprived of all property by the Soviet government, and most of them were driven into exile, or else executed or imprisoned. This was a terrible tragedy for the individuals concerned, and it would be glossing over human cruelty to forget this. But the vast majority of people in Russia had no property anyway, and were not much affected by this change. All they were aware of was that property formerly owned by the monarchy, the aristocracy, the Church, the small middle class, and the big landowners, became the property of the Soviet state. The Kremlin has always been careful to point out to the people that *they* are the state, and that therefore it is *they* who now collectively, if indirectly, own Russia's forests, and fields, and mines, and factories, and that they must never permit these resources to pass into the hands of individuals or groups uncontrolled by the state.

The Soviet government does not, however, attempt to practice the Marxist principle that all goods produced in the state should be distributed to all "according to their need." It encourages workers in factories and peasants on collective farms to turn out more or better work, and as an incentive offers them an opportunity to increase their piecework wages, or receive bonuses or decorations like the Order of Lenin, or enjoy special privileges, such as vacations in state sanatoriums in the Crimea and the Caucasus. Thus today people in Russia are remunerated not according to their "need" but according to their "work."

It would therefore be mistaken to think that there is a dead level of economic and social conditions for all the population. Whatever may have been the original conceptions of Marx or Lenin, this is far from being the case in Russia today. A famous actor or a highly trained engineer or an experienced industrial manager receives a salary which, in relative terms, would compare quite favorably with the salaries of similar individuals in the United States. On this salary the engineer, or manager, or actor in Russia can enjoy a higher standard of living than the unskilled worker or the unskilled peasant. He will probably be unable to obtain many of the luxuries and even necessities that the average worker can obtain in the United States—because Russia does not as yet produce sufficient consumer goods to meet even the simplest needs of the civilian population. But of the goods that are available, he will be able to buy more than men and women who are less well paid than he. He will also enjoy special privileges, such as better housing, the use of a car, and so on. Under no circumstances, however, will he be able to invest a part of his salary in private enterprise.

3. RISE OF NEW MIDDLE CLASS

As a result of this differentiation in wages, which has become more and more pronounced during the past decade, Russia for the first time in history was witnessing on the eve of World War II the appearance, on a large scale, of what we would call the middle class. It will be recalled that, before 1917, Russia had only a small middle class, wedged in between the monarchy and aristocracy at the top, and vast masses of landless peasants and underprivileged factory workers at the bottom. In Western countries the presence of a middle class, constantly replenished from the ranks of workers and peasants, served to cushion the shock of revolutionary movements in the nineteenth and twentieth centuries. The lack of a considerable middle class in 1917 made it impossible for Russia to effect an orderly transition from absolutist monarchy to a political system patterned on that of Britain, or the United States, or republican France. Paradoxical as it may seem, Russia, after jumping over the stage of social and economic development that, in the West, saw the rise and flowering of the middle class, has been developing such a group since 1936.

This new group, like the middle class in Western countries, is composed of engineers, actors, government officials, industrial managers, administrators of collective farms, professional men like doctors and teachers, and highly skilled workers known as Stakhanovists, in honor of Stakhanov, a worker who set new records of production. Like the middle class in Western countries, this is a fluid group which is being constantly enlarged by the promotion of younger and still younger workers and peasants to posts of authority and responsibility. With the rise of this group has also come a way of life which had seemed alien to many of the early Bolshevik leaders, but is comparable to the way of life of what they had once contemptuously called the "bourgeoisie" of other countries. From contempt for the privacy of the home (which is in any case often unavailable owing to a grave shortage of housing in urban centers), the Russians have swung toward respect for home life, and an attempt to embellish the room or two they may have with furniture of the Grand Rapids style, and antimacassars and aspidistras reminiscent of the Victorian age. From an extremely elastic attitude toward marriage, which allowed wide latitude for divorce and abortion, the Russians have swung toward an attitude of respect for marriage, encouragement of large families, and prohibition of abortion. From a policy of urging defiance of parents and teachers by children, they have changed to strict concepts of discipline at home and in school.

This does not mean that the new group of engineers, managers, government officials, professional men, and skilled workers has become "frozen" into a caste, and that there is no further opportunity for the economic and social progress of other groups of the population. On the contrary, as has been pointed out, this group is constantly being expanded. This is one of the principal advantages of the Soviet system from the point of view of former landless peasants and underprivileged factory workers, many of whom, under Czarism, seemed condemned to a narrow, impoverished, and, as they called it, "dark" existence. Today in Russia—as has been true in the United States in periods of prosperity, and especially during the opening up of the continent in the nineteenth century—the sky is the limit for men and women of ability. The son of a peasant may become an engineer, or an industrial manager, or a general. Napoleon's phrase, that every one of his soldiers had a marshal's baton in his knapsack, applies in Russia to all spheres of endeavor.

This freedom of opportunity is a recent development. For many years after the Bolshevik revolution the Soviet government, which still feared counter-revolution, discriminated against the children of priests (who in the Russian Orthodox Church were allowed to marry), of Czarist officials, of industrialists, and later of Trotskyists. These discriminations, however, have been gradually abandoned. The post-war young generation is relatively free from the heritage of hatred and prejudice which Russia had accumulated during centuries of one form of absolutism or another, and every young man and woman feels that, if he or she is bright and hard-working, exciting opportunities of achievement lie ahead in a country much of which is still undeveloped. This feeling of opportunity and elbow-room has been an important factor in creating enthusiasm on the part of the younger generation, and the Soviet government has been active in promoting young people to positions of responsibility.

4. PERSONAL VS. STATE PROPERTY

But how can these opportunities for advancement amount to much, some people ask, if extra earnings cannot be translated into property? For the abolition of *capitalism* in Russia has been taken by many Americans to mean that the Russians cannot own any *personal property* whatever. That is not true. The Soviet leaders draw a sharp distinction between ownership of capital for private gain, and ownership of various forms of personal property—houses, books, domestic utensils, clothes, furniture, automobiles, and so on— for private use. What a Russian cannot do is accumulate money from his wages and then put this money into a private enterprise, even a small shoe shop or stationery store, and hire people to work for him as an individual. This is strictly forbidden. All the financial resources in Russia are owned by the state, and are invested by the state in various enterprises —from the steel mills of the Donets Basin and the tractor factories of Rostov to the stores in which people buy their shoes, clothes, and furniture.

A Russian, however, can use his wages to buy himself a house in town or a place in the country. And he can buy as much in the way of furniture, clothes, books, and bric-a-brac as he can afford or—what is more important—can find in the shops. Theoretically, he could buy an automobile, a washing-machine, a refrigerator, and so on—if such things were on the market for private purchase. Actually, however, the Soviet government has concentrated the country's industrial resources on production of heavy equipment, especially for war purposes, and has drastically cut down production of consumer goods. Russia had been preparing for war for many years before its invasion by Germany in 1941, and the steel and other materials as well as labor that might have gone into private automobiles had gone instead into tanks, into airplanes, into all the weapons that the Russians then effectively used against the Germans.

The shortages of consumer goods in Russia—even ordinary things like soap and toothbrushes—are due not to the desire of the government to prevent people from owning private property, but to its desire to prevent diversion of the country's resources from war production to peace production. The Soviet leaders have often indicated that, once the shadow of war had been lifted, and Russia's productive forces could be applied to peacetime needs, they would want to have every man, woman, and child in Russia provided with as many amenities of life as possible. In other words, the Soviet ideal is not to have the population condemned forever to an ascetic mode of existence, but to raise the standard as rapidly as external conditions permit. A Russian can also use such part of his salary as he does not spend on consumer goods for the purchase of government bonds, thus returning part of his salary to the government for investment in state enterprises, and he usually receives interest on these bonds. He can also transmit his house, furnishings, books, and so on to his children by inheritance.

What has just been said about ownership of personal property by Russians who draw wages in factories or salaries in offices is also true of peasants working on collective farms. The number of individual farms has been reduced to less than 1 per cent of the total. Most Russian peasants are members of collective farms, and share in the net profits of the farms as a return for the tasks they perform—whether these be plowing, or milking, or harness-mending, or clerical work in the farm administration. These profits are paid part in cash, and part in the produce of the farm. But, in addition, the peasant can own his own house, and can have a garden of his own, in which he is free to raise vegetables, as well as pigs, rabbits, and fowls. He can also sell the produce of his garden—vegetables, eggs, chickens, and so on—in what is called the "free market." That is, he can take them to the nearest town and sell them to the townspeople without having to pass through government-operated stores. The right to own a garden and sell the produce of that garden was a concession made by the government to the peasants after collective farming had become an accepted thing.

Thus, theoretically at least, the average Soviet citizen has the right to own personal property—though not private investments—in a way which does not greatly differ from the right to own personal property in other countries.

5. A PLANNED ECONOMY

The second feature of Soviet economy that strikes Americans is that it is an economy whose development is planned by the state—not, as in this country, by a myriad of private producers.

The Soviet government, in the midst of civil war, undertook the gigantic task of transforming Russia from a backward agrarian country into a modern industrial state organized on socialist lines. This transformation was intended to accomplish three principal aims: liberate Russia from dependence on advanced industrial states for capital and manufactured goods; establish a basis for the collaboration of industrial workers and peasants in a socialized economy; and eventually enable Russia to attain and, if possible, "surpass" the economic level of capitalist countries like the United States and Germany, meanwhile protecting it against "capitalist" attack.

Such comprehensive transformation, according to Lenin, could be successfully achieved only by a proletarian dictatorship, under a system of planned economy which would permit the state to regulate the use of natural resources and means of production, planning both production and distribution over a period of years. The system of planning, which had received preliminary trial in the field of electrification, was finally embodied in the first Five-Year Plan, inaugurated on October 1, 1928. This plan, first of a series of plans the fourth of which, launched in February 1946, is now in operation, contained detailed programs for the development of every branch of national economy as well as all fields of social activity, such as housing and education. When the plan was originally introduced, its magnitude was regarded as fantastic not only abroad, but even among the more cautious members of the Communist party. Ten years of actual planned economy before World War II, however, demonstrated the practicability of the system, especially as concerns capital investment and certain branches of heavy industry.

The first Five-Year Plan, necessarily experimental in character, was used more as a goal to be exceeded whenever possible than as a norm to regulate national economy. Spurred by the desire to attain socialism in the shortest possible time, the various planning bodies constantly tended to raise production estimates above those set by the government, even when fulfillment of such estimates appeared doubtful in the light of past experience. Political pressure was brought to bear on both planners and individual industries to achieve economically impossible objectives, at a serious cost in terms of wear and tear on men and materials.

As a result of this process the virtues usually ascribed to economic planning—symmetrical coördination of various branches of economy, accurate correlation of production and distribution, elimination of waste—were repeatedly sacrificed to political and military considerations. Collectivization of agriculture, for instance, was forced to outrun the estimates of the plan for 1928–1930, and neither transportation nor the manufacture of agricultural machinery managed to keep pace with collective farming. Similarly, in 1932–33 peasant opposition to grain collections caused a decline in agricultural production, and a serious food shortage which reacted unfavorably on industry. Yet application of planned economy has been sufficiently elastic to permit of rapid adjustments to altered political or economic conditions — even if these adjustments have often resulted in sharp zigzags, throwing production temporarily out of gear.

The task of planning is performed by a special organ, the State Planning Commission (*Gosplan*), which coördinates the plans of the several republics as well as all enterprises and undertakings in the Union, drafts "a common Union perspective plan" in collaboration with a whole network of regional and local planning bodies, and supervises execution of the plan.

The industrial reorganization begun in the fall of 1937 had as one of its aims transformation of the individual commissariats (now ministries) in control of industry from mere administrative departments into actual "operative centers of national economy." At the present time individual industrial plants and undertakings controlled by those ministries are grouped into trusts which, in turn, are organized into over thirty so-called combines, such as coal, oil, rubber, agricultural machinery, industrial machinery, and others. The combines appoint the directors of the trusts, control the supply of raw materials assigned to these trusts, regulate the distribution of government credits among them, and assist the State Planning Commission in the preparation of annual plans for their respective industries.

Under the first three Five-Year Plans the efforts and resources of the Soviet state were concentrated on the development of heavy and defense industries. Soviet leaders declared that, once the country was equipped with adequate facilities for the manufacture of means of production, it would become independent of capitalist states, and could then turn its attention to light industry—the production of consumer goods. Heavy industry, including the production of armaments, consequently made the greatest relative gains during the period 1928–1939, while light industry lagged far behind.

6. WAR DESTRUCTION

The German invasion of 1941 shattered Russia's economy, still in the throes of growing pains. Few people in this country, where the war resulted not in wholesale destruction of industry and agriculture, as in Russia, but in large-scale expansion of all production facilities, can imagine the damage inflicted on Russian economy by the war. The Nazis were determined to deprive the Soviet Union of its newly created industries and reduce it to the status of a producer of raw materials and foodstuffs for the vast industrial empire they intended to build on the European continent. They systematically destroyed plants, and disorganized collective farms by removing or damaging tractors, which had become the life-blood of collective farming. They flooded mines, gutted oil refineries, stripped factories and laboratories of machinery and tools, leveled homes, schools, and hospitals to the ground, destroyed means of transportation. A few figures illustrate the scale of the disaster suffered by Russian economy. The War Damage Commission of the U.S.S.R. estimates that 65,000 kilometers of permanent way, 4,100 stations, and 15,000 bridges were destroyed; 15,800 locomotives and 428,-000 cars broken up, damaged, or removed; 1,400 seagoing vessels and 4,280 river craft sunk or destroyed. In the field of housing, the Soviet authorities are confronted with the destruction of 6 million buildings, with the number of homeless persons estimated at 25 million. The output of oil in the Baku region has dropped to about half of its pre-war volume. The rehabilitation of the Donets coal basin is not expected to be completed until 1949.

The Soviet government is thus confronted with the gigantic task, at one and the same time, of reconstructing the devastated areas, and of resuming the process of industrialization on which it had been engaged before 1941. This twofold program must be undertaken at a time when the Russian people, who for a quarter of a century had literally contributed "blood, sweat, and tears" to the development of their country's resources, always hoping that at the end of the series of Five-Year Plans they would be able to enjoy not luxuries, but the bare necessities of life, are faced with the grim prospect of greater and still greater sacrifices and further postponement of their need for consumer goods. When Stalin, in his speech on the eve of the February 10, 1946 elections spoke of fear of "capitalist encirclement," he was not rousing the Russian people to fight the rest of the world, as some commentators in Western countries assumed. He was trying to stir people mortally weary from years of grueling labor and war into the display of energy essential for the fulfillment of the fourth Five-Year Plan. Fear of "capitalist encirclement," however, apparently did not act as a stimulant. Seven months later Stalin, who is a shrewd judge of the temper of the Russians, took the occasion offered by a questionnaire submitted by a British newspaperman, Alexander Werth, to declare that he did not believe there was any real attempt at "capitalist encirclement," and did not anticipate war in the near future. This statement appears to have been intended primarily for home consumption, to relieve the Russians of fear of another war, and assure them that they have at least a substantial breathing-space ahead for domestic recovery at home. Stalin's reassurances were followed by measures of demobilization, with the object of bringing back some of the Russian forces stationed in occupied countries to fill the urgent need for manpower in factories, in mines, and on farms.

7. GOALS OF FOURTH FIVE-YEAR PLAN

The dimensions of the tasks of reconstruction and economic progress envisaged by the Soviet government can be judged from the blueprint outlined in the fourth Five-Year Plan.* This plan, embodied in "The Law on the Five-year Plan for the Restoration and Development of the National Economy of the USSR for 1946–1950," adopted at the first session of the Supreme Council of the U.S.S.R. on March 18, 1946, set the goals to be achieved by the country's economy during the next five years. According to the law, the principal aims of the fourth Five-Year Plan are "to rehabilitate the devastated regions of the country, to recover the prewar level in industry and agriculture, and then considerably to surpass that level." To achieve these aims, the law declares,

* For complete text of the fourth Five-Year Plan, see "Special Supplement on the 4th 5-year Plan," *Information Bulletin* (Washington Embassy of the Union of Soviet Socialist Republics), June 1946.

it is necessary, among other things, to give priority to the restoration and development of heavy industry and railway transport; to promote agriculture and the industries producing consumer goods "in order to raise the material well-being of the people of the Soviet Union and to secure an abundance of the principal items of consumer goods in the country"; to promote technical progress in all branches of the national economy, "as a condition for a powerful increase of production and a rise in the productivity of labor, which will necessitate not only catching up with but surpassing scientific achievement outside the U.S.S.R. in the near future"; "to further enhance the defensive power of the U.S.S.R. and to equip its armed forces with up-to-date weapons"; to attain a high rate of capital accumulation, "fixing for this purpose the centralized capital investments for the rehabilitation and development of the national economy of the U.S.S.R. in the Five-Year period at 250,300,-000,000 rubles and putting into operation rehabilitated and new enterprises to a total value of 234 billion rubles (in 1945 estimated prices)"; and to strengthen the currency and improve credit arrangements in the national industry.

Plans for industrial reconstruction and development will be based on the principle of rational distribution of productive forces of the different regions of the country, in order to bring industry as close as possible to the sources of raw materials and to avoid overlong hauls by the transport services. The Soviet government lists, among targets to be achieved at the end of the next five years, the annual production of 19.5 million tons of pig iron, 25.4 million tons of steel, 17.8 million tons of rolled metal—35 per cent above the pre-war output. The plan also provides that in the five-year period "the output of copper shall be increased 1.6 times, that of aluminum doubled, magnesium increased 2.7 times, nickel 1.9 times, lead 2.6 times, zinc 2.5 times, wolfram concentrates 4.4 times, molybdenum concentrates 2.1 times, and tin 2.7 times." Coal production for 1950 is fixed at 250 million tons, as compared with 166 million tons in 1940. Oil refineries, left in a critical condition as a result both of prewar over-exploitation by the Russians and of German destruction, and electric power stations are to be rebuilt and expanded. The engineering industry is to give priority to the production of equipment for the iron and steel, power, coal, and oil industries, of electrical machines, railway rolling stock, motor vehicles, tractors, agricultural machinery, equipment for the building industry, and equipment and instruments for the chemical industry. The output of building materials is to be vastly increased to meet the needs of housing reconstruction in war-damaged areas.

The general agrarian structure of the U.S.S.R. is retained under the fourth Five-Year Plan, which calls for maximum consolidation of the collective farm system, the strengthening of the role of the state farms as models of productivity, and the expansion of machine and tractor stations as factors of organization and mechanization. According to the Five-Year Plan, the total annual farm produce of the country by 1950 should be 27 per cent above the figure of 1940. The Five-Year Plan declares that the productivity of labor is to be increased, and costs of production are to be reduced. The transportation system, one of the keystones of the country's economy, is to be rehabilitated and expanded. Provision is made in the Five-Year Plan for increase of total freight carried by rail, road, and water from 480,000 million ton-kilometers in 1940 to 657,500 million in 1950, an increase of 36 per cent. The plan provides also for doubling the stocks of motor vehicles and for building 11,400 kilometers of improved motor roads. The civil air fleet is to be built up, and the airline network is to be enlarged to 175,000 kilometers.

Of the 250,300 million rubles which are to be invested in the country during the next five years, about 115,000 million are allotted to reconstruction of the devastated regions, and about 135,000 million to other parts of the Union, in particular Siberia and the Far East. It is expected that the industries of these eastern areas, greatly expanded during the war years through the transfer of labor and equipment from the western regions occupied by the Germans, will now in turn contribute to reconstruction of the west. The industrial production of the country will thus also be decentralized with a possible view to its dispersal as a defense measure, especially against the atomic bomb.

Even this brief summary of the main goals of the fourth Five-Year Plan indicates that the recovery of the country's economy from the damage wrought by war requires, first of all, development of heavy industry and transport and, above all, of the engineering industry, which must supply machinery and tools for other industries as well as tractors for mechanized agriculture. It is not surprising that, in view of plans for vastly increased expansion of industrial production and transportation, the Russians have displayed a lively interest in the possible peacetime uses of atomic energy, which, they believe, can be more rapidly exploited in a state-controlled economy than in an economy like that of the United States, where private utilities might fear government competition.

8. BOTTLENECKS OF A DEFICIT ECONOMY

Russia, too, like most countries of the world, has been experiencing a post-war economic crisis. In contrast to the United States, its main problems are not those of production in excess of domestic demand, with the potential danger of a slump and resulting widespread unemployment. Its problems are due to underproduction, with the potential danger that persistent disparity between the growing needs of the population and the quantity of available goods may lead to demoralization, resulting by a vicious circle in still lower productivity.

In the opinion of some American observers, Russia's internal economic problems are due in large part to concentration on military preparedness which, they contend, has led the Soviet government, during a quarter of a century, to divert the country's resources of manpower and materials to the development of heavy industry, and to neglect the production of consumer goods. As a result, in spite of the undoubted advances made by Russia in the direction of modern industrialization, the vast majority of the Russian people are forced to content themselves with a standard of living which is low even when compared to that of some of Russia's neighbors in Eastern Europe. It is true that, under the three Five-Year plans which preceded World War II, the Soviet government, regarding the prospect of war first with the "capitalist" world, then particularly with Germany and Japan, as inevitable, planned the development of the nation's economy with a view to making Russia as independent as possible of foreign sources of goods, and to provide its armed forces with adequate supplies of food and modern weapons. American observers believe that this atmosphere of feverish war preparedness which has characterized Russia's economic life since 1917 is now being created anew, with the United States and Britain represented as the potential enemies of the U.S.S.R.; and that the Soviet government is using the threat of another war, made more frightening by the possible use of the atomic bomb, as an incentive to bring about increased output.

While it is extraordinarily difficult to decide with dogmatic assurance whether Russia is preparing for a war of aggression, or is merely endeavoring to assure its own security against genuinely dreaded attack, it is clear that the Soviet government does intend to keep the country militarily ready for any eventuality by maintaining under arms forces now estimated at five million men. Yet the question can be fairly asked whether preparation for war or defense, as the case may be, is alone responsible for the determination of the Soviet leaders to create first a base for heavy industry, at the expense of the population's need for consumer goods, and, only when this goal has been achieved, proceed to the development of light industries. Actually the choice between devoting national resources primarily to the output of capital goods or consumer goods might face other countries emerging from the stage of backward agriculture and determined to develop modern industry with little or no financial aid from abroad. This form of economic nationalism is not peculiar to Russia, and has already been the subject of considerable discussion in countries which today face some of the decisions faced by Russia in 1917—notably China and India.

Some of Russia's post-war economic problems are frankly recognized in the report issued on January 21, 1947 by the State Planning Commission (*Gosplan*) of the U.S.S.R. "Concerning the Results of Fulfillment of the State Plan for Reconstruction and Development of National Economy in 1946." The report declared that in the first year of the fourth Five-Year plan the country's industry "basically completed the post-war reconstruction of industrial production," pointing out that the gross output of the entire industry for civilian production in 1946 increased by 20 per cent as compared with 1945. This increase may at first glance be considered an important gain, but if it is borne in mind that 1945 was the closing year of the war, when production had not yet been shifted to a peacetime basis, the increase must be regarded as disheartening. Even less encouraging was the year's record with respect to agriculture, the output of certain basic raw materials, and serious bottlenecks in housing, transportation, and labor productivity. In the devastated areas it is officially estimated that industrial output "did not even reach half the pre-war production."

In agriculture, which in spite of the growth of industry

since 1917 remains the principal occupation of the Russian people, the Soviet government has been aiming at three main targets: restoration of collective (*kolkhoz*) and state farms in occupied areas which in many cases had been broken up by the Germans; expansion of agricultural production; and increase in the output of tractors and other farm machinery on which the collective farms had become peculiarly dependent since completion of collectivization in 1933. The Nazis, who planned to draw on the agricultural output of the Ukraine to supply food and raw materials for their projected German industrial empire, had indicated that under their rule collectivization would be replaced by return to individual land ownership. It will be recalled that peasant opposition to collectivization during the early 1930's, especially in the Ukraine, where individual land ownership was more widespread than in other parts of Russia, had brought about a bitter internal struggle terminated only by forcible deportation of recalcitrant peasants, and famine conditions due in part at least to passive resistance. Post-war reports from some of the occupied areas, chiefly the Ukraine, whose people are historically known for their strong nationalism and spirit of independence, imply that peasants have in some instances proved reluctant to resume collective farming. To cope with this situation, Lazar Kaganovich, long known as the government's "trouble shooter," was appointed in 1947 Secretary of the Communist party in the Ukraine, replacing the former secretary, Khruschev who, however, remained Ukrainian prime minister. It was also officially stated by A. A. Andreev, member of the *Politbureau* who in October 1946 became chairman of the newly established Soviet for Kolkhoz Affairs, that collective farms and collective farm property had been "misappropriated." From available information it would appear that out of the 12,000,000 acres of collective farm land "misappropriated," 10,000,000 had been taken over during the war, with government permission, by factories, offices, and organizations for the benefit of their employees and workers, and that these factories and offices have been reluctant to return the land to the government. According to the London *Economist*, less than 1,500,000 acres—or 0.5 per cent of the sown acreage —were "misappropriated" by the peasants themselves.

Resumption of collective farming, however, has been hampered by the shortage of tractors and other farm implements, destroyed or removed by the Germans. So critical is this shortage, in a country which depends on domestic production for food and technical crops like cotton and flax, that manufacture of tractors and farm implements is regarded as one of the most urgent tasks on the Soviet list. Some airplane factories have been reconverted to tractor manufacture, and new models of tractors are being put into production, notably a caterpillar tractor known as *Kirovetz*. Production of tractors, however, was 22 per cent below the plan in 1946, and there is a serious shortage of tractors and parts. Great stress has also been laid on proper organization of machine and tractor stations—central distributing points which service collective farms in a given area; on prompt and efficient repair of machinery; and on adequate supplies of spare parts. The ultimate objective of these attempts to restore agriculture is to assure high and, what is regarded as more important, steady production, through scientific rotation of crops and the application of improved agricultural methods.

In spite of all governmental warnings and admonitions, the disorganization of agriculture produced by war and German depredations, the shortage of skilled agricultural labor, and the lack of mechanized farm equipment created cumulatively unfavorable conditions, further aggravated by the drought of 1946 which particularly affected the normally rich grain-growing regions of Moldavia, the Ukraine, and the right bank of the Lower Volga. As a result, Russia during the past year experienced a severe shortage, in some areas approaching near famine, of two of its basic food crops, wheat and rye—making it impossible to abandon rationing of bread in 1946, as anticipated in the fourth Five-Year plan. While official Russian figures are not available, it has been estimated that in 1946 Russia produced only half the grain and vegetable oil seeds and only about one-third the sugar beets produced in 1940, with a population to feed probably larger in relation to cultivated territory than that of 1940. Early crop reports for 1947, however, were said to be encouraging, and in June William L. Clayton, American Under-Secretary of State for Economic Affairs, declared that Russia might be in a position to export some food this year, particularly to its neighbors in Eastern Europe. In spite of the dire need for manpower at home the Soviet government has been reluctant to withdraw its armed forces, estimated at approximately a million, from occupied countries where they have been living "off the land," to that extent helping to relieve the food situation in the U.S.S.R.

Emphasizing some of Russia's agricultural problems, the Central Committee of the Communist party, in a directive "On Measures to Expand Agrarian Economy in the Postwar Period" issued on February 28, 1947, ordered immediate steps to restore and expand agriculture. The main objectives of this directive were an "abundance of food" for the population; the production of technical crops, such as cotton, flax, rubber, and soya beans for Soviet light industry; and accumulation of stocks of food and raw materials. The area of grain crops, wheat and rye, was to be increased by 15,750,000 acres in 1947 over 1946, and by an additional 15,250,000 acres in 1948 over 1947. This increase is expected to assure a gross grain harvest of 127,000,000 tons in 1950, at the end of the current Five-Year plan, as compared with an estimated 42,000,000 tons in 1940. It should be noted, however, that meanwhile the population of the U.S.S.R., through natural growth and inclusion of new territories, has risen from about 170,000,000 in 1940 to about 200,000,000 in 1947.

The February 28 program called for improvement in supervision of agriculture by government and Communist party organizations; liquidation "to the very end" of violators of collective farm work that "hinder the productivity of labor"; a decisive improvement in the work of machine and tractor stations to bring about higher efficiency; the organization of wide training and retraining of personnel for agriculture; and equipment of agriculture with new machinery, trucks, fertilizer, and fuel. *Pravda*, organ of the Communist party, in an editorial of March 31, stressed the importance of the 1947 harvest to Russian economy, and made it clear that it is "the most important sector on the economic front," resorting to military terminology to spur the population to greater exertion. Not only, said the editorial, is "the battle for high crops" the most important factor in the nation's economy, but also "each heroic deed performed on that front is as dear and important as martial and heroic deeds were dear and important to us during the war." The editorial declared it was necessary "that the masses realize that this question is not one of a struggle for isolated, although significant successes, but a battle for a radical improvement of the whole agricultural economy, a powerful advance in our agriculture."

In keeping with this tone of military campaign, the title of Hero of Socialist Labor is to be awarded to leaders of field teams, chairmen of collective farms and other officials whose farms produce unusually large crops per acre of wheat and corn. This award will also be given for increased production in sugar beets, cotton, and rye. The Order of Lenin is to be awarded for specified increases in the production of wheat and other crops. Indicative of the heightened tempo of production expected from collective farms was the provision in the February 28 program that a collective farm with 1,000 acres of arable land must make its 1947 deliveries to the state on the basis, not of the area actually sown, as in the past, but on the basis of its entire arable area, even if only 800 acres, for example, are sown because of lack of tractors, manpower, or seed. A determined drive is also to be made to increase livestock, drastically depleted as a result of the war. For example, in the Ukraine—again, it should be noted, one of the most productive regions of the U.S.S.R.—it is estimated that on collective farms only 6.5 per cent of the horses, 6.2 per cent of the cattle, and 1.8 per cent of the sheep survived the war. By 1950, the fourth Five-Year plan proposes to increase the number of horses by 46 per cent, cattle by 39 per cent, goats and sheep by 75 per cent, and pigs to three times their number in 1946. To coördinate and streamline agricultural production, three Ministries concerned with agrarian activities were merged in 1947 into a single Ministry of Agriculture headed by I. A. Benediktov.

9. INDUSTRIAL BOTTLENECKS

The fourth Five-Year plan, like its predecessors, places chief emphasis on development of heavy industry, which includes the production of armaments. It is in this field that the major gains were registered in 1946, with some increases, inadequate though they were, in the output of various kinds of capital equipment and machinery. The *Gosplan* report complained of a lag in the output of materials essential for modern industry, especially coal, iron, steel, copper, and oil. This lag, however, was not in terms of the plan, which in most instances was either fulfilled or even exceeded, but in terms of the needs of post-war national economy, apparently not fully anticipated by Soviet planners. The 1946 plan for coal, for example, was fulfilled: although the Asiatic coal mines fell short of their target by 3 per cent, the European mines, now producing half of Russia's coal, produced 5 per cent more than was planned.

To remedy the present lack of certain raw materials urgently needed in industry, the Soviet government in 1947 anounced a drive to tap the country's mineral wealth. According to this announcement, "more than eight hundred expeditions, involving some 60,000 scientists, engineers, technicians, and workers fitted out with the most up-to-date equipment, will be engaged in the work on a territory stretching from the 69th parallel on the Kola Peninsula to the 40th parallel in the mountains of the Greater Gissar mountain range in Tajikistan, and from the island of Sakhalin to the Transcarpathian region of the Ukraine." Exploratory drilling is to be carried out in various parts of the country in search of unprospected reserves of coal, nonferrous metals, iron ore, mica, lignites, and so on.

Over the long run, increased output of raw materials would require rehabilitation of mines, plants, and refineries damaged or destroyed by the Germans, and installation of new machinery. Such rehabilitation, however, could be promptly effected only if the Soviet government were able to obtain the necessary equipment and machinery from abroad. The country's need for industrial equipment of all kinds explains in part Russia's stubborn demand at the Moscow Conference for $10 billion worth of reparations out of the current production of the western, highly industrialized, zones of Germany. The Soviet government has also pressed for delivery of machinery and other goods which were in our lend-lease "pipeline," but not yet delivered, on V-J Day. The machinery and other goods, some built to Soviet specifications, included oil refinery equipment, farm implements, tractors, telephone and telegraph poles, and so on, and were valued at approximately $25 million. The Soviet Union, like other recipients of lend-lease material

in the "pipeline" on V–J Day, had agreed to pay, on final
accounting, 90 per cent of the cost of the material plus
expenses of transportation, and payment was to be made
on a thirty-year basis, at an interest rate of 2⅜ per cent.
However, the Soviet government's long-continued reluctance to negotiate a final lend-lease settlement with the
United States aroused growing concern in Washington and,
in spite of pleas from the Department of State, Congress refused to authorize delivery of the "pipeline" material, then
estimated at only $15 million. When the Soviet government,
in April 1947, made known its decision to negotiate a final
lend-lease settlement, this announcement was interpreted as
a possible prelude to a request for a substantial American
loan. In its abortive 1947 trade negotiations with Britain,
Russia is reported to have requested a £55 million credit for
the purchase of electrical equipment and other machinery.

The industrial problems of the U.S.S.R. were bluntly
pointed out in a statement issued by the Council of Ministers on March 1. This statement called for an average rise
in production norms of 20 to 25 per cent—a rise which, it
is hoped, will increase per capita production and lower labor
costs. All Ministries were instructed to revise their production norms during March and April to assure the average
raising of norms by these percentages in all engineering
and manufacturing enterprises and in auxiliary undertakings
and shops. The Council of Ministers pointed out that, in
spite of the investment to date of 17.5 billion rubles in capital construction in the regions liberated from the Germans,
including the Don Basin (Donbas), the volume of industrial
production in these areas in 1946 "has not reached even one
half of pre-war level." Industrial deficiencies were summa-
rized as follows: (1) slow growth of the coal industry, which
delays the development of various branches of heavy industry and transportation; (2) deficit in the production of consumer goods; (3) failure to fulfill the plan for housing

construction which, in turn, delays the organization of the permanent labor force and holds back labor productivity; (4) failure to open a number of new mines and ferrous metallurgical plants for production in 1946, leaving a considerable amount of uncompleted construction on hand; (5) a "serious" lag in the production of electrical equipment and agricultural machinery; (6) failure to produce enough tracks and wheels for railroads, pipes for the petroleum industry, and sheet metal for automobiles; (7) a considerable gap between stocks of building materials on hand and the national housing requirements, mostly as a result of slow development in lumbering.

An important feature of the fourth Five-Year plan is its formalization of the geographic shift in industrial development effected by the war. This shift had already been under way before 1941 as a result of the government's decision to decentralize industry, both for reasons of security (since the pre-1917 industrial and agrarian centers located in the Ukraine and the Donbas were peculiarly vulnerable to enemy attack), and of accessibility to their sources of raw materials. The fourth Five-Year plan provides for reconstruction of industry in the devastated areas, former center of Russia's industrial production—the Ukraine and the Donbas—where some important rebuilding has already taken place, notably the partial restoration of the Dnieprostroy dam, blown up by the Russians as part of their "scorched earth" policy. Reconstructed, as well as new, factories will be equipped with new machinery, while machinery removed during the war from this region to safety in the Urals and other parts of the country will remain where it is. Industrial enterprises evacuated to the Urals, the Volga, Siberia, Kazakhstan, and the Russian Far East will be permanently located in these areas, speeding up their economic development, and it is planned to continue the construction of plants east of the Urals. Moreover, the Five-

Year plan calls for the creation of industrial centers in the north of European Russia, beyond the Arctic Circle, where the Pechersk coal basin is to become the nucleus of a new coal and metallurgical combine. When this vast program of industrial decentralization has been eventually fulfilled, the U.S.S.R. will be a less lopsided country than in the past, when its industry was concentrated in the West and South, and vast regions of its continental expanse were left relatively or wholly undeveloped.

The shift of industrial production from west to east is indicated by some comparative figures collected in 1947 by the diplomatic correspondent of *The Times* of London. According to this estimate, "in 1913 little more than a tenth of Russian coal came from beyond the Urals; by 1936 the proportion had risen to nearly a third; in 1940 it was 36 per cent; by 1950 it should be almost half—47 per cent. The same shift is seen in steel: far less than a fifth in the early years of the revolution the proportion to be produced beyond the Urals by 1950 is to be 51 per cent. And in spite of many delays and false starts, the same process is seen in oil: in 1913 less than 5 per cent came from the eastern areas; in 1940 it was 12 per cent; by 1950 it should be 36 per cent. Light engineering and chemical industries are to have their main bases even more securely established in the eastern regions."

Transportation by rail and road, although improved since the days of the Czars—when inadequacy of transportation gravely hampered Russia in the Russo-Japanese War and World War I—remains a bottleneck, with the added complication that expanding industry is placing an even greater strain on the country's transportation facilities. The fourth Five-Year plan provides for development and improvement of transport by road, by rail, by water, and by air. Particular stress is laid on the creation of an improved railway system, through new construction, reconstruction of existing lines, modernization of operation, production of railway equipment, and accelerated freight handling.

As under previous five-year plans, the main emphasis is on construction or restoration of railways connecting "principal production centers with each other and with raw-material bases." Projected new lines, totaling 4,493 miles, are to include the Stalinsk-Magnitogorsk trunk line, now called the Southern Siberian trunk line, which will contribute to completion of the Trans-Siberian route; and a line from Mointy, northwest of Lake Balkhash, to Chu, which will make Karaganda coal available to all industrial centers in Central Asia. The construction of these lines again emphasizes the marked eastward shift of Soviet economy. Meanwhile, railways in occupied areas torn up by the Germans are to be reconstructed.

Plans are also underway to modernize Soviet railway transport by various methods, including electrification, notably in the Urals and in the Krivoi-Rog and Donbas industrial regions, both in the Ukraine. The output of rails, ties, locomotives and railway cars, both freight and passenger, is being speeded, and tank factories are being reconverted to locomotive production.

10. OUTLOOK FOR CONSUMER GOODS

A distinctive feature of the fourth Five-Year plan, as compared with earlier plans, is the emphasis it places on the desirability of increasing the production of consumer goods, urgently needed—as in other countries devastated by war—to raise the morale of workers and peasants, and hence their labor productivity. While some gains had been registered during 1946 in the output of consumer goods by state enterprises, the current production of such essential goods as textiles, shoes, and household utensils does not begin to meet the Russian consumer demand long postponed in favor of the development of heavy industry. This demand, moreover, has been recently sharpened by the material losses of the war and by contact, on the part of over two million Russian soldiers, with higher standards of living in occupied countries. To supplement the production of state-managed light industry, which is still the stepchild of Soviet economy, the government on November 9, 1946 issued a decree designed to expand and improve the activities of the country's coöperatives. At the present time it is estimated that there are 18,000 consumer coöperatives, which function mostly in rural areas, and 11,000 producer coöperatives, which include small workshops and factories.

The purpose of this decree is to assure the population more food and consumer goods at lower prices, and to raise the volume and character of retail trade. Consumer coöperatives are directed to buy up food surpluses in remote villages which, because of poor transport, have not been sending food to markets in towns—and for this and other purposes are allotted the use of 7,000 trucks as a start. Consumer coöperatives are allowed to open their own shops, booths, and stalls in urban areas, at railway stations, steamer piers, and so forth and to sell at prices prevailing in the free market but not above the prices of the government's commercial shops almost every kind of food—bread, meat, fish, fats, milk, eggs, and so on.

Producer coöperatives are urged by the government to expand their production of household utensils, shoes, hosiery, toys, and clothing, and are warned to display greater "initiative" in obtaining the necessary raw materials and in arranging for distribution of their output. The government, for its part, undertakes to provide the producer coöperatives with the necessary tools and equipment, and local authorities have been instructed to find the requisite technicians and skilled labor and to furnish adequate premises. Special stress is placed on the employment in producer cooperatives of disabled veterans. Soviet newspapers have expressed the hope that this "healthy competition" with the state on the part of producer coöperatives will improve the lot of the consumer, who in the past has often received cavalier treatment in state shops, and have urged that retail trade adopt "cultured" methods in dealing with customers. Judging by discussions in the Soviet press, the Russian customer, for the first time in a quarter of a century, has at least a chance of being recognized as "always right."

In spite of the publicity given to producer coöperatives, the state-controlled light industries remain the principal source of such consumer goods as are made available to the population. For example, by 1950, the state-managed shoe industry is scheduled to manufacture 240,000,000 pairs of shoes as compared with the 13,500,000 to be manufactured by the coöperatives in 1947, and state-managed textile factories are to produce 3,738,000,000 yards of cotton fabrics as compared with 29,000,000 yards to be produced in 1947 by the coöperatives. While the fourth Five-Year plan makes no reference to foreign trade, Russia's various foreign economic arrangements indicate that it may intend to fill at least some of its requirements for consumer goods from the light industries of neighboring countries—notably Poland, Hungary, Finland, and Czechoslovakia—through war reparations, joint economic undertakings, barter trade, and other methods.

An equally important part in the government's plans to satisfy the needs of consumers is played by the housing program. The problem of housing, acute "The Whole World Over" as indicated by Konstantin Simonov's play on this universal subject, is particularly serious in Russia, where even before the war the building of homes had lagged far behind the growth of the population and had not adequately met population shifts from rural areas to urban centers resulting from intensive industrialization. The endless human conflicts generated by lack of adequate living quarters, which are only now beginning to harass the Western world, have been a constant feature of Russian life since the 1917 revolution, and have raised many sociological issues, such as the size of families and the advisability of abortion.

As a result of large-scale war damage, the government is confronted with the task not only of providing new homes for the 25,000,000 made homeless by the war, but also of rebuilding schools, hospitals, factories and farms in the devastated areas, before it can even begin to plan for new housing or industrial units and civic institutions. Several of the country's principal cities have been partly or almost wholly destroyed—among them Stalingrad, Sevastopol, Minsk, Odessa, Kiev, Novorossiisk, and Rostov—and are to be replanned and in part rebuilt. The fourth Five-Year plan provides for the construction of 100,000,000 square meters of dwelling area, 72,500,000 of which will be built by the government under a central plan, and the balance by factories, housing coöperatives and individuals, at a total estimated cost of 52,300 million rubles—42,300 million to be used for government construction and housing, and 10,000 million for credits to individuals and group builders. While this program seems staggering in scope, it has been estimated that, even if it is completed, it will not assure more than four square yards per person by 1950 to the 25,000,000 citizens left homeless—and before the war the population was increasing at the rate of about 3,000,000 a year. At the present time, moreover, lack of cement, bricks, and timber seriously hampers the housing program. Efforts are being made to supplement the work of professional builders through labor contributed without compensation by voluntary "Saturday-Sunday workers" in various communities, who concentrate especially on rebuilding and repairing schools, and other structures of civic importance.

11. PROBLEMS OF LABOR PRODUCTIVITY

One of the principal bottlenecks in industrial production, it is freely admitted by Soviet officials, is that of labor productivity. Like other countries in the process of transition from backward agriculture to an economy attempting to combine large-scale agriculture with intensive industrialization, Russia has not had, and in the immediate future does not expect to have, problems of unemployment. On the contrary, its problem is that of shortage of skilled men and women to run its new industries, mines, and refineries. This problem, which already was acute before the war, has been greatly aggravated by wartime manpower losses (estimated at between 10,000,000 and 20,000,000 men, women, and children, divided between the armed forces and the civilian population); by retention of nearly 5,000,-000 men under arms; and by the need to reconvert production to a peacetime basis, with consequent difficulties in transferring labor from some sectors of the nation's economy to others.

In attempting to remedy the manpower shortage, the Soviet government has resorted to a wide range of methods. It has successively demobilized thousands of men in the armed forces, including troops occupying the Russian zones of Germany and Austria and the Axis satellites, returning them to work in mines and factories and on farms. It has resorted to the use of forced labor, using both Russian political prisoners whose terms run as long as twenty-five years, and German war prisoners whose numbers are estimated by the Russians at 896,000 and by Western observers at between 2,000,000 and 3,000,000. The Soviet government has also demanded the return of persons originating in territories now included in the U.S.S.R. from DP camps in Germany, and has contended that resettlement of

DPs overseas would deprive Russia of much needed manpower. At home the government has inaugurated intensive programs for the training of young people in various industrial skills by establishing a large number of lower, middle, and higher technical schools, as well as training programs in factories. In 1940 it inaugurated a program calling for annual mobilization of 1,000,000 of 14–17 year-olds into technical and trade schools, and created a Bureau for National Manpower Reserves (reorganized in 1946 into the Ministry of Manpower Reserves) to direct the training of these students. The fourth Five-Year plan estimates the number of workers needed by 1950 at 33,500,000, while in 1946 the number of workers available was estimated at 27,-000,000—the figure attained in 1937.

The Soviet government, however, apparently does not intend to increase hours of labor. Since the end of the war the eight-hour day has been restored, and the number of overtime hours restricted. To meet the need for new man-power, the government proposes to draw 4,500,000 new workers from the villages, 1,000,000 from the cities, and about 2,000,000 from the technical schools, and to retrain workers to new skills. Among measures taken to shift manpower from occupations regarded as less important to more important ones has been the effort, reported particularly favored by Stalin, to reduce the number of workers in government offices and to transfer them, following retraining at government expense, to factories, mines, and farms. Far-reaching plans have also been made to promote mechanization in industry and agriculture, and to train and utilize disabled veterans. Meanwhile, restrictions on the unsupervised transfer of workers remain in force, but eyewitness reports indicate that workers continue to move from job to job, and from one part of the country to another in spite of restrictions.

In addition to measures designed to increase the numbers

and standard of efficiency of workers in industry and agriculture, the government offers moral incentives to stimulate individual achievement and, when these prove ineffective, resorts to threats. Special measures are being used to get workers now in relatively "soft" jobs to undertake hard tasks in the mines and on the farms. For example, the salaries of agricultural experts employed on administrative tasks in offices will from now on be 25 per cent less than those of agronomists working in the field. Those who refuse to comply are threatened by the withdrawal of ration cards. Privileges hitherto enjoyed by members of the government bureaucracy have been reduced, and administrative personnel, whenever possible, is being transferred to the industrial and agricultural "fronts." Increased emphasis has been placed on Stakhanovism. The policy of paying workers on the basis of results and of adopting progressive piece rates, in effect since the inauguration of Stakhanovism in 1935, has been further extended. Still higher rewards are being offered for output above the standard norms which, in turn, are being raised. This means, in practice, that workers have to work harder in order to keep the rate of pay they formerly had. Output below the new, higher norms, moreover, is to be penalized through decreasing scales of payment. A striking change has also been made in the payment of agricultural wages, which in the past had been a combination of time and piece work, with the time rate being paid for the "working day," calculated as equal for all. The uniform payment per working day has now been abolished, and henceforth all agricultural wages are to be calculated on the basis of efficiency, thus approximating work on farms to that in factories. The "carrot" and the "stick" are both being used to increase labor productivity.

12. WAGES AND PRICES

In the U.S.S.R. wages and prices are controlled by the government, which is thus in a position to adjust both in accordance with existing political and economic requirements. The scarcity of consumer goods which has characterized Russia's economy during the past quarter of a century has been further aggravated since 1941 by near-suspension of consumer goods output in wartime and by four years of German destruction. Meanwhile, during the war, compensation to workers in various forms was increased, and special bonuses were granted to skilled workers and specialists. As a result there are today in the U.S.S.R. more people with money they want to spend on urgently needed goods than there are goods for them to buy. Only drastic government controls have prevented the inflationary trend latent in Soviet economy from assuming runaway proportions.

The Soviet government fixes the prices of all industrial products manufactured by state enterprises, as well as the prices of all agricultural products delivered by state and collective farms. In this way the government is able to exercise effective control over the prices of the bulk of available basic foodstuffs and manufactured consumer goods. In spite of price controls and reductions in prices of foods sold in commercial stores, prices since the end of the war have been kept high or have even been raised. What is most significant is that the prices of rationed foods, which represent the minimum necessities of life for the majority of the population, have been drastically raised. Prices of some industrial consumer goods, however, have been reduced. Stringent efforts have been made to keep rents relatively stable, but anyone seeking to obtain living space finds that an illegal fee must be paid.

At the same time the government has given consumers with extra cash in their pockets an opportunity to supplement their rations by purchases of scarce goods at high prices—through "free markets," and through commercial government stores first established during the war in 1944. To the "free markets" in the cities collective farmers can bring the produce of their personal plots of land—eggs, pigs, chickens, vegetables, rabbits—either as individuals or as members of consumer coöperatives. In the commercial government stores consumers can purchase better quality clothing, shoes, luxury goods, furniture, radios, perfumes, and other scarce products. By this method the government limits the size of the otherwise flourishing black market, satisfies at least some of the demands of high-salaried workers and technicians who might have little or no incentive to exert special efforts for unexpendable monetary rewards, and obtains from the better-paid groups of the population some of their excess earnings through the turnover tax levied on all purchases.

So far as can be judged from available information, take-home wages in the U.S.S.R. have risen considerably since 1938, partly because of the increase in hourly wages, and partly because of high overtime rates paid during the war for work in excess of the peacetime legal seven-hour day for manual labor and six-hour day for intellectual work. In July 1945 the eight-hour day was introduced pending return to pre-war conditions, but with the proviso that the reduction in hours of work should not involve any reduction in nominal wages. As a result, it has been estimated that, if 1938 is taken as 100, the index of increase in nominal wages is between 165 and 175, depending on categories of work. Owing to the continuance of high prices, however, and to various curbs recently placed on individuals' purchases, real wages have actually undergone a sharp decline.

On September 16, 1946 the government overhauled the

price system for both rationed and unrationed goods. A new category of rations at a lower level was established for dependents—apparently in order to get more people to go to work and produce more goods. The prices of certain essential rationed goods were sharply raised on an average of 180 per cent over previous prices—with the effect of further draining off money in circulation. By contrast, prices of unrationed goods in commercial government stores were reduced by 30 to 35 per cent. On December 14, 1947 the Soviet government announced a triple-barreled program of currency devaluation, termination of rationing of foodstuffs and industrial consumer goods, and introduction of a single-price system with reduction of prices for bread, cereals, and beer. Since the government controls both production and distribution, however, abolition of rationing does not have the same significance as in countries whose economies are subject to limited controls. There are to be different price scales for urban and rural areas, with advantages for the former, as well as for three different geographic zones, with advantages for the devastated regions.

As already indicated, the range of wages varies widely—"fanwise," to use the phrase of a French writer—depending on the social value of a given task from the point of view of Soviet economy. To nominal wages must be added payment for piecework, now widespread in the U.S.S.R., which is calculated on the basis of improvement in working skill, saving in time and materials, and so on. In addition, all workers receive some form of "collectivized salary"—that is, various privileges such as free medical services, old-age pensions, maternity benefits, special grants to large families (beginning with the third child), free education in elementary and secondary schools and, for some students, also in the universities, use of libraries, vacations in government resorts, and so on.

Out of his wages the worker, in addition to payment for

rent and food for himself and his family, must pay an income tax; if he has no more than two children, a tax on small families; a special tax if he is a bachelor or childless; and trade union dues. The principal tax he pays, however, is the turnover tax. This tax, levied on every item every time it changes hands—not only when it is purchased by a consumer but when it passes from one enterprise to another in the course of production—yields 60 per cent of the national revenue. All workers, moreover, are expected to contribute to internal state loans, four of which were offered during the war, bringing in a total of 76 billion rubles. In May 1946, in connection with the fourth Five-Year plan, the government launched a twenty-year loan "for the restoration and development of the national economy of the U.S.S.R.," totaling 20 billion rubles, which was subscribed in four days. For interest payments this loan substitutes lotteries, to be held every year until 1950, with a large number of prizes of 200 and 500 rubles, and a limited number of prizes between 1,000 and 50,000 rubles. Since the bonds bear no interest, bondholders who win no prizes will lose the twenty-year interest on their investment.

13. WILL THE SOVIET SYSTEM CHANGE?

Information available from Russian sources concerning economic developments in the U.S.S.R. since the end of the war reveals no fundamental departure from the system of state-controlled and state-planned economy established during the past quarter of a century. Practical necessities, however, have to some extent tempered Soviet economic theories or altered their concrete application. "Initiative" and "competition," as used in Soviet terminology, are being stressed in state undertakings, and in collective farms and producer and consumer coöperatives, to an extent that may come as a surprise to those who had assumed that the Soviet system would completely stifle the spirit of enterprise. The growing differentiation in economic rewards, with wages calculated on the basis of the individual's efficiency—not his need, as in earlier Marxist slogans—is equally surprising to those who had assumed that the Soviet system would produce an equalitarian society. The geographic decentralization of industry, due both to security and transportation considerations, has brought about increasing decentralization in administration. Greater emphasis is placed on the responsibility of local government organs and industrial managers for fulfillment of plans laid down by the State Planning Commission, whose own calculations, in turn, are based on reports of actual fulfillment it receives from enterprises throughout the country. With the expansion of industry and agriculture, the Soviet leaders are more acutely aware than ever of the need to recruit and train able managers, government administrators, and skilled workers through intensified technical education and material compensation sufficient to create the highest possible incentive.

Russia's economy in the post-war period continues to be beset, as it was before the war, by the profound maladjustments of a society which is striving to pass from backward agriculture to modern industrialization at maximum speed without substantial foreign loans. There appears to be nothing intrinsic in the character or capacities of the Russian people to prevent them—given capable managerial and technical leadership—from creating an economy comparable to that achieved by many Western countries. At the present time, however, the economy of the U.S.S.R. is a deficit economy as compared with the surplus economy of the United States. Only when the U.S.S.R. has reached the point where it will be producing surpluses above domestic needs—a point which, in the opinion of competent American experts, will not be reached for some fifty years—will it stand comparison with the economic achievements of this country.

The test the Soviet government faces in the immediate future is whether it can expand industrial and agricultural production under peacetime conditions—not in the feverish and militant atmosphere of preparedness for war which has marked the country's activities for a quarter of a century; whether it can not only create a base for heavy industry, but also satisfy the consumer needs of its vast population and bring about a standard of living that would encourage greater productivity, and hence further advances in terms of human comfort and welfare.

The Soviet leaders are acutely aware of Russia's backwardness and wartime destruction as compared with Western nations untouched by war, especially the United States. Their attitude toward this country is characterized both by envy, and by hope that another major depression will reduce the economic advantages now commanded by the American system. Moscow's feeling of envy might conceivably be reduced by an American loan for rehabilitation of the economy of the U.S.S.R.—and Washington observers believe that the Soviet government would welcome foreign loans if unaccompanied by political and economic conditions. Moscow's hope of an American depression would be most effectively challenged by determination on our part to make our own political and economic system succeed, and to give all possible assistance to needy nations, as proposed by Secretary of State Marshall in his Harvard University address on June 5, 1947.

It is conceivable that the Russian people might enjoy a higher standard of living today if for the past quarter of a century their economic activities had not been strictly controlled by the state. But this, again, is "iffy" speculation. The generation now actively engaged in operating the Soviet state is for the most part unfamiliar with other types of economy, except for the relatively small number of officers and soldiers who have had some contact with the Western world during the period of occupation of Germany, Austria, and the Axis satellites. Not all of them are by any means satisfied with their present economic condition, and many aspire to improvement in their standard of living—but apparently even they for the most part believe or hope that such improvement can be achieved through the Soviet system. Some may wonder whether citizens of Western countries enjoy greater comfort or personal happiness. But Soviet propaganda has so constantly stressed the precarious character of capitalist economy, with its recurring depressions, large-scale unemployment, and sense of insecurity, that it is doubtful whether such comparisons as citizens of the U.S.S.R. may draw with other nations are in favor of the West.

The political and economic concepts of the Soviet state have had a profound influence on its foreign policy, both political and economic. The main aspects of Russia's attitude toward the outside world must now be considered before analyzing Russo-American relations in various geographic areas where the interests of the two countries overlap, coincide, or conflict.

PART III

RUSSIA AS A WORLD POWER

6. Main Threads of Russia's Foreign Policy

To many Westerners the seemingly sharp oscillations of Russia's foreign policy—from revolutionary internationalism to more-Czarist-than-the-Czars nationalism and back again —appear incomprehensible and, for that very reason, sinister. In the early years of Soviet rule the West feared the spread of Bolshevik doctrines about property, religion, and the relationship of the individual to the state through the propaganda of the Third or Communist International established by Lenin in Moscow in 1919. The Western powers were shocked by the Soviet government's repudiation of the foreign debts contracted by the Czarist and Kerenski régimes, which threatened to undermine all contractual obligations between states. They were alarmed by Lenin's abrogation of Czarist treaties assuring Russia special privileges in countries like China and Iran, which challenged the privileged position of colonial powers in backward areas.

At that time, however, Russia, still in the throes of civil war, which, if the struggle for collectivization is included, did not end until 1935, and still in the initial stages of industrialization, did not loom as a military or economic menace to the advanced industrial nations of the West. It is only since World War II, when Russia demonstrated—with powerful aid, it is true, from the industrial resources of the United States and Britain—that it was capable of holding at bay and defeating Germany, and then proceeded to station military forces in occupied territories, that the Western countries began to fear Russia's national aspirations as well as its revolutionary international activities. When, moreover, the Soviet government gave aid, direct or indirect, to "friendly" régimes in neighboring countries, and denounced the policies of its wartime allies with increasing violence, many Westerners who had been warmly sympathetic to Russia during the war, and had looked forward to friendly peacetime coöperation, began to wonder whether they had checked the menace of Nazism only to foster the menace of Communism.

1. CLAIMS TO GREAT POWER RANK

Perhaps the most difficult psychological hurdle for Westerners to overcome in judging Russia's foreign policy is the widely prevalent misconception that Russia is not a great power on the same plane as the United States and the British Commonwealth of Nations. This misconception is due to the fact that the Russia familiar to the generation that grew up during the inter-war years was an industrially backward nation, rent by civil strife, which lived for many years in a condition of semi-isolation, partly because of the hostility it had aroused outside its borders and partly because of its own reluctance to establish contacts with countries it regarded as hostile. Many Westerners consequently came to think of Russia as a second-rate country which, however dangerous the doctrines of its leaders might be to democracy and private enterprise, was not destined to play a decisive part in world affairs. This mental picture of Russia neglected to take into consideration the role Russia played before 1914, when for two centuries no important events took place in Europe and Asia without its participation. To correct this picture one need only to recall Russia's role during the Napoleonic wars, when Russian armies stopped Napoleon at Moscow as Russian armies stopped Hitler at Stalingrad, and Czar Alexander I demanded as great a share in the making of the peace as Stalin has in our day.

Any discussion of Russia's foreign policy must therefore start with recognition of the fact that Russia has emerged from World War II as a great power, and that the Soviet government intends to claim all rights and privileges claimed by other great powers—which means the United States and Britain, now that Germany and Japan have been militarily and industrially disarmed. The Soviet leaders have left no page unturned in the history of the Czarist Empire. Every advantage, great or small, obtained by the Czars for Russia before 1914—in Manchuria, in Iran, in the Black Sea area—has been claimed anew; and to these ancient claims have been added new ones based on modern concepts of air and atomic bomb strategy—in the Kurile Islands, on Spitsbergen, in Africa. In contrast to the policy adopted by Lenin, who repudiated on behalf of Russia the special privileges gained by the Czars in backward areas and aligned Russia on the side of colonial peoples against the advanced Western nations, Stalin and his associates have sought restoration of the world position occupied by the Czarist empire before its defeat by Germany in 1917. In this respect, they have profoundly disappointed admirers of Russian Communism who had been particularly impressed by its anti-imperialism and its sympathy for colonial peoples. At the same time Soviet leaders have won the support of some Russian nationalists who, however great their distaste for Soviet doctrines and methods, are in sympathy with the Kremlin's concern for the interests of the Russian national state.

The Soviet government has already gone beyond the limits reached by the Czarist Empire, and has carefully matched, move for move, every step taken by the United States and Britain to strengthen their respective strategic and economic positions in the wake of World War II. The Russians, as is well known, are passionately interested in chess, the most popular national sport. Russia's activities on the world scene since the end of hostilities in Europe and Asia have had something of the intellectual precision and delicately balanced calculation of well-matched opponents in a chess game. Whenever the United States or Britain makes a move in any direction on the globe, the Russians are right there to counter them with a comparable move. When Britain, for example, asked for one of Italy's colonies in Africa, Russia demanded a trusteeship in Tripolitania. Countering the development of the oil resources of southern Iran by a British company which now shares its oil with an American concern, Russia made a claim for an oil concession in northern Iran, on terms similar to those granted by Iran to the British. The demand of the United States for national control of certain Pacific islands, some of which had been administered by the Japanese under a mandate from the League of Nations, was matched in advance by Russia's acquisition of the Japanese-controlled Kurile Islands. War-time American bases in Iceland, formerly linked to Denmark, and in Danish-controlled Greenland, were matched by Russia's attempt to obtain a base on Norwegian-controlled Spitsbergen. When the British and Americans in 1947 announced economic unification of their zones in Germany and aid in the recovery of German export industries, Russia announced a vast increase in the level of German industrial production for its zone. When the Western powers objected to Russia's demand for control of the Dardanelles, and demanded international administration of the Danube, the Russians countered by demanding internationalization of the Panama Canal, Suez, and Gibraltar. These Russian claims have been criticized in Western countries as a regrettable throwback to rough-and-ready methods of earlier ages when great powers ruthlessly grabbed what they wanted all over

the world—methods which, it is contended, have become obsolete in this new age, dedicated to international coöperation
and the rule of law. The Russians, however, have taken the
view that, since other great powers have not relinquished
most of the gains they made in past ages, there is no reason
why Russia should not act as they once did.

Nor does Russia intend to be left out of any international
negotiations, no matter how remote the subject may seem to
be from its immediate interests. When the Western powers
decided to call a conference in 1945 on the status of Tangier,
Russia insisted on being included in that conference—and
only those who had forgotten that the Czarist government
had been represented at the Algeciras Conference of 1906
or had not known of the Potsdam agreement on the Tangier
zone were tempted to express surprise. This does not mean
that Russia, once it has been invited to participate, invariably
presses for acceptance of its views, or that it has clearly defined views on every subject. For example, the Russians,
having asserted their right to be represented at the conference on Tangier, attended the meeting, but took no
further action on the matter. What the Soviet leaders insist
on is that Russia, as a great power, must be automatically included in discussions of all international problems, and accorded equality of treatment with other great powers.

This "me-too" attitude appears childish and recurrently
annoying to the United States and Britain—even though the
great Western powers would be both surprised and alarmed
if other nations should question their right to play any part
they may see fit in all world developments which, in their
opinion, affect their interests. There is, of course, a simple
way in which the Western powers could counter Russia's
"me-too" attitude—the simple but admittedly drastic way of
refraining from further claims to the rights and privileges
of great powers. Then, having adopted a policy of abnegation, they would be in a strong strategic position to demand

similar selflessness from Russia. But as long as the United States and Britain act on the theory that they are entitled to special treatment in world affairs because they are great powers, they must not be surprised to find Russia following the same course. As it is, Russia's claims have already had the effect of enforcing a degree of abnegation on the part of other great powers. For example, when Russia in 1945 demanded a UN trusteeship over Tripolitania, Britain, rather than have Russia receive one of Italy's African colonies, refrained from pressing its demand, with the result that the Italian peace treaty of 1947 left the disposal of Italy's colonies to further consideration by the Council of Foreign Ministers. If that body fails to arrive at a decision within a year, it must refer the matter to the General Assembly of the United Nations and abide by its recommendation.

2. RUSSIA AND INTERNATIONAL ORGANIZATION

Russia's determination to be treated as a great power is reflected in its attitude toward international organization. So far as can be determined, the Russians are just as genuinely interested as other nations in the success of the United Nations. They have persistently contended, however, that since a primary function of the UN is to prevent military aggression and assure the security of all nations, those members of the UN which bore the brunt of winning the war, and must now bear the principal responsibility for preserving the peace, should be vested with special authority as compared with smaller nations which do not possess the requisite military and industrial resources. From the Russian point of view it is not only logical, but essential, that the great powers—a category to which Russia only reluctantly agreed to admit France and China—should have the final say about all arrangements concerned with security by having the right of veto in the Security Council, the organ the Russians regard as the keystone of the UN. Any attempt by other nations to divest the great powers of the veto, as Australia and Cuba repeatedly proposed, or to whittle it down with respect to certain matters, as Bernard M. Baruch urged in the case of punishment of violations of the proposed convention for control of atomic energy, is viewed by the Russians as a direct threat both to its newly asserted position of great power and to the practical capacity of the UN to assure the security of its members.

The veto is also important to Russia because, without the veto, it might be repeatedly outvoted on issues affecting its security. The experience of Russia at the 1946 Paris Peace Conference, where decisions on a number of occasions were taken by majority vote, and in the General Assembly of the UN, where the great powers have no veto, has indicated that, at the present time at least, Russia could not muster more than the five votes of the Ukrainian and Byelorussian republics, and the Slav countries, Poland, Czechoslovakia, and Yugoslavia, in support of its proposals, out of a total membership of fifty-five nations. Difficult as the Russians, unaccustomed to political opposition at home, have found this situation in the General Assembly, they would regard it as intolerable in the Security Council, which must decide on questions susceptible of leading to war, and thus of endangering the security of Russia.

It is security which, in the opinion of the Russians, is the *raison d'être* of international organization. Their interest in other aspects of the work of the UN and in the specialized international agencies clustered around the UN is in direct ratio to the benefit that may accrue to Russia. The Russians have shown interest in the World Health Organization—as they had in the health work of the League of Nations during the inter-war years—and in the Narcotics Commission. For months they were cool to plans for economic reconstruction of Europe discussed in the Economic and Social Council, suspecting they might camouflage an attempt at formation of a United States of Europe which would exclude or even threaten Russia, but finally in March 1947 they agreed to the formation of a European Economic Commission. They have also taken an attitude of aloofness toward agencies which, without offering Russia much aid, might in one way or another invoke its membership as justification for inquiry into its internal affairs—such as the International Bank and the International Fund set up at Bretton Woods, and the Civil Aviation Organization. They have indicated no desire to take part in the work of UNESCO, apparently because of fear that this organization might be used by the Western nations as a channel for propagation of their ideas in the U.S.S.R. At the same time the Russians have indicated a growing interest in the General Assembly, which they had at first regarded as an unnecessary appendix to the Security Council, and have taken every opportunity to use this "town meeting" of the world as a forum for the presentation of their ideas on controversial subjects such as disarmament and treatment of dependent peoples, as well as for criticisms of the views of the Western powers on these subjects.

3. A WEAK GREAT POWER

Russia, however, is not only a great power which will continue to insist on being treated like the United States and Britain; it is also—and this perhaps has not been sufficiently understood in the Western world—a weak great power. As has already been pointed out, Russia has at its disposal vast resources of man power and strategic raw materials, and is in a geographic position to decentralize its industries in such a way as to reduce the country's vulnerability to the atomic bomb. Yet it is twenty-five to fifty years behind the United States in many aspects of industrial production, and it suffers from the intrinsic weakness of being a landlocked coun-

try without facilities for the creation of a large-scale navy
—a weakness that can be alleviated but not altogether overcome by the future development of an air force and of jet-
propelled weapons. The size of Russia's large and still growing population as compared with that of the United States
has caused some alarmists to assume that, because the Russians can raise a large land army, they constitute an insuperable danger.

One must not forget, however, that it is not the size of a
population, but also and especially the degree of its skills and
aptitudes, which determines the role it may play in world
affairs in this age of industrial warfare. Russia has the poten-
tialities of becoming a great power comparable to the United
States, but the potential must not be confused with the
actual. Russia is now developing industrially, but the United
States, which has already reached the highest stage of industrial production in the world, is not standing still, and unless this country abandons scientific research or succumbs to
political and economic paralysis the margin of difference now
existing between Russia and the United States may be expected to persist for years to come.

It is because the Soviet leaders are fully aware of Russia's
weakness as a great power when compared with the United
States and the British Commonwealth of Nations combined,
that they remain concerned about the attitude the Western
nations may take toward Russia. The picture of the "scared
men in the Kremlin" drawn by some writers is a caricature
in the sense that the Soviet leaders, who have shown themselves ruthless and undaunted by adversity at home, are not
apt to become jittery when confronted by danger abroad.
But it has an element of truth in the sense that the Russians
remain genuinely convinced that the struggle against Nazism
and Fascism is not over, and that it is therefore dangerous
for Russia to relax vigilance—while at the same time aware
that reconstruction requires a certain measure of relaxation.

Constant vilification of the Western powers by the Soviet press and radio is a measure of defense rather than attack. To most Americans and Britishers the military defeat of Germany and Japan was equivalent to the defeat of Axis ideas and practices. This view is not shared by the Russians, who believe that the roots of Nazism and Fascism remain very much alive, and that some groups in all countries outside of the U.S.S.R. are prepared to foster their growth because of hostility toward the Soviet system. The Russians, for example, have contended that the Americans and British delayed thoroughgoing measures of denazification in their zones of Germany in the hope of aligning former Nazis and conservatives on their side for ultimate opposition to Russia—while the Western allies have taken the view that the creation in the Russian-controlled zone of Germany of the Socialist Unity party, combining Socialists and Communists, was designed by Moscow to implant Communism throughout Germany. The Russians have also claimed that the Big Three pledge at Yalta that they would assist "the peoples liberated from the domination of Nazi Germany and the peoples of the former Axis satellite states of Europe to solve by democratic means their pressing political and economic problems" has served the interest of native Fascist elements in some of the countries of Eastern Europe and the Balkans who, taking advantage of democratic procedures, have tried to challenge Communist-controlled or Communist-influenced régimes which the Russians regard as "democratic" or "progressive." The Russians have carried their intolerance of political opposition at home over into their relations with neighboring countries, arguing that the existence of native "Fascist" elements is a menace to the security of Russia and, in effect, of the world. They have sharply questioned the intervention of the United States and Britain in Hungary, Bulgaria, Romania, Poland, and Yugoslavia—where the Western powers, under the Yalta agreement, have insisted on "the earliest possible establishment through free elections of governments responsive to the will of the people"—on the ground that opposition groups like that of Mikolajczyk in Poland or Maniu in Romania represented "Fascist" tendencies, a phrase used by Moscow with great elasticity to describe all groups opposed to Russia or to native Communists.

4. COMMUNISM AS A WEAPON OF FOREIGN POLICY

From the point of view of Westerners, Russia's efforts to set up and aid "friendly" governments in neighboring countries is only another phase of the revolutionary international activities at one time conducted by the Third International. It is a matter of general knowledge that the Soviet leaders had used the Third International (Comintern) for the dissemination of their ideas abroad, expecting at first that revolutions patterned on their own would occur elsewhere, bringing to power governments sympathetic to their aims. At the height of its influence in the 1920's the Comintern was composed of representatives of Communist parties in fifty-eight countries. Theoretically, the Russian Communist party was only one of the component groups. Actually, however, the Russian Communists from the outset played a dominant role in the Comintern. This was due partly to the fact that the Third International had its headquarters in Moscow, but most of all to the position of the Russian Communist party, the only one which had succeeded in establishing and maintaining political control of a country—and a country that was also a great power.

The success of the Russian Communist party, as compared with the relative weakness of Communist groups in other nations, endowed it with enormous prestige in the eyes of Communists throughout the world. The political, economic, and social system established by that party in Russia became for all Communists, irrespective of their nationality, the prototype of what a Communist (or, as Stalin still calls it, a socialist) state should ultimately be. In this sense the Russian Communist party, although representing a country far less advanced industrially than, for example, Germany or the United States, exercised a determining influence on the policies of other Communist parties, which unquestioningly followed the "party-line" laid down in Russia. Moscow became the Mecca of Communists throughout the world.

The proclaimed object of the Third International, as set forth in its program, was to replace world capitalist economy by a world system of Communism through force and violence. Its supreme organ of authority was the World Congress, which met annually in the first years of its existence, always in Moscow, but after 1924 assembled only twice—in 1928 and 1935. Between sessions the World Congress delegated its powers to an elected Executive Committee of fifty-nine members. Of the ten members then composing the *Politbureau,* steering committee of the Russian Communist party, two—Stalin, Secretary-General of the party, and Andrei Zhdanov, at that time secretary of the party's Central Committee and chief of its propaganda section—were members of the Executive Committee of the Third International. The decisions of the Executive Committee were binding on all Communist parties represented in the Comintern, as well as on individual Communists throughout the world. The Russian Communist party, like other member groups, contributed dues to the Third International. It was difficult to prove that the Comintern received financial aid and other support from the Soviet government, but since it did receive financial and other support from the Russian Communist party it would have been splitting hairs to say that the Third International had no connection with the Kremlin—as was often asserted by Soviet spokesmen when Moscow was accused by other countries of backing the activities of the Comintern.

With the fiasco of revolutionary movements in Europe and Asia in the 1920's, the death of Lenin in 1924, the gradual eclipse of Trotsky, advocate of "permanent revolution," and the emergence of Stalin, who was determined to concentrate Russia's resources on "building socialism in one country" instead of dissipating them on revolutionary activities, the Third International was relegated to the background, although it retained its importance as a rallying-point for the Communists of other countries, many of whom received their training in Moscow. The Third International, under the influence of the Russian Communists, acquiesced in Stalin's thesis. This indefinite postponement of world revolution was denounced by Trotsky and his followers as unwarranted surrender to capitalism and betrayal of Lenin's ideas. The Third International, however, turned its back on Trotskyism, and became a mouthpiece of Stalinism. In spite of this, factional disputes within the Russian Communist party were duplicated in Communist parties throughout the world, which split up into Stalinists, Trotskyists, and other splinter groups.

As more and more nations established diplomatic and trade relations with the Soviet government, culminating in recognition by the United States in 1933, and the world's spotlight shifted from the menace of Russia to that of Germany, the Soviet leaders were no longer under such pressure as in the civil war years to rely solely on the support of Communist parties abroad. Instead, parallel to the reconciliation with non-party elements at home, they began to urge the cooperation of all "democratic" forces against Fascism, and the creation of a "Popular Front," especially on the question of Spain. In this Popular Front Communists were ordered to work with all other anti-Fascist and anti-Nazi groups, no matter what might be their political views. Communist parties thus switched from denunciation of Socialist and "bourgeois" parties to an urgent demand for formation of Popular Fronts in all countries. This course was probably determined by sincere abhorrence of Fascism and Nazism. But it was at least in part determined by Stalin's desire to strengthen the security of the U.S.S.R. against possible attack by Nazi Germany, and in this sense was dictated by Russia's national interests as much as by the ideological convictions of the Russian Communists. The Communist demand for formation of the Popular Front coincided with the Kremlin's effort to develop closer relations with France, which it had once denounced as a stronghold of the "bourgeoisie," and with France's allies in Eastern Europe. Following Germany's departure from the League of Nations in 1934 after Hitler's rise to power, Russia, on the proposal of France, was admitted to the League, which it had previously denounced as a "league of capitalists," and the Soviet government found Geneva a more universal sounding board for its ideas than the congresses of the Third International.

This combination of Communist hostility toward Nazism and Russia's concern to avoid war with Germany was reflected in the subsequent activities of the Third International. Like the Soviet government, the Comintern denounced Italo-German intervention in Spain during the civil war of 1936, and urged aid to the Spanish Loyalists. When Britain, France, and the United States persisted in a policy of nonintervention in Spain, the Soviet Union—and the Comintern —began to recede from their previous support of the Popular Front, which had disappointed their expectations of a genuine concerted struggle against Nazi Germany. Following the Munich surrender to Hitler in 1938, the Communist parties of the world followed Moscow's lead in denouncing Britain and France for their policy of "appeasement." When Russia's negotiations with the Western powers in the summer of 1939 for a military alliance against Germany failed to bear fruit, the Comintern supported Stalin's decision to conclude a nonaggression pact with Hitler, who had been previously branded as the archenemy of both Communism and Russia. During the first year and a half of World War II, in accordance with the new "line" of the Russian Communist party, Communists in other countries abstained from attacks on Germany, and to some extent collaborated with Nazi groups abroad. At the same time they bitterly criticized Britain and France for waging an "imperialist" war. The moment Germany invaded Russia, however, all Communist parties again switched their "line," since it had then become Russia's national interest to coöperate with Britain and the United States. These abrupt changes of policy have been severely criticized by non-Communists as indicating the hypocrisy and unreliability of Communists. It is difficult to escape the conclusion, however, that Russia was correct in its appraisal of the international situation when it pointed out the danger of Nazi and Fascist activities in Spain, and expressed fear that the Western powers might be willing to let Germany expand eastward provided it left them untouched, especially if this expansion were to weaken the position of Russia and of Communism. If Russia—and the Third International—seemed subject to sudden conversions, the Western powers, too, were not always consistent when they first "appeased" Germany and then, once Hitler, as a result of their concessions in the east, had girded Germany for expansion to the west, belatedly sought Russia's aid against the Nazis in 1939. The conflict between Western nations and Russia about Germany was temporarily suspended after 1941, when West and East worked in much closer collaboration than could have been anticipated in view of their previous divergences. During that period the Soviet government, finding the Third International more of a liability than an asset, officially terminated its existence in 1943.

The Russians, however, had learned the value of propaganda as an instrument of foreign policy, especially for a country like Russia, which lacked some of the other attributes of modern power in a measure comparable to Germany or the United States. The moment the war was over, Russia resumed the use of ideas as weapons—this time not through an international Communist organization, but by aiding directly or indirectly the activities of Communists and other Leftist groups in neighboring countries intent on carrying out internal changes similar to those effected by the Bolsheviks in Russia a quarter of a century before. Russians, however, had learned, especially from the fiasco of the Finnish Communist régime they had sponsored in 1939, that the conditions of Russia in 1917 may not be exactly duplicated elsewhere, and that the ideas formulated by Russian leaders on the basis of Marxist principles as applied to Russia may not prove applicable to other peoples unless they are carefully adapted to local circumstances. Russia's ideological influence on neighboring countries has unquestionably been greatly strengthened by its military power—which, if not comparable to that of the United States, is incomparably superior to that of the rest of Europe—and by the advantages Russia offers for barter trade in the post-war period of economic readjustment. But its influence is due primarily to the interest aroused by the actual operation of the Soviet system. In this respect Stalin proved right in assuming that, once Russia had succeeded in "building socialism" at home, it would exercise far greater influence than if it persisted in stirring up revolutions abroad. Contrary to fears expressed in 1919 about the threat of Communism to Western industrial nations, Soviet doctrines have appealed primarily to backward agrarian countries which are struggling with the problem of reconverting their economies to modern industrial conditions, and wonder whether the experience of Russia, shorn if possible of the excesses of political dictatorship, is not better suited to their needs than that of the Western nations.

5. COMMUNIST—OR RUSSIAN?—DYNAMISM

What the Western nations, which would like to enjoy a breathing space after their wartime exertions, find most harassing about the Communists in all countries is that they seem never to weary of action, and, having won one objective, press on without pause to the next, or having failed to win by one method turn energetically to another. This dynamism may be inherent in the tenets of Communist faith and in Communist technique. But one wonders whether any new movement of revolt against established institutions and values may not be similarly dynamic—whether the early Christians may not have seemed equally harassing to imperial Rome, or the French revolutionaries of 1789 to the monarchs of Europe. Although the Communists give the impression of being "monolithic" and impregnable to internal dissension, they actually display as many divergences as any other group of believers in a given doctrine, and do not wholly escape the influence of the national environment in which they function. Even in Russia, where the Soviet dictatorship has succeeded in maintaining iron discipline over the party as well as the nation, the cleavages on foreign policy familiar to Czarist times have reappeared, causing a recurring tug of war between those who favor some degree of cooperation with the Western world, and those who oppose it, between those who in our terms would be regarded as internationalists and those who would be regarded as isolationists.

Like many other doctrinaires, the Communists are most intransigent toward those who share some of their beliefs and want to achieve some of their objectives, but are determined to do so by parliamentary methods. In consequence, the most bitter ideological struggle in the post-war world promises to be the struggle between Communists and Socialists, with the Communists bent on absorbing the Socialists, or at least influencing them to accept their ultimate objectives. This situation is illustrated by the difficulties experienced by the British Labor government in its efforts to arrive at a workable agreement with Russia, and by the creation, in the Russia-controlled zone of Germany, under Moscow's sponsorship, of the Socialist Unity party, designed to achieve the fusion of Communists and Socialists. The majority of European Socialists find it impossible to accept the political dictatorship and arbitrary disregard of the rights of the individual practiced in Russia, and countenanced by Communist parties abroad. Yet many of them admit that some of the most important economic and social reforms now urged by Communists outside Russia had been envisaged in Socialist programs before the second World War, although they had not yet been translated into practice by "reformist" methods. The Socialists, as well as groups that can be described as liberals, are therefore faced with the grave dilemma of either coöperating with the Communists at the risk of having eventually to subscribe to a system of political dictatorship, or opposing them, at the risk of retarding reforms and being denounced by the Communists as "reactionaries."

The questions most frequently asked about Russia's foreign policy are: Is it imperialistic? Is it revolutionary? Is it defensive? Is it aggressive? The most accurate answer to these questions would be that Russia's foreign policy is both imperialistic and revolutionary, both defensive and aggressive. There is no reason to assume until proved by experience that Marxism is synonymous with imperialism, and that a country situated under conditions other than those existing in Russia during the past two decades would, if ruled by Communists, necessarily have Russia's great-power aspirations, which existed under the Czars as they do under the Soviets. The policy of Lenin, anti-imperialist and anti-Western, may have been more representative of Communist ideals than that of Stalin, who has superimposed nationalism on Marxism, and has reconciled to his own satisfaction sympathy for the downtrodden colonial peoples with the demand on behalf of Russia for special rights and privileges at their expense. But, again, such reconciliation of apparently conflicting elements is not characteristic of Russia alone. Other great powers have found nothing incompatible between democracy and imperialism, between concern for human welfare and the urge to acquire political influence or economic resources in other countries. And if it should turn out that other Communist-controlled governments, like that of Russia, adapt themselves to the traditional concepts of foreign policy of the nations over which they rule, then the international aspect of Communism may come to be obliterated by the recrudescence of nationalism, as Trotsky had anticipated and feared. In fact, seasoned observers of the European scene believe that since any form of effective socialism implies controls over at least portions of national economy, the establishment of socialist—let alone Communist—governments in a number of countries might conceivably spell a period of extreme nationalism, contrary to the previous expectation that socialism (or communism) would be synonymous with expansion of internationalism.

What marks out Russia today is not so much that it is either uncommonly nationalistic or uncommonly propagandistic in its foreign policy, but that it is employing at one and the same time, with considerable efficiency, the methods of nineteenth-century diplomacy and twentieth-century propaganda, and that in foreign affairs, as in domestic affairs, it is telescoping developments which in Western countries were spread over centuries. As a result, its impact on the world has all the force of a delayed explosion. The complex skein of old nationalist aspirations and modern ideological concepts runs through all of Russia's policies on international political and economic problems.

7. Russia's Political Stake in World Affairs

As pointed out in the preceding chapter, Russia has for at least two centuries played an active role in the affairs of Europe, Asia, and the Near and Middle East. Again and again it has swung from one continent to the other, becoming more active in Europe when it felt hard-pressed by other great powers in the Middle East and Asia, and turning to Asia as it encountered resistance to its objectives in Europe. Just as Germany once planned its military preparations in terms of a "two-front" war, and the United States in World War II organized its naval strength for a "two-ocean" conflict, Russia had to take into consideration the protection of far-flung frontiers in two continents. Owing to the lack of an adequate overland transportation system, this has meant that Russia could not undertake to wage war in Europe unless it had made arrangements to safeguard its territory in Asia, as it did in 1941 by concluding a nonaggression pact with Japan on the eve of the German invasion; and, conversely, it could not undertake to wage war in Asia unless it felt secure from attack on the European border, as in 1945 when it waited for the defeat of Germany before joining the Western powers in their struggle against Japan. Preeminently a land power, Russia has traditionally feared attack by naval powers—once Britain and France, now the United States. For centuries an economically backward na-

tion, it has feared attack by advanced industrial nations—
once Germany and Japan, now the United States.

1. FACING BOTH WEST AND EAST

Russia's relations with the three main geographic areas
where its political interests are concentrated have been
shaped in considerable measure by its attitude toward the
peoples of these areas. Russian leaders from Ivan the Terrible and Peter the Great to Lenin and Stalin have been
keenly aware that Russia was technically inferior to the
Western world—which in our time includes the United
States. This made them eager to have Russia learn all the
lessons it could from more advanced nations, and at the same
time apprehensive that through inefficiency or inexperience
they might fall short of this goal and incur the contempt and
hostility of Westerners. The fear of being made either a
laughingstock or a target for armed attack has caused the
Russians to adopt an outward façade of Westernization
whenever subjected to the scrutiny of foreigners, while inwardly rejecting Western culture as alien to the Russian
spirit—somewhat as the Arabs, for example, profess to despise
the very progress they want to achieve. The Westernization
forced on a still Byzantine Russia by Peter the Great at the
end of the seventeenth century left an inner cleavage which
in varying forms has persisted into our own times. This is a
cleavage between a group, hitherto in a minority, who
favored the adoption of Western ideas, whether those of
Voltaire or Karl Marx, and the masses of the Russian people,
physically isolated from Europe, and strongly susceptible
to doctrines that combined isolationism and nationalism with
a messianic sense of national mission, whether Pan-Slavism
in the 1870's or international communism in the 1920's. The
Bolshevik revolution brought all these deep-seated trends to a
dramatic culmination, forcing Russia to undergo a highly

accelerated process of industrialization, and at the same time to forego the development of political institutions which in the West had owed their flowering to the material progress fostered by the Industrial Revolution.

While Russia remained for the most part outside the main stream of Western civilization, it was profoundly affected by the political ideas of the French—both of the French Revolution as imprinted on Napoleonic France, and of the Paris Commune of 1871—and of the Germans, especially the philosophy of Hegel and, of course, the theories of Karl Marx. The Russians have had and still have great admiration for French culture and German industrial skill. Russia drew heavily on German administrative talent under the Czars; also on German technical knowledge both after World War I, when defeated Germany alone of the Western countries did not treat Russia as an outlaw, and since the end of World War II, when the Russians, under the head of reparations, have utilized not only German tools and machinery but German technicians and skilled workers as well. Germany, however, under Hitler, as under the Kaiser, has coveted the food and raw material resources of the Russians, and has sought to obtain them by force. If it had not been for this, and for the German feeling of racial superiority toward Slavs, it has sometimes seemed that the two peoples whose characters are in many respects complementary might have achieved a high degree of fruitful coöperation. This cannot be said of Russia's traditional relations with Britain, which under the Czars as under the Soviets has been regarded as an actual or potential opponent at all key points of Russian interest—in the Baltic, at the Dardanelles, in the Near and Middle East. Although Russia has again and again fought on the same side as Britain, in the Napoleonic wars as in the two world wars of the twentieth century, it has distrusted Britain, traditionally denounced as "perfidious Albion," and has been little affected by British concepts of political democracy. For this reason, if for no other, the Russians have been hostile to any British plans, such as that championed by Churchill, for a United States of Europe that would exclude Russia but presumably include or be closely linked to Britain—especially since the Russians believe that they have more of a stake in the European continent than the British, and a clearer perception of the main forces that are shaping it today.

While Russia's relations with Western Europe have been alternately affected by admiration for its technical achievements and revulsion against Westernism, its relations with Eastern Europe, even with Poland, for centuries an outpost of Roman Catholicism and Western culture, have been relatively free from a feeling of inferiority. This was due in part to the heritage of Slav traditions which the Russians shared with the Czechs, Slovaks, Serbs, and Bulgarians, and in part to the conspicuous role Russia played in the nineteenth century in the liberation of the Slav peoples belonging to the Orthodox Church from Ottoman rule and the final withdrawal of Turkey from Europe. Through the Pan-Slav movement, Russia became intimately associated with the political aspirations of the Southern Slavs, an association which has been renewed with fresh vigor since World War II through Russia's close coöperation with Yugoslavia and Bulgaria. Sympathy for the Slav peoples of Eastern Europe and the Balkans has also colored Russia's attitude toward the three powers in Europe which at one time or another attempted to coerce or subjugate the Slavs—Turkey, the Austro-Hungarian Empire, and Germany under the Kaiser as well as under Hitler.

In its relations with the peoples of the Near and Middle East and of Asia, most of whom are either at the political and economic level of Russia in 1917, or lag behind in varying degrees, Russia has alternately acted like one of the advanced Western powers, claiming special rights and privileges of an imperialistic character in China and Iran, and again as one of the "colonial" countries oppressed by Western "capitalist exploiters," refusing to have any part of the heritage of Western empire. Because Russia itself partakes of two civilizations—the advanced industrialism of the West and the backward agrarianism of Asia—it is both a bridge between the two continents and a microcosm, within its own borders, of their complex political, economic, and spiritual development at different historical levels. The seemingly chameleon-like way in which Russia assumes one role or the other in the East, and the support it has given to the demands of colonial peoples, have been denounced in the West as a mere propaganda device for attack on the United States and Britain. Actually, however, Russia, which itself has millions of Asiatics among its population, is both genuinely concerned with the destiny of Asia and conceivably more aware than the Western nations of the problems and aspirations of peoples whose experience it has shared.

2. EASTERN EUROPE AS A BUFFER

In Europe the focal points of Russia's interest since World War II are Germany and the Danubian basin. When Germany surrendered unconditionally on V–E Day, Russia, although gravely weakened by terrible losses of man power and material, stood at the highest peak of power and influence it had achieved in Europe, except at the close of the Napoleonic wars. The military defeat of Germany and the territorial losses imposed on it at Potsdam have also opened a new phase in the struggle that has raged for over a hundred years concerning disposal of nations in Eastern Europe and the Balkans which at one time or another formed part of four great empires whose interests conflicted in that area—the Ottoman, Russian, German, and Austro-Hungarian empires. Of the thirteen nations involved, all of which had achieved independence by 1919 only to lose it in several instances during World War II—Finland, Estonia, Latvia, Lithuania, Poland, Hungary, Czechoslovakia, Austria, Romania, Yugoslavia, Bulgaria, Albania, and Greece—all have found themselves objects of direct concern on the part of Russia, the only empire on the European continent that survived the two world wars.

While Russia is interested in the economic resources of its neighbors in Eastern Europe and the Balkans, which can usefully supplement its own, especially during the difficult years of reconstruction when it is suffering from an acute shortage of consumer goods, and has historical affinities with the Slav peoples of this area, its policy of trying to establish "friendly" governments along its western border is determined primarily by strategic considerations. The Russians may not have paid much attention to Mackinder and Haushofer, but geopoliticians in this country have pointed out that the only practicable way of attacking by land "The Heartland"—which to Mackinder meant Russia—is through the eastern border territories, which offer few points of natural defense. These border territories have both isolated Russia from the Western world (and this long before the concept of the *cordon sanitaire* had been propounded at the Paris Peace Conference of 1919 by a French official), and provided a traditional highway for invasion of Russia from the West. Some Western observers, analyzing Russia's postwar activities in Eastern Europe and the Balkans, have thought that the object of the Russians was to create a base in that area for eventual westward expansion into Europe, possibly as far as the Atlantic. It seems more probable that its chief purpose is to make sure that neighboring countries can never be used against Russia either by a remilitarized Germany or by embattled Western powers which have enlisted Germany on their side. At the same time, Moscow has lost no opportunity to foster Communist movements abroad.

It should be recalled that at the Peace Conference of 1919 the Big Four of that time agreed to prevent Germany from entering into relations with Russia and to build up Poland as a barrier against Russia and a check on Germany. In its efforts to foster the creation, along its Western border, of "friendly" governments, the Kremlin has used every weapon in the armory of a modern world power. Appeals on ideological grounds, economic inducements, military pressure, political suasion, have all been tried, in varying mixtures thought best adapted to local conditions and national temperaments. The influence of Communism has been blended with that of the Russian Orthodox Church; and Pan-Slavism, revived during the war as a powerful antidote to Pan-Germanism, has been invoked to rally the Slavs of Poland, Czechoslovakia, Yugoslavia, and Bulgaria to the support of Russia. For strategic reasons Ruthenia was acquired from Czechoslovakia in 1946. What Moscow has been building in Eastern Europe is more like a *cordon sanitaire* of its own than a base for westward expansion. In this task it has enlisted the coöperation of political leaders in neighboring countries who during the interwar years had lived in Moscow and worked with the Comintern—notably Boleslav Bierut of Poland, Marshal Tito of Yugoslavia, Matyas Rakosi of Hungary, Georgi Dimitrov of Bulgaria, and Klement Gottwald of Czechoslovakia. It would be unrealistic, however, to assume that these men and others associated with them are mere stooges of Russia, unconcerned with the welfare and problems of the peoples they govern. Bierut, for example, was long active in Poland in opposing the pre-1939 government, and during the war participated in the resistance movement against Germany.

Russia's policy has had mixed results. As of May 1948, the governments of all countries along Russia's western border were Communist-controlled. To the surprise of the Western world, Czechoslovakia, regarded as a bulwark of democracy and free private enterprise in Eastern Europe, cast 40 per cent of the votes in the 1946 elections for the Communist party—the highest Communist vote registered in the entire area. In February 1948 the Communists seized control of the government.

Many reasons explain the large vote cast for the Communists in the one country of Eastern Europe which had had notable experience with political democracy. The Czechoslovak state, since its formation after World War I, had been riven by conflicts between its component national groups—notably between the Czechs and the Sudeten Germans. The Socialist party, which under more favorable circumstances might have proved a bulwark against Communism, was deeply split between right-wing and left-wing elements. The Munich settlement had left in its wake profound disillusionment with the West; and even Czechs who were bitterly opposed to Communist doctrines believed that their country had to maintain close ties with Russia as the only reliable safeguard against German resurgence.

The sources of at least part of Russia's influence in Yugoslavia and Bulgaria are also not difficult to ascertain. Whatever may be the political character of the régime in Moscow, Serbs and Bulgarians nurture a deep feeling of gratitude to Russia for its assistance in their liberation from the Turks in the nineteenth century, and have a closer affinity for Russian ideas and practices than for those of the West, although they are not all by any means prepared to tolerate political dictatorship or agrarian collectivization. In Poland, which has historic reasons for hostility to the Russians, whether under the Czars or under the Soviets, Russia's influence through Polish Communist leaders trained in Moscow has in considerable measure been counteracted by unabated Polish nationalism, by the persistent individualism of the Poles, and by the deeply rooted traditions of the Catholic Church. In Hungary and Romania, which do not have the links of either Slav kinship or religious affiliation with Russia, the Russians have encountered determined opposition on the part of political groups which in the past had identified themselves with the interests of the peasants, notably the Smallholders' party in Hungary and the Peasant party of Julius Maniu in Romania. While in Romania the presence of King Michael, beloved by his people and for that reason respected by the Russians, has prevented an open conflict, in Hungary the Russians, spurred by the realization that they would have to evacuate the country three months after ratification of the peace treaty signed in February 1947, have sought to suppress recalcitrant elements of the Smallholders' party. Russia's political intervention in liberated countries and former Axis satellites east of Germany has brought mounting criticism from the United States and Britain, which have charged the Soviet government with repeated violations of the Big Three pledges at Yalta concerning free elections, and with attempts to suppress democracy and institute Communist dictatorship. The Soviet government has retorted by accusing the Western powers of giving political and financial support to "reactionary" or "Fascist" elements opposed to what it considers as "progressive" or "democratic" régimes established under its tutelage. Moscow's contention that Fascism is still a force to be reckoned with is confirmed by non-Russian observers—for example the London *Economist*, which in May 1947 stated that "the symptoms of a Fascist revival are undoubtedly visible" in that area, adding that "the social bases of a Fascist revival are the dispossessed bureaucracy and commercial class and the discontented peasantry," together with some of the leaders of the Catholic Church. The resulting clash between West and East has wiped out the already precarious middle groups in Eastern Europe and the Balkans, and has forced liberals either to the Right or to the Left.

A similar situation, only in reverse, developed in Greece, traditionally regarded as within the British sphere of influence, where Britain, during and after the war, rendered military and financial assistance to Greek governments denounced by the Russians as "Fascist" and "anti-democratic" in their efforts to suppress armed opposition from the Left. This Left opposition, according to some Greeks, was furnished arms, training, and funds by neighboring Slav countries, Yugoslavia and Bulgaria, allegedly aided, in turn, by Moscow. In the view of pro-government Greeks, the guerrilla warfare fostered by the Slav countries had the twofold purpose of overthrowing the existing government in Athens established following the foreign-supervised elections of 1946 and replacing it with a Communist régime, and of detaching from Greece strategic territories which were to be incorporated into Yugoslavia and Bulgaria. These contentions were denied by Leftist spokesmen outside the government, notably former Foreign Minister John Sofianopoulos, who argued that the Greek guerrillas were for the most part inspired not by Slav or Communist propaganda but by genuine opposition to the political and economic practices of the Athens régime, and were merely seeking to bring about a broader coalition government capable of inspiring general confidence, restoring internal order, undertaking the country's economic reconstruction, and achieving reconciliation with Greece's Balkan neighbors and with Russia, while maintaining friendly relations with Britain and the United States. The United Nations Balkans Investigation Commission, after an inquiry in Greece, came to the conclusion that while Greek guerrillas had received aid from neighboring countries, particularly Yugoslavia and Bulgaria, internal conditions in Greece were also responsible for the existing unrest. It is important to bear in mind that Greece, a non-Slav country bordered by Slav peoples, had been engaged in previous bitter contests with its Balkan neighbors during the Balkan wars of 1912-13.

3. THE TRUMAN DOCTRINE

Without entering into the intricate complexities of Greece's internal politics, it suffices to say that, while the United Nations Commission was investigating charges and countercharges about Greek guerrilla warfare, Britain, faced with a rapidly deteriorating economic situation at home, announced that it would be forced to terminate its financial aid to Greece on March 31, 1947—at the very time when aid previously rendered through UNRRA was also drawing to a close. Fearing that Greece, deprived of outside assistance, would become easy prey to pressure from Russia and from the Balkan Slav countries, and that Communism would become entrenched at one of the focal strategic points in the eastern Mediterranean, the United States intervened with an offer of financial aid to Greece, to be used in part for economic reconstruction and in part for the strengthening of Greek military forces. In his address of March 12 to Congress, which has been compared to enunciation of the Monroe Doctrine, President Truman justified American aid to Greece on the ground that Britain was being forced to withdraw its financial assistance, that lack of such assistance might plunge Greece into chaos, but, above all, "that it must be the policy of the United States to support free peoples who are resisting attempted subjugation by armed minorities or by outside pressures." Although Mr. Truman did not explicitly name Russia as the source of the danger he believed to be threatening Greece, he stated bluntly that "the peoples of a number of countries of the world have recently had totalitarian regimes forced upon them against their will" —then naming Poland, Romania, and Bulgaria. Irrespective of the questions whether or not the United States is to become heir of the British Empire, or whether American aid should be rendered to Greece unilaterally or through United Nations channels, the main issue raised by what has become known as the Truman Doctrine was that of a direct challenge by "free peoples," as represented and supported by the United States, to "totalitarian regimes" as represented and supported by the U.S.S.R.

The prolonged and often embittered debate about the character of governments in Eastern Europe and the Balkans reflects the fundamental controversy between Russia and the Western powers about the meaning of "democracy." From the point of view of the United States and Britain, free elections mean unrestricted participation by all parties, except avowed Nazis or Fascists, in elections similar in form to those familiar in Western countries. The emphasis is on civil liberties and on the freedoms usually associated in the West with political institutions. From the point of view of Russia democracy means acceptance by all groups of the population of economic and social concepts and practices which the Russians regard as essential for the creation of governments "friendly" to the U.S.S.R. This means emphasis on the struggle against local "vested interests," native or foreign, socialization of national resources, introduction of "socialist" rights and duties—not necessarily carbon copying of the Russian system, but rather its adaptation to local circumstances. In fact, in many instances, local Communists, in the economic and social programs they advocate or carry out, have not gone much beyond the programs urged, but as yet not put into effect, by socialists in that area before World War II—with the all-important difference that the Communists have not hesitated to set aside the political rights and civil liberties previously enjoyed by individuals whenever that seemed necessary to achieve their ends.

The West-East debate about democracy has been complicated by the vast differences in actual conditions and historical experience between Eastern Europe and the Western world—differences that are not always sufficiently recognized in the United States and Britain. For example, the question is often raised whether Mikhailovitch was really a traitor, as claimed by Tito, or a patriot as claimed by his adherents, and, if the latter, whether his execution was not a gross act of injustice. The most cogent answer one can give is that, so far as can be ascertained, both Mikhailovitch and Tito were patriots, but while the former sought to conserve the forces of Yugoslavia, very much as the Czechs conserved their forces during the German occupation, Tito favored a dynamic struggle against the Germans, irrespective of the losses it might involve. Mikhailovitch did not consider himself a traitor to Serbia, but he did collaborate with the Germans. Moreover, by the standards of desperate guerrilla warfare in which "he who is not with us is against us" he had inflicted grave injury on Tito, and from Tito's point of view deserved to be punished. Similarly, throughout this area where the unsparing cruelty of the Nazis provoked equally unsparing resistance, and collaboration with the enemy, or even mere acquiescence in his misdeeds, was a mortal sin, there is as yet little room for that spirit of tolerance toward political opposition, from whatever source it stems, with which we are familiar in the West. Under those circumstances it might have been wiser for the Western powers not to have insisted on the holding of elections before the fires of wartime political conflict had subsided. Moreover, it has been easy for Russia and its supporters abroad to point out that governments of a nondemocratic character are tolerated by Western powers in other areas—such as the Franco régime in Spain, the Kuomintang régime of Chiang Kai-shek in China, which, according to Secretary of State Marshall, has been dominated by reactionaries and militarists, and many of the régimes of Latin America, most conspicuously that of Perón in Argentina. And ideological controversy frequently obscures what are fundamentally strategic conflicts, as in Greece, between the land power of Russia and the naval power of Britain and the United States.

4. ECONOMIC PREREQUISITES FOR DEMOCRACY

No matter what pledges are made about democracy, however, or what institutions are established to meet the demands of the Western powers, democracy in the Western sense cannot be expected to flourish in Eastern Europe and the Balkans unless economic and social conditions are fundamentally improved. Most of Russia's neighbors in Europe are today at an economic and social level comparable to that of Russia in 1917. Finland, Czechoslovakia, and, to a lesser degree, Poland, had made notable progress toward industrialization before 1939—and it is significant that although the first of these was among the Axis satellites, Russia has treated all three since the war with marked respect for their economic achievements. By contrast Romania, Yugoslavia, Bulgaria, and to a lesser extent Hungary, which has developed light and extractive industries, are still primarily agricultural countries which in the past have exported food and certain raw materials, paying in this way for the consumer goods and machinery they were as yet unable to produce within their own borders. The pre-war standard of living of this region (sharply reduced by war destruction) was dangerously low, as indicated by an inadequate level of nutrition, and the resulting high incidence of deficiency diseases, such as pellagra, anemia, scurvy, and rickets, as well as a high rate of infant mortality. To raise their standard of living these countries would have to increase materially their production of food. The breaking-up of large estates which, except for areas of Hungary, had been carried out on an extensive scale during the inter-war years, does not of itself promise solution of the agricultural output problem, as the Russians discovered after they had parceled big estates in 1917—and the Poles are discovering now as they divide up lands seized from the Germans. What is needed is more efficient utilization of land through such measures as scientific crop rotation, use of fertilizer, substitution of modern agricultural machinery for the ancient plows and harrows which too often are still the only tools available to the peasants, land reclamation and drainage, agronomic research, animal breeding stations, and improved methods of marketing agricultural products.

The mere recital of these needs calls to mind the series of reforms which the Soviet government effected between 1933, when peasant resistance to collectivization was ruthlessly suppressed, and the invasion of Russia by Germany eight years later. It is true that in Eastern Europe and the Balkans, where private ownership of land was far more widespread than in Russia before the Bolshevik Revolution, collectivization similar to that undertaken by the Soviet government may prove impracticable; and it is significant that the governments of these countries, even when directly inspired from Moscow, have been cautious about proposing collectivization, and have emphasized their respect for private property provided it is put to social use. Yet Russia's agricultural experience offers a pattern for this area possibly better adapted to its needs than the farming methods developed in Western Europe or the United States under entirely different political and social conditions.

The industrial problems of these countries call for measures in which the experience of Russia may also prove helpful. Owing to the low standard of living throughout this area, the demand for consumer goods was limited to primitive needs for shoes, cheap textiles, paper, soap, sugar, salt, and matches. Poland is the only country of the area which has large resources of coal, increased by the assignment to it at Potsdam of Germany's Silesian coal mines. It can therefore look to the development of large-scale industry, such as Czechoslovakia has successfully developed. Romania and Hungary, however, have important resources of oil; and Yugoslavia has copper, lead, and chromite. The area has considerable resources of water power which have not been sufficiently utilized, and could maintain a variety of consumer goods industries.

The creation of these industries is at present hampered by an acute shortage of skilled labor and supervisory personnel (who for a long time might have to be recruited abroad) and shortage of capital. Conceivably these countries could develop their resources with little or no capital from abroad, by forcing their exports, but this could be done only by decreasing their standard of living still further—as Russia discovered under its series of Five-Year plans. And Russia, it must be recalled, had large resources of gold to pay for the services of foreign technicians and for imported machinery, and could draw on a huge reservoir of man power not available to its small neighbors.

If the countries of Eastern Europe and the Balkans are to emerge in the near future from their backward condition, and create the economic and social climate for democratic political institutions, they must be able to obtain foreign capital and technical assistance. In the past, however, foreign capital has tended to go into extractive industries (American, British, French, and Belgian capital has been invested in the oil wells of Romania, French capital in Yugoslav copper, British in Yugoslav lead), or else it has been offered only on condition that the borrowers purchase armaments in the lending country. This was particularly true of France's loans during the inter-war years to its allies east of Germany—Poland, Czechoslovakia, Romania, and Yugoslavia. What is needed most urgently is capital for the development of industries that could produce consumer goods, raise the standard of living, and incidentally liberate these countries from their previous excessive economic dependence on Germany.

A certain measure of economic progress might be achieved

through economic unification of the countries of this area, as had been repeatedly proposed during the inter-war years in various plans for Danubian union or federation—plans which were in effect seeking to restore the economic advantages offered by the Austro-Hungarian Empire. None of these Danubian plans came to fruition before 1939 because of the network of political conflicts between the great and small nations of Europe which vitiated any attempt at economic coöperation. Projects for such coöperation have again been revived since the war—some in the form of a federation, mostly Slav, that would embrace Yugoslavia, Bulgaria, and possibly Albania, and some for a broader Danubian union that would also include Romania and Hungary. All these projects are linked with greater utilization of the Danube by countries through which it flows. Even if these projects are inspired from Moscow, they should not be automatically rejected by the Western powers, provided they are not discriminatory in nature, and are eventually geared into proposed world arrangements for the liberalization and expansion of world trade.

In the long run, however, the agrarian countries of Eastern Europe and the Balkans will need broader contacts than those offered to them by a Slav or Danubian federation. It is at this point that the possibility of joint undertakings by the United States, Britain, and Russia, possibly under the supervision of the United Nations, for the development of Eastern Europe and the Balkans deserves serious consideration. Russia's present suspicions of the objectives and methods of the Western powers may make such undertakings difficult for the time being. But before we criticize Russia's attitude we must remember that the United States and Britain, in the heyday of their influence in that area, showed little or no interest in the welfare of the native peoples, and were concerned primarily with the short-term advantages to be gained from investments in oil or other raw materials.

The day for foreign investments that disregard the interests of local inhabitants has passed, as many of us have learned from our relations with Latin America. From now on the first test of investments is whether, in the long run, they will benefit the borrowing countries and, by benefiting them, also increase the well-being, and hence the security of the rest of the world. An interesting model for investment favorable to native welfare can be found in the projects sponsored by the Rockefeller brothers in Brazil and Venezuela.

It should not be assumed offhand that the peoples of Eastern Europe and the Balkans, great as is their dependence on Russia for security and certain economic advantages, are irrevocably committed to a purely pro-Russian orientation. On the contrary, their contact with Russian occupation troops has in many cases produced profound disillusionment about both Russia and Communism, and has led to reappraisal of the value of political liberties. The very fact that governments "friendly" to Russia have found it increasingly necessary to resort to force in order to check the opposition, as in Poland and Hungary, is an indication of the growth of that opposition. Russia's policy of drawing neighboring countries into its orbit may have the effect—not anticipated in Moscow —of arousing intense nationalism directed against the influence of all foreign powers, including the U.S.S.R. At the same time, we must not discount the drawing power of Russia's multinational society on the mixed populations of Eastern Europe and the Balkans. For centuries the nations buffeted between the four great empires that once dominated this area have vainly sought to find some way in which they could preserve their heritage of culture, valiantly defended against encroachments by Turks, Austrians, Germans, and Russians, and at the same time achieve a measure of political and economic security. The League of Nations proved a vain hope because of the refusal of the great powers to defend the interests of the small. The United Nations Organization now has an opportunity to succeed where the League failed. But if the small nations should again find themselves at the mercy of the ambitions and conflicts of the great, the possibility must not be excluded that the U.S.S.R. will make a strong bid for the inclusion within its elastic framework of some of its small neighbors, especially those inhabited by Slavs.

5. GERMANY THE KEY IN EUROPE

Moscow, however, is not so much concerned with the fate of its neighbors as with the use that might be made of them by a resurgent Germany hostile to Russia. It is Germany which is the key to Russia's post-war relations with the other nations of the continent. Nazi documents have clearly established that it was Russia—not the Western "plutodemocracies"—which was the principal target of Hitler. The Russians cannot forget his *Mein Kampf* program: "When we talk of more ground and room in Europe, we can in the first place think only of Russia and the border states depending on her." Yet from the outset Soviet spokesmen, Stalin first among them, insisted that a distinction should be drawn between the Nazis and their supporters among big industrialists and Junkers, and other Germans. Non-Russian observers agree that, after the initial period of occupation before V–E Day, when individual Russian soldiers committed acts of murder and looting, often with the avowed desire to avenge personal losses suffered at the hands of the Germans, the Russian military authorities in their zone of Germany limited measures of denazification to the top ranks of the Nazi hierarchy, and left many lesser administrators, factory managers, and others at their posts, irrespective of their previous Nazi affiliations. Instead of seeking to eliminate all persons connected in one way or another with the Nazis—a policy which would have disorganized administrative and industrial activities in the Russian zone—the Russians, once they had purged the Nazi leaders on their black list, vigorously encouraged the organization of groups they regarded as "friendly" by the creation of the Socialist Unity party combining Communists and left-wing Socialists. Had this party succeeded in establishing its control in the Russian zone, it is entirely possible that the Soviet government would have sought its extension to the other three zones of Germany in the hope of promoting the establishment of a central German government sympathetic to the U.S.S.R. This prospect was at one time seriously feared by Russia's Western allies. Another possible alternative that aroused concern in the West was that, failing the creation of a central Socialist Unity government for Germany, Russia might detach its zone from the already truncated state and include it within its federal framework, harnessing the resources, skilled workers, and technicians of the zone to the Russian industrial system. It was thought at that time that, in an effort to win German support, Russia might even repudiate its wartime pledge to Poland, and offer to return to the Germans the eastern German territories assigned, on Russia's demand, to the Poles at Potsdam, pending final determination of Germany's eastern border. The Poles, however, did not believe that it would prove practicable for Russia to retreat from the position it had previously taken on the question of the eastern border. As they see the situation, Russia is determined to turn the tables on Germany by erecting Poland as an eastern outpost to the west, instead of having it remain a western outpost to the east. The Poles are also convinced that a Russian "Munich" would irrevocably shatter the whole structure of the Slav buffer area painstakingly erected by Russia since the war.

Whatever may have been the various alternatives contemplated by Russia, the failure of the Socialist Unity party to win a controlling position in the Russian zone in the 1946 elections, in spite of unstinted Russian aid, and Russia's growing need for capital equipment out of current production in the western zones of Germany, brought about a reconsideration of Russian policy toward Germany. After initial resistance to American and British plans for economic unification of Germany, Russia expressed alarm that the fusion of the Anglo-American zones in January 1947 would exclude it from access to the resources of the Western zones, and became a strong advocate of both economic and political unity for Germany. At the same time the Russians sought to conciliate the Germans by promising them vastly increased industrial production in their zone, and by putting out feelers for negotiations with the Social Democratic party, which they had previously opposed.

During the Moscow conference of 1947 there appeared to be little substantial difference between Russia, the United States, and Britain concerning the need for economic unity of Germany. The Russians, however, looked with suspicion on newly advanced plans in the Western countries for political decentralization and federalization of Germany, contending that these plans were designed to include the western German areas containing the Ruhr coal and the country's principal heavy industries in a western block directed against the U.S.S.R. The Russians also insisted that fundamental changes should be effected in the economic and social composition of German society before political unification was undertaken. In their opinion, the British and Americans had been too mild in their treatment of the big industrialists, the Junkers and the German conservative nationalists who, given favorable circumstances, might once more gird Germany for expansion to the east. Only after Germany has been purged of these elements will it be possible, in the opinion of the Russians, to set up a central German political administration and to permit a relatively high level of industrial production without fear that a centralized government and increased industrial output would be utilized for renewed military preparations.

On the crucial question of the economic future of Germany, Russia has so far been at odds with the Western powers, as revealed by the stalemate reached at the Moscow conference. The Soviet government, confronted by a serious shortage of consumer goods, and aware, from the experience of the past two years, that removal of German factories and machinery to Russia is an unsatisfactory method of increasing its own production, demanded, in addition to the reparations it has already collected in its zone of Germany under the Potsdam agreement, an additional ten billion dollars' worth of reparations out of the current production of the western zones administered by the United States and Britain. The Western powers, especially after the Moscow negotiations, recognized Russia's need for goods to repair the material losses it suffered as a result of the war. They believed, however, that reparations out of current production from the western zones on the scale claimed by Russia—a claim which, in the opinion of Washington and London is in any case contrary to the Potsdam agreement—would jeopardize the economic recovery of Germany, regarded as essential for the recovery of all of Europe. The program proposed by former president Herbert Hoover in February 1947, on the eve of the Moscow conference, stressed the immediate need for relief of the German people at an estimated cost of $475,000,000. This amount was to be made a first charge on the economy of Germany and repaid from any future net German exports (which were to be encouraged by the United States and Britain), taking priority over reparations Germany owes to the countries it conquered and devastated. The issue was thus squarely joined between the Western powers and Russia in terms of German relief and recovery versus further reparations to victims of German conquest.

At the Moscow conference where, instead of pointing out the effects of German destruction on Russia's economy, Foreign Minister Molotov castigated the Western powers, thus arousing their understandable resentment, no substantial progress was made toward breaking the reparations deadlock. Secretary Marshall, however, outlined a formula, repeated in his report to the nation on April 28, 1947, which may contain the seeds of a possible settlement. He said that the United States would be willing to study "the possibility of a limited amount of reparations from current production to compensate for plants, previously scheduled to be removed as reparations to various Allied countries, which it now appears should be left in Germany; it being understood that deliveries from current production are not to increase the financial burden of the occupying powers or to retard the repayment to them of the advances they have made to keep the German economy from collapsing." In other words, provided that removal of factories from Germany was terminated, the United States proposed to combine limited reparations—possibly spread over a long period of years —from current production, with measures to aid the recovery of Germany. This proposal, however, was superseded by the subsequent deadlock at the London conference of November 1947, the creation of Bizonia by Britain and the United States, and growing tension between the Big Four, highlighted by Russia's efforts to force withdrawal of the Western powers from Berlin.

Russia's policy toward countries of Europe bordering on Germany in the north, west, and south, where the Russians cannot directly exercise their influence as they do in Eastern Europe and the Balkans, is determined primarily by the attitude of these countries toward Germany, which has become the litmus test, for Moscow, of their attitude toward Russia as well. Any attempt to tolerate German groups which might conceivably be willing to fight Russia, or to increase German productive resources without adequate

Allied military and political safeguards, or to establish a "bloc" of western nations that might include the western areas of Germany arouses an automatically hostile reflex in Moscow. Equally disturbing, from the Soviet government's point of view, are attempts to create a socialist bloc—composed of the Labor government of Britain, the Socialists of France, and the Social Democrats of Germany—unless socialists indicate willingness to coöperate with the Communists. And, as already pointed out, plans for a United States of Europe that would exclude Russia and would inevitably come to be dominated by the Germans, even if Germany had previously been broken up into several federated states, is anathema to Moscow. Because of Russia's traditional distrust of Britain, to which has been added, in the post-war period, Communist distrust of Socialists, the Soviet government has centered its suspicions of some sort of anti-Russian Western combination primarily on the British. Winston Churchill's speech at Fulton, Missouri in 1946, proposing an Anglo-American "fraternal association," added fuel to these suspicions.

The Russians believe, or profess to believe, that the British are ready to use the heavy industry resources of Germany as either a shield or a gun-emplacement, as the case may be, against the U.S.S.R. Since the United States, in an attempt to reduce the burden of American taxpayers for the relief of the Germans in the western zones, has undertaken to help finance the revival of German export industries, the Russians associate this country with the sinister purposes they attribute to the British. The Russians consequently insist that their twenty-year alliance of 1942 with Britain should be revised in such a way as to exclude the possibility of a western bloc. In this connection Mr. Byrnes's 1946 proposal for a twenty-five year four-power military alliance to prevent Germany's military resurgence appeared to the Russians as yet another move by the Western powers to gain control of Germany without effecting the internal economic and social changes which, in the view of the Russians, would alone make Germany safe for Europe. On the question of security against renewed German expansion the Russians are closer to the French, who want to make Germany incapable of attacking them once more, than to the British and Americans; but Russia, being far stronger militarily and industrially than France, is seeking to achieve security not by crippling Germany's industrial and political activities but by removing from the scene German groups who, in Moscow's opinion, either actively or potentially favor renewal of German militarism. The danger anticipated in Moscow, as well as in London and Washington, is that, unless a definite settlement is soon reached, Germany may yet succeed, as it did after 1919, in playing off West against East, in oscillating between a new Rapallo and a new Locarno, and emerge again out of defeat to more decisive victory than the victors.

While Russia's divergences with Britain and, to a lesser extent the United States, have been focused since the end of the war on Germany, Russia and Britain have also found themselves at odds along the periphery of Europe—in Spain, in Italy, in Austria, in Greece. From the point of view of the Russians any country which openly or secretly aided Germany during the war was as much an enemy as if it had actually taken up arms against Russia. The Soviet government has consequently remained adamant in its insistence on the need to overthrow the Franco régime, and has had no patience with British and American attempts to temporize on an issue they regard as fundamental to the peace of Europe. The Western powers, for their part, have come to feel that the danger of Communism in Spain, Europe's gateway to the Atlantic, is greater than any threat now offered by Franco. In Italy, too, the Russians have felt that the Western powers have been unduly tolerant of former Fascists, and have allowed themselves to be affected by the anti-Communist views of the Vatican; while the British and Americans, in turn, have sought to stem the rise of the Italian Communist party, led by Palmiro Togliatti, by various concessions to Christian Democratic Premier de Gasperi. The struggle between East and West for political influence in Italy reached a climax with the Italian national elections of April 18, 1948. Both Russia and the Western powers sought to sway Italian voters by offering Italy advantages of various kinds. The clear-cut victory for the Christian Democrats, and defeat for the Left bloc, composed of Communists and Pietro Nenni's left-wing Socialists, merely gave the de Gasperi government a breathing-space in which to carry out fundamental social and economic reforms. Otherwise, continued poverty and wide discrepancies in the lot of the few rich and the many poor would foster unrest favorable to the growth of Communism.

The future of Carinthia, a province of Austria claimed by Yugoslavia, has so far proved one of the stumbling-blocks to conclusion of the Austrian peace treaty. Austria, which even in the truncated form dictated by the peacemakers of 1919, still is a wedge reminiscent of the Austro-Hungarian Empire in the predominantly Slav-populated Danubian region, has become a focus of controversy between West and East. The Russians have little hope of permanently bringing westernized Austria within their orbit except by force, yet resist its inclusion in Germany through some new Anschluss which would leave it in the orbit of the western powers, especially as they consider Austria the birthplace of Nazism. Greece, pressed from the north by Slav peoples and occupying a key strategic position on the Mediterranean, has also become a bone of contention between Russia, which claims that the British are supporting reactionary forces in that country, and the British, who for the protection of the Mediterranean "life line" if for no other reason are determined to prevent Greece from being dominated by Com-

munists or Communist sympathizers who would be subject
to the influence of Moscow. Reconciliation of British and
Russian differences in countries along the periphery of Europe would require reconciliation of ideological conflicts between the two vastly different socialisms of Britain and
Russia, as well as alleviation of the two nations' historic
strategic antagonisms in the eastern Mediterranean.

6. ANCIENT STRUGGLE FOR THE DARDANELLES

For, while in Eastern Europe Russia clashed again and
again with the Germans, Austro-Hungarians, and Poles for
control of disputed border lands, in the eastern Mediterranean it found itself repeatedly in conflict with Turkey and
Britain over the approaches to the Black Sea through the
Dardanelles. From earliest times Constantinople played an
important part in Russia's history, first because of its importance as a center of lucrative trade, then as the capital of
Byzantine Christianity fallen under the rule of the infidel
Turk. Medieval Russian princes dreamed of nailing their
shields to the gates of Czargrad (Constantinople), as Western
Crusaders dreamed of liberating the Christian world from
the Moslem yoke. With the rise of Russia as a modern state
under Peter the Great, the Ottoman Empire came to be regarded not only as a religious challenge but also as an obstacle
to the growth of Russia's nascent naval power.

Although Russia won notable victories over the Turks
in the first part of the eighteenth century, it lost most of its
gains under the treaty of Belgrade of 1739, in the negotiation of which the Sultan had the support of the French. At
that time the Turks were able to prevent Russian ships
from entering the Black Sea and the Sea of Azov. Access
from the Black Sea to the Mediterranean became a matter of
urgency for Russia in the nineteenth century, with the development of the rich grain-growing regions of Novorossia

(New Russia), which needed outlets for grain exports, and Russian conquest of Transcaucasia, previously controlled by the Turks. The Russians began to talk of the Straits of the Dardanelles as the "gates to our house," and the gradual disintegration of Turkey made it both tempting and urgent for Russia to seize control of these gates or at least share their control with the Turks. Throughout the nineteenth century counsels in St. Petersburg were divided between those who favored a policy of expansion and the ejection of Turkey from Europe, and those who advocated friendly coöperation with Turkey as the least of possible evils, fearing that the disappearance of the Ottoman Empire would leave Russia at the mercy of the superiór naval power of Britain and France. On the eve of World War I, Foreign Minister Sazonov said to the Czar that "the Straits in the hands of a strong state mean the full subjection of the economic development of southern Russia to that state."

With the outbreak of World War I, Russia's "immemorial and sacred" dream of obtaining Constantinople seemed closer to realization than it had been for centuries. By the secret treaty of 1915 Britain and France, which in 1856 and 1878 had opposed Russia's claims to the Eastern Mediterranean, agreed to its acquisition of Constantinople and the Straits, as well as eastern Thrace, and two islands off the Dardanelles from Turkey, then an ally of Germany and Austria-Hungary. Russia's defeat by Germany abruptly ended these dreams, and Lenin denounced all Czarist secret treaties providing for annexations and indemnities. With Turkey in a state of collapse, and Russia in the throes of civil war, Britain and France obtained control of the Dardanelles and the Black Sea, and at one time, while supporting the anti-Bolshevik forces of General Denikin in southern Russia, Britain sought to gain hold of the oil fields of Baku, and France of the Crimea. The Treaty of Lausanne (1923), by which Britain and France made peace with Turkey, left

Constantinople and the Straits to Turkey but demilitarized them under international supervision. This treaty challenged the traditional Russian policy, perpetuated by the Soviet government, that the entrance to the Black Sea should be closed to other powers than Russia and Turkey. True, it provided that in time of peace no non-Black-Sea state should send into the Black Sea a force larger than the Soviet navy, but since the U.S.S.R. feared a "capitalist" coalition which would inevitably command superior naval power, this made Russia feel peculiarly vulnerable in the Black Sea.

Thirteen years later, at the Montreux Conference (1936), the status of the Straits was once more reconsidered, this time with the participation of Russia. Britain and France, fearful of the rise of Nazi Germany and Fascist Italy, were then no longer opposed to Russian and Turkish claims in the region of the Straits. Under the Montreux convention, which is still in force, Turkey was granted again the right to fortify the Dardanelles and the Constantinople district and, as desired by Russia, limitations were imposed on the tonnage of light warships which non-Black-Sea states could send through the Straits in time of peace. Such states could send no large vessels, submarines, or aircraft carriers, and belligerents, for the most part, could not use the Straits. Commercial vessels, whether of belligerents or nonbelligerents, however, were to be permitted as in the past to pass freely provided Turkey itself was not at war. At the Montreux Conference Soviet Foreign Commissar Litvinov laid particular stress on two concepts that represent the essence of Russia's views on the Straits: that the Black Sea, unlike the Mediterranean or the Caribbean, is a "closed sea," over which the coastal states should have paramount control; and that Russia is more interested in preventing the entrance of hostile fleets into the Black Sea than it is in obtaining an exit for its own naval and merchant vessels.

During World War II Russia, which had fought eleven

wars with Turkey between 1676 and 1918, primarily about the Straits, was not opposed by the Turks—partly because a long period of relatively friendly relations during the inter-war years had served to reduce long-standing friction be-tween the two countries, partly because Turkey, disillusioned by its defeat at the side of the Central powers in World War I, had signed a defensive alliance with Britain in 1939, and resisted Hitler's pressure to enter the war. In the opinion of the Soviet government, however, Turkey showed con-siderable sympathy for Germany's invasion of Russia—a view supported by German documents published since the war. Russia therefore felt no compunction in applying in-creasing pressure on Turkey, once the war was over, to obtain revision of the Montreux convention governing con-trol of the Straits, cession of certain strategic points on Turkish territory close to the Dardanelles, and return of the areas of Kars and Ardahan in Transcaucasia which the Rus-sians had wrested from the Turks in the nineteenth century but had been forced to cede under the Brest-Litovsk Treaty of 1918. Britain, which retains its defensive alliance with Turkey, has traditionally opposed Russian control of the Straits, which today would upset the already precarious balance of power in the eastern Mediterranean and the Near East. When Britain in 1947 was forced by internal economic difficulties to curtail its commitments in this strategic area, in which the United States has become increasingly interested as a result of its growing naval power and its need for ad-ditional sources of oil in the Near and Middle East, Presi-dent Truman, in the same address in which he requested Congressional approval for aid to Greece, urged financial assistance to Turkey for maintenance and modernization of its armed forces. Such modernization, Mr. Truman said, is necessary "for the maintenance of its national integrity"; and "that integrity is essential for the preservation of order in the Middle East."

The United States and Britain have both officially taken the view that the Montreux convention, if it is to be revised at all, should be revised at an international conference attended by all the signatory powers, not through bilateral negotiations between Russia and Turkey. Yet the 1945 Potsdam agreement of the Big Three on "The Black Sea Straits," published only in March 1947 following Mr. Truman's address, stated that the Montreux convention "should be revised as failing to meet present-day conditions"; and it was agreed that "as the next step" (in the Russian version the phrase is "the proper course"), the matter should be "the subject of direct conversations" (in the Russian version the phrase is "negotiations") between each of the three governments and the Turkish government. While it is understandable that the United States and Britain would object to Russian pressure on Turkey as a method of obtaining revision of the Montreux convention, the Potsdam agreement would appear to permit bilateral conversations (or negotiations) on that subject between Russia and Turkey. It is possible that, as a result of recent moves and counter-moves, the United States may suggest, instead of further negotiations with Turkey on the part of the Big Three, an international conference whose objective would be the creation of a United Nations régime for control of the Straits. Again, as in the case of Greece, irrespective of the questions whether the United States is to take up "the white man's burden" laid down by Britain, or share it with the United Nations, the Truman statement on Turkey squarely joined the issue between the United States and Russia as to their respective future roles east and west of the Straits.

7. OIL AND IDEOLOGY IN THE MIDDLE EAST

Russia's interests in the eastern Mediterranean have long been linked to its interests in the Near and Middle East, an area where it has also repeatedly clashed with Turkey and Britain. Peter the Great had already looked as far afield as Central Asia, and had led a campaign against Persia in 1723. It was as a result of this campaign on the shores of the Caspian that the Shah of Persia, then struggling like Russia against the Turks, surrendered Baku with its rich oil fields and his country's eastern and southern seacoast to Russia. By 1735 Russia had been forced to relinquish these territories to Persia, but it had at least succeeded in preventing the Turks from obtaining a foothold in this strategic area, and subsequently continued to benefit by conflicts between Persia and Turkey. Early in the nineteenth century Russia began its conquest of Transcaucasia by absorbing the kingdom of Georgia, over which Persia had claimed suzerainty, into the Russian empire; and at the close of the Napoleonic wars in 1813 Persia recognized Baku and most of eastern Transcaucasia as part of Russia. Following a bitter war in 1826–1828 Russia obtained control of Azerbaijan and Persian Armenia, and established its frontier a hundred miles from Tabriz, second largest city of Persia. By 1831 it had recovered Kars from Turkey and had obtained the port of Batum, Black Sea outlet of Transcaucasia. But not until the end of the nineteenth century did Russia pacify this turbulent area, whose revolts were immortalized in the poems of Lermontov and in Tolstoi's tale, *Hadji Murad*.

Having subdued Transcaucasia, the Russians turned to the Middle East and to Central Asia where they soon found themselves in conflict with Britain in Persia, Afghanistan, and India. The British in the 1860's talked of the Russian "threat to India," and the "bear that walks like a man," while the Russians commented acidly on British oppression of the Indian people, denouncing Britain's alleged hypocrisy and unbridled territorial ambitions. Russian nationalists demanded "a free exit to the Indian Ocean," and objected to the division of Persia into spheres of influence, insisting that

Persia must remain the object of Russian "material and moral protection." But Russia's defeat in its war with Japan, which strengthened the opposition of Asiatic peoples, including the Persians, to the imperialism of western powers, including Russia, caused the Czarist government to abandon its policy of intransigence; and in 1907 it concluded an entente with Britain covering the interests of the two countries in Persia, Tibet, and Afghanistan. Russia recognized Britain's position of predominance in Afghanistan, thus removing the "threat to India." Persia was divided into Russian and British spheres of influence, north and south respectively, with a neutral zone between, preserved for the Persian government. The question of oil fields did not arise at that time, and it was not until 1912 that the Anglo-Persian (now Anglo-Iranian) Company, in which Persian interests have a 49 per cent share and British interests 51 per cent, was created for the exploitation of oil resources in the British sphere.

With the advent of the Soviet government, Russia relinquished all the special rights and privileges which the Czarist government had acquired in Persia. By the 1921 treaty, however, Russia specifically provided that the privileges it surrendered would not be accorded to other countries, and reserved the right to send armed forces into Iranian territory if that territory were made a base of hostile operations—the contingency then envisaged being operations by counterrevolutionary White Russians with the aid of foreign states. Preoccupied for a quarter of a century with internal problems, the Soviet government displayed no active interest in the affairs of Iran until World War II. When it proved necessary, after the German invasion, to find a route over which American war materials could be sent to Russia without fear of interference by the Axis, the devious route established through the Persian Gulf and across the territory of Iran to Russia's Caspian ports brought Iran once more to the forefront of Russia's interests.

At the Teheran Conference (1942) Russia, together with Britain and the United States, guaranteed the independence of Iran; and by the Anglo-Russian-Iranian treaty of 1942 pledged itself to withdraw its troops from Iranian territory six months after the end of hostilities—later interpreted as six months after V-J Day, or March 2, 1946. Meanwhile, however, Soviet Azerbaijan had begun to develop close relations with the neighboring Azerbaijan territory of Iran, and a coup there for the establishment of an autonomous Azerbaijan republic, staged in 1946, was attributed by Teheran to instigation on the part of Moscow. Following the withdrawal of British forces and American technical personnel by March 2, 1946, Russia continued to maintain troops in northern Iran. In 1944 Britain and the United States had sought to obtain oil concessions from the Iranian government and Russia followed suit. To avoid the danger of a three-power clash about oil, Iran had then declared that it would consider no request for oil from any quarter until the end of the war had brought about the departure of foreign troops, and Britain and the United States were reported to have withdrawn their requests.

When Iran, in February 1946, appealed to the Security Council of the United Nations against the continued presence of Russian troops on its territory, asserting that it constituted a threat to international peace and security within the meaning of Article 34 of the United Nations Charter, Russia proposed that the issue be left to direct negotiations between Moscow and Teheran. These negotiations, conducted in Moscow by Iranian Premier Ahmed Ghavam Sultaneh, proved fruitless, and the Security Council, overriding Russia's objections, once more inquired into the dispute. The Iranian Ambassador to the United States, in the course of his answers to the Council's questions, revealed that Russia had attached two conditions to withdrawal of its troops from Iran: that Teheran recognize the autonomy of the province of Azerbaijan, and that a Russo-Iranian joint stock company be formed for the exploitation of oil resources in northern Iran, with Russia controlling 51 and Iran 49 per cent of the shares—the same control ratio as that of the concession held by the Anglo-Iranian Company. Russia eventually withdrew its troops from Iran in May 1946, and the proposal for an oil concession to Russia remains to be considered by the Iranian parliament (Majlis) which was in process of being selected during the opening months of 1947. Meanwhile a brief revolt in Azerbaijan against the central government at Teheran was promptly suppressed by Iranian forces in December 1946 at Ghavam's direction, with no stronger public reaction by Russia than a diplomatic protest, and the Tudeh party, favorable to Russia, went into eclipse.

Both Britain, which has extensive military, political, and economic interests in the Near and Middle East, and the United States which has become increasingly concerned in that area through its desire to obtain additional sources of oil, have viewed Moscow's demands in Iran as an entering wedge for extension of Russian influence in the Middle East, and an attempt to undermine the position of Britain. Russia, for its part, has regarded the presence of British troops in Palestine (a British mandate), in Iraq (former British mandate which received independence in 1936), in Trans-Jordan (former British mandate whose independence Britain unilaterally recognized in 1946), and at the Suez Canal as a threat or obstacle to its influence in that area. Moscow's apprehensions were heightened by the announcement in 1946 of a defensive alliance between Iraq and Turkey, both of which have alliances with Britain; and by the news in 1947 that the British had undertaken to train Iraq military forces. Nor have the activities of American diplomats and oil experts in Saudi Arabia, or the agreement (1946) between British and American oil companies to share the product of the Anglo-Iranian Company's fields in Iran, passed unnoticed in Moscow. Russia had once sought to win sympathy among the Arabs by opposing Zionism, but in the UN in 1947 it came out for partition of Palestine, and in May 1948 recognized the new state of Israel. Communism has so far made slight gains in the Near East. As in Eastern Europe and the Balkans, Russia's ideas and practical achievements, modest as they seem to westerners, may exercise a growing attraction on neighboring peoples in the Near and Middle East who feel that they have hitherto had little opportunity either to govern themselves (and thus have no particular cause to admire democracy), or to derive material benefits from the natural resources of their lands (and therefore have little attachment for foreign or native capitalism). In the Near and Middle East, as in Eastern Europe, the best hope for stabilization lies in joint undertakings by the Big Three within the framework of the UN for development of the resources of the area, the most important of which is oil, needed by Russia as well as by Britain and the United States.

8. RUSSIA'S STAKE IN ASIA

While Russia, in modern times, has had Germany as its chief antagonist on the continent of Europe, and Britain as its principal opponent in the eastern Mediterranean and in the Middle East, on the continent of Asia it has had to contend primarily with Japan, allied in the early part of this century with Britain. The United States had already persuaded Japan to open its doors to foreigners in 1853–54 and Britain had acquired Hong Kong and obtained special privileges for its traders in China by the time Russia, about 1860, began to take an active part in Asiatic affairs. During the Crimean war the Russians defeated British forces sent to occupy Kamchatka, and in 1858–1860 obtained from China the Amur region and a portion of the Chinese seacoast down to the boundary of Korea. In this coastal region

Muravyov-Amursky, one of Russia's leading colonizers who foresaw a great future for Siberia, founded the port of Vladivostok, ice free most of the year, which in World War I became a major point of entry for Allied war materials. During that period Russia and Japan had a controversy over the island of Sakhalin, lying across the Gulf of Tartary close to the Siberian mainland, and in 1875 Russia took possession of the island.

(A) JAPAN RUSSIA'S OPPONENT

With the inauguration, in 1891, of the Trans-Siberian Railway, which opened up the Russian Far East to large-scale colonization and development, Russia, it will be recalled, embarked on a drive to the Pacific comparable to the opening up of the American West.

This drive to the Pacific received the wholehearted backing of one of Russia's outstanding pre-revolutionary political figures, Count Witte, who became Minister of Finance and Communications in 1892. Witte had far-reaching plans to transform Russia into a great industrial and naval power by funneling the rich raw material resources of Siberia into the heavy industries he hoped to see established, and also by constructing naval facilities on the Pacific coast. In its efforts to strengthen its position in Asia, Russia collided with Japan, which had plans of its own for domination of the strategic coastline facing the Japanese islands. When Japan defeated China in the Sino-Japanese war of 1894–95, and under the Treaty of Shimonoseki obtained the Liaotung Peninsula, Russia, aided by France and Germany, forced Japan to surrender this territory. Russia also guaranteed a loan to China by establishing the Russo-Chinese Bank, a joint stock concern, and concluded an alliance with China against Japan by which it obtained the right to build across northern Manchuria a broad-gauge railway known as the Chinese Eastern Railway, thus materially shortening its communications with Vladivostok. The Chinese Eastern, whose construction was practically completed by 1904 (as compared with the Trans-Siberian not completed until 1917), was controlled entirely by the Russian government, which enjoyed wide rights of administration over the adjoining railway zone in Manchuria. In 1898 China granted to Russia a twenty-five-year lease on the Liaotung Peninsula which Japan had been forced to surrender. Of particular importance to Russia was the port on the peninsula, Port Arthur, open to navigation all the year round, which the Russians transformed into a strong fortress and naval base. Not satisfied with this acquisition, however, Russia displayed increasing interest in near-by Korea, where it hoped to obtain an ice-free port less remote from Vladivostok than Port Arthur.

Count Witte, a diplomat as well as a man of political vision, had sought to obtain special privileges for Russia in Asia by negotiations, but extremist nationalists found his policy too cautious, and urged the use of force to wrest an unchallenged position for Russia on the Pacific. The Japanese, for their part, were determined to prevent Russian domination of the mainland, where they hoped to obtain raw materials for their growing industries. When Japan saw that Russia had become entrenched in northern Manchuria and was contemplating further penetration in Korea, it concluded an alliance with Britain (1902), the strongest naval power of that time in Europe. It then delivered a surprise night attack on the Russian fleet at Port Arthur in February 1904, comparable to its attack nearly forty years later on Pearl Harbor. Not until May 1905, fifteen months later, did Russia's Baltic fleet, which had had to travel all the way around the world, arrive in the Sea of Japan, only to be destroyed by the Japanese in the Straits of Tsushima—a disaster which demonstrated in a tragic manner the grave naval weakness of the country and the lack of adequate facilities on the Pacific coast for the operation of a major fleet.

Under the treaty of Portsmouth of September 1905, Russia abandoned Port Arthur on the Liaotung Peninsula as well as southern Manchuria, acknowledged Japan's control over Korea which Tokyo annexed in 1910, ceded to Japan the southern half of Sakhalin, and accorded to Tokyo valuable fishing rights along the coast of Siberia. In spite of these concessions, however, Russia aligned itself with Japan in opposition to the policy of the "open door" in China proclaimed by American Secretary of State John Hay in 1899–1900. It also came to terms with Japan in defining respective spheres of influence in China, as it had done with Britain in the Middle East and Central Asia. Under this arrangement Russia was to exercise domination in northern Manchuria, Outer Mongolia, and Sinkiang, and Japan over southern Manchuria and Inner Mongolia. Following the Chinese revolution of 1911, which deposed the Manchu dynasty in Peking, Russia forced China to concede full autonomy to Outer Mongolia—a move that foreshadowed the policy of the Soviet government which, in 1921, established close relations with the Mongolian People's Republic whose internal system was closely patterned on that of the U.S.S.R.

Although the first World War was waged primarily in Europe, it created a serious threat for Russia in Asia when Japan, one of the Allied and Associated Powers, took advantage of Allied intervention in Siberia (1918–1922), ostensibly to check Germany but actually to oppose the Soviet government, and tried to oust Russia from the Siberian mainland. It required vigorous action by the United States to obtain the removal of the 70,000 Japanese troops sent to Siberia, which were not finally withdrawn until 1922. In 1925 Japan recognized the Soviet government and evacuated the northern portion of Sakhalin, obtaining in return oil concessions in that area as well as extensive fishing rights. In 1917 the Soviet government had repudiated in the Far East, as elsewhere, all special rights and privileges acquired by the Czarist régime, including extra-territoriality. By this measure Russia sought to range itself on the side of dependent peoples against the imperialism of Western colonial powers.

During his brief tenure of power Lenin had established close relations with the leader of the Chinese revolution, Dr. Sun Yat-sen, who in his testament and his *Three Principles of Democracy* expressed ideas in some respects similar to those of Lenin. Sun Yat-sen's People's Party (Kuomintang) had looked to the Soviet government as a source of inspiration in a common struggle against Western imperialism, and had received ideological and technical assistance from Moscow which, at that time, hoped that Communism would triumph in other countries. The newly formed Chinese Communist party was seen as a hopeful portent of the spread of international communism by Russian leaders like Trotsky, who advocated "permanent revolution." But a break within the Kuomintang in 1927, two years after the death of Sun Yat-sen, between right-wing and left-wing elements resulted in a setback for the Chinese Communists, who had been committed to thoroughgoing revolution.

The Chinese Communists, although defeated both in their hopes for national domination and in their coöperation with Moscow, developed a practical program which drew its inspiration chiefly from the traditions and existing conditions of China. During China's long-drawn-out war with Japan the Chinese Communists established themselves firmly in the provinces of Yenan and Shansi, close to the Russian border, ruling over a population estimated at ninety million out of China's four hundred million. The extent of Moscow's influence and material assistance to the Chinese Communists remains a matter of dispute. The program of the Chinese Communists, whose policy is affected by the predominantly agrarian character of the country's still backward economy, differs in many respects from that of the Soviet government. Nor can it be assumed that the Communist leaders of China are prepared to accept unquestioningly the *diktat* of Moscow. At the same time there is little doubt that a greater affinity of past experience, present objectives, and future expectations exists between the Chinese Communists and Russia, than between the former and the Western powers.

Following the invasion of China by Japan in 1931, however, Russia gave material aid to Chiang Kai-shek in the form of arms and airplanes exceeding, at that time, the aid of the United States, which was then still selling war materials to Japan. Russia also urged the Chinese Communists to join forces with the Kuomintang in a "national front" of resistance to Japan. Alarmed by Japan's invasion of Manchuria, Russia, feeling unequal to an open clash with Tokyo, retreated from that area and in 1936 sold its rights in the Chinese Eastern Railway to the Japanese-controlled government of Manchukuo.

In accordance with Stalin's policy of "building socialism in one country," Russia was meanwhile strengthening its own base of operations in Asia by industrialization of the country east of the Urals, the double-tracking of the Trans-Siberian Railway, and the construction of a second rail connection north of the Amur River, out of range of Japanese attack. This improvement in communications across the vast reaches of Siberia was intended to remedy the grave defect in transportation which had been one of the principal reasons for Russia's defeat in 1904–05. By 1939 Russia, no longer willing to accept further encroachments by Japan, vigorously resisted Japanese efforts to press northward in the vicinity of Outer Mongolia with which Moscow had concluded a pact of guarantee in 1936. After a sharp military clash the two countries signed an armistice in 1939 at the outbreak of war in Europe. In April 1941, as Germany was preparing to strike in the Balkans, Russia concluded a non-aggression pact with Japan.

During the first two years of that war Russia and Japan remained on guard along their fifteen-hundred-mile border, with Russia reported as maintaining a Far Eastern army of one million men, and Japan a force in Manchuria estimated at close to that figure. In spite of Russia's unconcealed aid to China, Japan, rejecting the counsels of its army leaders who advised war against Russia, yielded to the advice of its naval spokesmen, and struck without warning at the United States on December 7, 1941. Just as Russia by its non-aggression pact with Tokyo had obtained a safeguard against Japanese attack in Asia while it was fighting for survival in Europe, so Japan, by that pact, had obtained a safeguard against an attack from the north while it sought to achieve domination in southern Asia and in the Pacific. Under the nonaggression pact Japan had recognized Russia's sphere of influence in Outer Mongolia, and Russia that of Japan in Manchuria.

(B) RUSSIA AND POST-WAR CHINA

The United States, faced as late as the Potsdam Conference of July 1945 with the prospect of a prolonged, indecisive, and bloody struggle against the Japanese islands, vigorously urged Russia's entrance into the war in Asia even before the war in Europe had come to an end. To obtain Russia's aid, President Roosevelt and Prime Minister Churchill, in a secret treaty concluded at Yalta in February 1945, promised to assist Moscow in obtaining special rights and privileges from China. As it turned out, the United States, having mastered the secret of manufacturing the atomic bomb, was able to shorten the war materially by delivering two staggering blows at Hiroshima and Nagasaki. Russia which, in accordance with its undertaking, had denounced its nonaggression pact with Tokyo in April 1945 and had declared war on Japan three months after V–E Day (the time regarded as necessary to transfer Russian forces from the

West to the East), invaded Manchuria only to find Japan suing for unconditional surrender a week later.

Meanwhile, Russia and China had opened negotiations in Moscow for a thirty-year pact of friendship and alliance, concluded on August 26, 1945, which embodied the main terms agreed on by the Big Three at Yalta. The most significant features of the treaty and its supplementary agreements are the recognition of a special position for Russia in Manchuria and the explicit pledge of the signatories "to act according to the principles of mutual respect for their sovereignty and territorial entity and non-interference in the internal affairs of both contracting parties." This clause was assumed to mean that the U.S.S.R. would deal only with the Chinese Central government and would not extend aid or recognition to the Chinese Communists in Yenan. Shortly after, conversations looking toward establishment of national unity were opened in Chungking by Generalissimo Chiang Kai-shek and Mao Tse-tung, leader of the Communists, with General George C. Marshall, former Chief of Staff of the United States, in the capacity of mediator. These conversations, however, proved abortive, and civil war flared up anew in the autumn of 1946.

The Russo-Chinese treaty did not fully restore Russia to the position it occupied before the Russo-Japanese war of 1904–05. The rights granted to the U.S.S.R. by China are much more limited than those possessed by Czarist Russia, and no attempt was made to restore extraterritoriality. Russia and China are to have joint control of the Chinese Eastern Railway and the South Manchuria Railway (built by Japan), which are to be combined under the single name of the Chinese Changchun Railway. The joint control, however, is to apply only to those properties in which the Russians previously had an interest, and other lines will apparently come under complete Chinese control. Port Arthur, from which Russia was ousted by Japan in 1905, is to be used jointly by Russia and China as a naval base "at the disposal of the battleships and merchant ships of China and the U.S.S.R. alone," while the near-by port of Dairen is to be "a free port open to trade and shipping of all countries." Ir Dairen various piers and warehouses were to be leased to Russia, and no import or export duties were to be levied on goods passing directly to or from the Soviet Union through that port. In both Port Arthur and Dairen the civil administration was to be Chinese, but the Russians were to exercise considerable authority, especially in Port Arthur.

The Soviet government also declared that it regards Manchuria as part of China and undertakes to respect China's full sovereignty over that area. According to a minute appended to the treaty, Stalin pledged that Russian troops would begin to withdraw from Manchuria three weeks after Japan's capitulation, the withdrawal to be completed within three months at the most. With regard to Outer Mongolia, which is non-Chinese in language, population, and historical background, but in theory has been under Chinese sovereignty, it was agreed that, if a plebiscite confirmed the people's desire for independence, China would recognize Outer Mongolia's independent status. Such recognition, Chiang Kai-shek stated in an address of August 25, 1945, was not only necessary for friendship, but would also be in harmony with the Kuomintang's principles of the equality and freedom of peoples. After a plebiscite held in October 1945 had resulted in an overwhelming popular vote for independence, the Mongolian People's Republic, with the support of Russia, sought, but without success, to obtain admission as a member of the United Nations Organization. With reference to Sinkiang, another disputed border area in which the Russians exerted great influence from 1934 until 1942, when they withdrew in favor of China, Russian Foreign Minister Molotov stated in connection with the treaty that the Soviet Union "has no intention to interfere with China's internal affairs."

Since the conclusion of this comprehensive Russo-Chinese treaty, relations between the two countries have shown rapidly increasing deterioration. The provisions of the Sino-Soviet treaty for joint Russo-Chinese control of the Chinese and South Manchuria railways have not been carried out, partly because of civil war conditions in Manchuria, where the central Chinese government has exercised only nominal control since the renewal of civil war in 1946, and partly because of the reluctance of the Kuomintang to permit Russian participation in administration of railways within the territories over which it does exercise control. Russia, for its part, has prevented the central Chinese government from entering upon "joint use" of the ports of Dairen and Port Arthur, as provided in the Sino-Soviet treaty, on the ground that the state of war with Japan has not yet been terminated, and that Dairen as well as the Port Arthur naval base area should still be subject to military supervision. In June 1947 the Chinese government, having apparently decided to adopt a strong line toward Russia, lodged a protest in Moscow, charging that the Soviet government had repeatedly refused to agree to the stationing of Chinese troops in Port Arthur and Dairen; and that Chinese Communists had formed strong armed forces in the vicinity of the two cities "to hinder the take-over of these regions by the Chinese Government."

Previously, Russia's delay in evacuating Manchuria—originally, at least, at the request of Chungking, which wanted additional time to bring up its forces, and thus prevent occupation of Manchurian centers by neighboring Chinese Communist troops—provoked protests not only from China but also from the United States and Britain; and Russia eventually promised to complete its evacuation by the end of April. By that time the United States, too, had agreed to remove its troops from Chinese territory. Russian troops did evacuate Manchuria but, before withdrawing, they stripped many factories and mines of machinery and other equipment. This action was justified by Moscow on the ground that the machinery had been used by Japan for war purposes and therefore constituted legitimate war booty—although no formal agreement had yet been concluded by the Big Three as to disposal of Japanese property in that area, or its possible application to a general reparations account. Moreover, some Americans contended that China, which had suffered most from Japanese occupation, should have first priority on reparations from Japanese sources, as against Russia, which had waged a war of but a week's duration in Manchuria. It is often forgotten in the United States, however, that throughout World War II Russia maintained a large army, estimated at one million men, along its border with China, thus immobilizing a Japanese army of comparable size which might otherwise have been deployed against the Chinese. The maintenance of this Far Eastern army represented a genuine sacrifice on the part of the U.S.S.R. to the common cause of the Allies, since this force might have been transferred to the West, possibly bringing the war with Germany to a close at an earlier date, with consequent saving of lives and material destruction.

Subsequent reports indicated that Russia's removal of industrial material from Manchuria was motivated less by desire to claim war booty or even to use this material in its own plants than by fear that the Chinese Central government, possibly with the aid of the United States, would utilize Japanese-built industries, left intact by war, to create a powerful base for future operations against the U.S.S.R. The United States and Britain were also alarmed by indications that Russia, taking advantage of the position it gained in Manchuria in its few days of military operations against Japan, was planning, in accordance with the policy of the Czarist

Empire, to oppose the "open door" in that area, and to seek special economic privileges from China, including Russian participation on a joint stock basis in Chinese industrial and mining enterprises.

(c) WILL U. S. REPLACE JAPAN?

The controversy over Manchuria is but a symptom of the uneasiness that developed between the United States and Russia in Asia upon termination of war with Japan. The fundamental change in the balance of power effected by World War II is that the United States has acquired a strategic position in the Far East which, taken in conjunction with our unequaled industrial and financial resources, gives this country a potentially far greater opportunity to determine the destiny of the Asiatic mainland than Japan commanded at the peak of its military successes. In this sense the United States has replaced Japan as a prospective contender with Russia for a position of influence on the Pacific shores of Asia. But if Moscow, even after a quarter of a century of industrial development, had much to fear from a militant Japan, the United States could be a still more formidable opponent for Russia during the period of that country's necessarily painful recovery from the damage wreaked on its economy by the Germans. To the casual reader of newspaper headlines it may have seemed, since V–J Day, that Russia was encroaching further and further on its Asiatic neighbors. Yet, so far, at least, the Soviet government has been merely retracing the paths of Russian penetration in the Far East blazed for over fifty years by the Czarist Empire. It is not so much that Russia's position on the Asiatic mainland has changed but that the United States, for the first time in its history, has emerged not merely as an interested party but as an active participant in Far Eastern affairs. While Russia's attitude toward the Chinese Communists, its relations with Outer Mongolia, its policy toward

Manchuria and Korea, may seem to constitute a threat to our interests, the stake we have acquired in the Orient as a result of the war may seem equally menacing to the Russians.

If we look at post-war developments in Asia from the point of view of Moscow, and not of Washington, what do we see? We see that the United States exercises paramount control over the Japanese islands, even though this control is qualified, on paper, by the existence of the Allied Control Council in Tokyo and the Far Eastern Commission in Washington, on both of which Russia is represented. This seems entirely proper to most Americans, who recall the sacrifices made by this country to defeat Japan. And it is understandable that General MacArthur should find Russia's attempts to question or challenge various aspects of his administration of Japan as irksome and unwarranted. It can also be argued that, while Russia undoubtedly bore the brunt of the fighting in Europe, its contribution to the winning of the war in Asia was relatively small, especially when compared to that of China or the United States. Yet the Russians, who can still remember the disastrous defeat inflicted on them by Japan in 1904–05, and the attempt of the Japanese to oust them from Siberia in 1918, feel that the future of Japan is of crucial importance for the security of their country—more crucial, perhaps, than it is for the security of the United States.

While some of the suggestions made by the Russians in the Allied Control Council in Tokyo for changes in Japan's political and economic structure can be discounted as propaganda, there is genuine concern in Moscow that the reform undertaken by the United States may leave more or less intact the very elements among the Japanese who did not hesitate to expose their people to the risks of war. The Russians, moreover, fear that the United States, sooner or later, may use force to dislodge them from the positions they have acquired in Asia. While this assumption may appear to some Americans as the figment of a distorted imagination, the Russians, measuring our policy by the yardstick of their anxiety, believe that the United States may use Japan as a base for air and naval attack on the Siberian mainland, now infinitely more vulnerable because of the possible use of the atomic bomb. The results achieved by this country at Hiroshima and Nagasaki have not escaped the attention of Soviet leaders. The Russians do not think it fantastic to expect that from Japan, which occupies a position with respect to the continent of Asia strikingly similar to that of Britain with respect to the continent of Europe, the United States, if it were so minded, could in short order destroy the laborious efforts Russia has made since the middle of the nineteenth century to establish itself on the Pacific. True, the Russians have sought to enhance their own security by obtaining outright the Kurile Islands off the northern coast of Siberia. But this acquisition, in Moscow's view, is more than matched by American control of the strategic Japanese mandated islands in the Pacific—even though these islands have by a trusteeship agreement been placed under the supervision of the Security Council of the United Nations. The problem of Russia's security in the Pacific will remain a cause of anxiety to any government in Moscow, whatever its political character, as long as Russia continues to lag behind the United States in air and naval power, and in the industrial capacity for mass production of airplanes, ships, and especially atomic bombs.

A comparable problem of security arises also in Russia's relations with the United States in China. There General Marshall, President Truman's special envoy, with the assistance, in later stages, of the American Ambassador, Dr. John Leighton Stuart, sought for a year to reconcile differences between the Central government of Chiang Kai-shek and the Chinese Communists. From the point of view of the United States, this constituted legitimate and, indeed, urgently necessary intervention to prevent the renewal of civil war in China, suspended but far from settled by the Japanese invasion. Many Americans, however, believe that American intervention, while intended to be impartial, in effect redounded to the benefit of the Central government, for this country continued to extend economic aid to Chiang Kaishek without waiting for the creation of a democratic régime representing all political parties which, according to President Truman's statement of December 15, 1945, was to have been a prerequisite of further assistance. Although it can be argued that the Chinese Communists might not in any case have found it possible to come to terms with Chiang Kaishek, the economic aid the Generalissimo received from the United States resulted in strengthening the reactionary elements in the Kuomintang, who were determined to crush the Communists once and for all, by civil war if necessary.

While the United States openly intervened in China, with the effect, unsought though it may have been, of consolidating the position of the Central government, Russia carefully refrained from giving any public indication of its attitude toward the contending groups—although there can be little doubt of where its sympathies lie. By deciding on unilateral intervention in China, the United States, as in Japan, avoided the innumerable complications that might have attended an attempt to reconcile its interests with those of Russia—complications that have unquestionably hampered joint Allied action in the liberated countries of Europe. But it has also gambled on having to assume sole blame for the failure of General Marshall's mission, in the eyes of the world, and, what is even more important, of the Chinese people. The danger was that this country, without conscious volition on its part, would appear to the Chinese as an associate, if not actually a supporter, of the reactionary elements in the Central government and, by that token, an opponent of the groups in China—not only Communists but also moderate reformers—who have been endeavoring to shape the country into the kind of progressive modern nation that many Americans say they want China to be.

The difference in approach to Asiatic peoples by the United States and Russia, which can only be guessed at in Japan and China, where the two great powers do not operate jointly, emerges into sharp focus in Korea, which is under their joint administration. It will be recalled that Korea, coveted by both Russia and Japan, was finally annexed by Tokyo in 1910, to be liberated only with the defeat of the Japanese in World War II. At the Cairo Conference, November 22–26, 1943, in which Russia did not participate, the United States, Britain, and China agreed that Korea should receive independence "in due course." At the Moscow Conference of December 1945 the United States, Britain, and Russia, with the approval of China, agreed on the formation of a provisional democratic government in Korea by a joint American-Russian Commission working in consultation with Korean democratic organizations, and the establishment of a four-power trusteeship for the country for a period up to five years, after which Korea was to achieve full independence.

Under the terms of this agreement the northern part of Korea has been administered by Russia, and the southern part by the United States, pending the outcome of negotiations for establishment of a provisional democratic government, which so far have proved fruitless. The Russians, in their zone, while pushing Communists to the fore, as might have been expected, have also used non-Communist elements who played an active part in resistance to the Japanese during the war. The American military government has relied primarily on Right-wing Koreans, including some former collaborators with the Japanese—a tendency that has not enhanced the prestige of Western democracy. The Russians, in their zone, proceeded to institute a land reform under which land, formerly a monopoly of the Japanese, was distributed on the basis of 5 hectares per farming family. The American military government has undertaken no land distribution in spite of the fact that our zone includes about 70 per cent of the cultivated area of the country and has preserved the principal Japanese industrial and agricultural combine, the Oriental Development Company, which owned more than half of Korea's entire wealth, renaming it the New Korea Company. The political stalemate has had as its corollary an economic deadlock, as a result of which the American zone, which contains well over half of the country's 30 million population and a major part of its foodstuffs, notably rice, the Korean staple, is cut off from the Russian zone, which contains the principal industrial and mining resources of Korea, notably coal. It has been argued with some truth that Russia's uncompromising attitude on the composition of the provisional government has proved an insuperable stumbling block to the development of Korea along the lines contemplated by the Allies in 1945. Yet agreement about the future of the country, whose strategic position is recognized with equal keenness by Russia and the United States, depends not merely on compromises by one or other of the two great powers, but on their ultimate success in achieving a fusion of their admittedly differing views about the political, economic, and social issues of our times. While the United States and Russia both have strategic and economic interests in Asia, it is possible that, pending the reconstruction of Europe and the development of the resources of the Near and Middle East, the Asiatic mainland may play a relatively less important part in relations between the Big Two than the European continent and the Eastern Mediterranean. Reconstruction of China involves far more complex problems and requires far greater expenditure of money and materials than that of the more productive areas of Europe and the Middle East, and may therefore receive a low priority in Washington, whose strategic and economic objectives in Asia may be better served by Japan. Meanwhile, the greater successes achieved by Chinese Communists as compared with Communists in Europe, and the strategic advantages already gained by Moscow under the Sino-Soviet treaty of 1946 may cause Russia to consolidate rather than to advance further—provided the United States, too, remains in *status quo* in China.

9. TWO FORMS OF INTERNATIONAL COÖPERATION

Russia, like the United States, has been in the paradoxical position of a country long isolationist in sentiment which, at the same time, has taken the leadership in advocating international organization. Its advocacy of coöperation among nations has taken two main forms: what might be described as vertical coöperation, between sovereign states, and horizontal coöperation, cutting across the territorial boundaries of nation states, and appealing to comparable groups in a few countries, as in Russia's support of Pan-Slavism, or all over the world, as in Russia's appeal to "toiling masses" through international communism. Russian leaders have sometimes alternated between these two forms, and sometimes have made use of them simultaneously, depending on current circumstances. Both Pan-Slavism and international communism have appeared alien and, on occasion, peculiarly sinister, to the non-Russian world. Yet Pan-Slavism is comparable to the emphasis frequently placed on the community of interests—Mr. Churchill called it "fraternal association"—created by Anglo-Saxon traditions. And international communism, while far better organized and more intensively pursued than the Holy Alliance of 1815 formed to combat any movement that challenged the authority of absolute monarchs, has displayed, in its reverse policy of opposing anti-Communist governments, a comparable tendency to subordinate nationalism to ideology.

As the fortunes of communism outside Russia declined in the early 1920's, the Soviet government began to turn to the more conventional form of international cooperation—coöperation between sovereign states. Russia had been excluded from participation in the Paris Peace Conference of 1919, as well as from negotiation of the Covenant of the League of Nations which was incorporated in each of the five peace treaties that brought World War I to an end. The Soviet government consequently not only felt no responsibility for the League of Nations, of which Russia was not a member, but strongly suspected that the League might be used by nations opposed to Bolshevism as the framework of an anti-Soviet coalition. In spite of this deep-seated suspicion, which the outspoken hostility of many League members toward Russia did nothing to dispel, the Soviet government in the wake of war and civil war coöperated with the League in four humanitarian tasks: the repatriation of war prisoners, the rehabilitation of Armenian and Russian refugees, the fight against epidemics, and the eradication of the use of opium.

Not only was the Soviet government determined not to work with "the League of Victors," considering Russia as among the defeated nations; it was even more opposed to collaboration with the International Labor Office, set up in 1919 as an autonomous body with headquarters in Geneva. The avowed aim of the ILO "to secure and maintain fair and humane conditions of labor for men, women and children," offered direct competition to the Soviet program for improving conditions of the workers of the world, and its work was denounced in Moscow as an "abominable masquerade to trick the proletariat." As a result the ILO, whose program was influenced by the ideals of evolutionary reformist socialists, and not by plans for violent revolution, found it difficult

to establish workable relations with the Soviet government
—although Moscow and Geneva did exchange statistical information on labor conditions.

Convinced that neither the League of Nations nor the
Permanent Court of International Justice could possibly
be impartial in considering any situations involving Russia,
the Soviet government steadfastly declined for fifteen years
to be associated with the international organization established by the League Covenant. In 1924 a Soviet spokesman,
in an interview given to an American newspaperman, suc-
cinctly formulated the policy of the Kremlin when, in connection with the League's handling of the Memel coup of
1923, he said, in words strangely familiar in 1947: "The
Soviet government is determined to lose no opportunity of
exposing to the world two points: first, the utter futility of
opportunist decisions by the 'Allied League of Nations';
and second, our fixed resolve that no matter interesting to
Russia shall be, or can be, settled without our participation
and approval. Outsiders may think our repeated insistence
on these points stupid and monotonous. Nothing is more
stupid and monotonous than drops of water falling, falling
—but they wear away solid rock, and neither the Allies nor
the League of Nations are solid rock." At The Hague Conference of 1922 Soviet Foreign Commissar Litvinov spoke
even more bluntly when he declared again in words that
presaged the West-East controversy after World War II:
"The world is divided into Russia and non-Russia, into Soviet
and non-Soviet systems, into a Third International and a
League of Nations. It is ridiculous to hope to find an insti-
tution or a person who would be 'impartial' in dealing with
decisions affecting these divisions of the world."

In spite of its attitude of mingled contempt and fear about
the League of Nations, the Soviet government presented its
own views in Geneva on two key problems which remain
unsolved to this day—disarmament and international eco-

nomic coöperation. During the sessions both of the Preparatory Commission for Disarmament (1927–1930) and the Disarmament Conference (1932–1936) Litvinov made it clear that Russia would be satisfied with nothing less than immediate, complete, and total abolition of armaments. This policy was understandable, since general disarmament not only lessened the danger of an anti-Soviet coalition of capitalist powers, but would also have deprived anti-Communist governments of weapons for the suppression of revolutions. The Soviet leaders, however, contended that one of the main reasons for their advocacy of disarmament was that it would reduce the economic burdens borne by the "toiling masses." In contrast to France's thesis that security had to precede disarmament, Litvinov contended that disarmament alone would create conditions of social justice and economic productivity that would assure security. On the eve of the Disarmament Conference in 1932, Anatol Lunacharski, Soviet Commissar of Education, said that the U.S.S.R. had no desire for war—not because it was in essence such a peaceful organization, but because it believed the real war was between classes, not between nations, and in that war victory had to be achieved by "peace construction" like that undertaken by the "great workers' state." At that time the Soviet government opposed the creation of an international police force, suggested by France, fearing that such a force might be used for an attack on the U.S.S.R.

With the rise to power of Hitler, Russia became more receptive to coöperation with other countries represented at the Disarmament Conference. Reversing Moscow's previous position, Litvinov began to urge the need of defining "the aggressor," against whom international sanctions might be applied. The definition he proposed was that the term aggressor could be applied to a nation which had been proved the first to take any of the following actions: (1) declaration of war; (2) armed occupation of territory; (3) bombardment or attack by armed forces; (4) military invasion without permission of the local government; and (5) naval blockade against another state. This definition was warmly supported by France, by France's allies in the Little Entente, and by some of Russia's small neighbors in Europe and the Middle East; and in July 1933, during the London Economic Conference, the U.S.S.R. concluded a nonaggression treaty embodying its definition with Afghanistan, Estonia, Latvia, Persia, Poland, Romania, and Turkey, as well as a similar agreement with the Little Entente (Czechoslovakia, Romania, and Yugoslavia). These nonaggression treaties foreshadowed the policy, intensively developed by the Soviet government since the end of World War II, of seeking to develop close security ties with neighboring countries.

Just as the Soviet government, in spite of its fundamental belief in the superiority of its system over that of "bourgeois capitalism," participated in disarmament discussions, so too it took part in a series of economic conferences in the inter-war years, from the Genoa Conference of 1922 to the London Economic Conference of 1933. For the Soviet government these conferences offered an opportunity to expound its own economic concepts, to seek safeguards against economic discrimination by other nations, and to obtain financial assistance for the purchase of tools and machinery abroad. The most interesting of these conferences, so far as the presentation of Soviet views was concerned, proved to be the International Economic Conference held at Geneva in 1927. At this gathering the Soviet representative, M. Obolenski, suggested a draft resolution stating that "with regard to the great importance of full participation of the U.S.S.R. in world trade, the conference recommends to all states to develop their relations with the Soviet Union on the basis of a pacific coëxistence of two different economic systems." By a paradox which has since become familiar, the Soviet representative accompanied this friendly-sounding resolution by a threat that, if the ideas he suggested were not accepted, the Soviet Union would have to withdraw. The conference met Russia's wishes in a resolution declaring that it regarded "the participation of members of all the countries present, irrespective of differences in their economic systems, as a happy augury for pacific coöperation of all nations." The Russian delegation itself had no doubts about the final outcome, one of its members predicting that competition between the two systems would end with the "happy elimination" of capitalism. "Time will prove," he asserted, "that of the two the socialist system is better calculated to eliminate economic inconsistencies and promote the development of potential productivity." Subsequent discussions, both at the International Economic Conference and at the London Economic Conference of 1933, revealed that the U.S.S.R., having a state monopoly of foreign trade, was not interested in the maintenance of tariffs and, on the contrary, being an exporter of grain, was particularly opposed to agrarian protectionism. At the same time it vigorously opposed cartels and industrial rationalization, on the ground that these measures injured the interests of the workers.

By the time Germany withdrew from the League of Nations in 1934, Russia, under Stalin's program of "building socialism in one country," had reached the point where, for the time being at least, it was less concerned with world revolution than with the twin needs of obtaining safeguards against German aggression and loans or credits from industrial countries for the purchase of urgently needed machinery and tools. During the five years of its participation in the work of the League of Nations (1934–1939), Russia, again represented by Litvinov, became the leading advocate of collective action against aggressor nations, urging such action against Japan in China, Italy in Ethiopia, and Germany when it started on its expansion to the east. Following the outbreak of World War II, Russia itself invaded

Finland in 1939 on the ground that that country was to have served as a base for German attack on Russian territory, and found that the League of Nations, which had refused to take any sanctions against Japan, Italy, and Germany, lost no time in expelling Russia as an aggressor nation. This action confirmed the early suspicions of Soviet leaders that the League was opposed to Russia and the Soviet system rather than to aggression in general.

In spite of Russia's unfavorable experience with the League of Nations, and its desire to limit international coöperation to a concert of the great powers patterned on the wartime conferences of Teheran, Moscow, and Yalta, Stalin was persuaded by President Roosevelt to have Russia participate in the negotiations of Dumbarton Oaks in 1944, which laid the groundwork for adoption at San Francisco in 1945 of the Charter creating the United Nations organization. Russia subsequently took an active role in the two parts of the first session of the General Assembly of the UN in London and at Lake Success in 1946.

10. OUTLOOK FOR THE FUTURE

To sum up, Russia considers that it has a stake in political developments not only in its sphere of influence, but all over the globe, and insists on being included in all international councils with the status of great power. Since it contends that the burden of responsibility for maintenance of peace must be borne by the great powers, and measures power by the availability of military strength and industrial resources, it consistently demands that all major decisions affecting security should be taken by the Big Four, and preferably the Big Two—Russia and the United States—leaving to small states only limited rights to present their opinions for consideration by the great.

The Russians are not convinced that the defeat of Germany and Japan has made an end of Nazism and Fascism, or has removed the threat of renewed aggression by the former Axis states. They believe, moreover, that the United States and Britain may decide in the future to use Germany or Japan or both to checkmate Russia. The traditional feeling of suspicious opposition to Britain has been increasingly extended to the United States as this country has forged closer economic and political links with post-war Britain. While Russia adheres to the United Nations organization, whose main function, in its opinion, is the maintenance of security, the Soviet government has tried to re-insure itself against possible renewed aggression from West or East by fostering the establishment of "friendly" governments along its far-flung borders. The fact that Russia, now that Germany and Japan are demilitarized, has at its disposal the largest and best-equipped land army in Europe and Asia has played an important part in causing Russia's neighbors to acquiesce in policies prescribed by Moscow—especially since Britain and the United States are geographically too far away to give them military aid against Russia. Many of these countries, however, had already been struggling before World War II with some of the political, economic, and social problems with which Russia has wrestled for a quarter of a century, and although by no means always ready to become slavish imitators of the Soviet system, have found Russia's experience of value in planning their own post-war reconstruction. In the long run, once the bitterness of civil strife which in practically every nation of Europe and Asia went hand in hand with war has somewhat abated, it will be the character and scope of economic recovery that will determine the political climate of war-torn continents. And in the economic, as in the political sphere, post-war Russia has indicated its intention of playing a decisive part.

8. Russia's Economic Stake in World Affairs

Probably one of the least expected results of World War II is the emergence of Russia as an economic challenge to the United States and, in lesser measure, other industrial nations as well. This challenge comes all the more as a surprise to the Western world because hitherto the principal competitors of industrial nations have been other industrial nations. Germany and Japan, for example, long before the war which brought about their downfall, vied with Britain and the United States for sources of raw materials and outlets for manufactured goods. While the U.S.S.R. has made great strides since 1917 in the direction of modern industrialization and agricultural collectivization, it still remains, judged by Western standards of production, technical skill, and labor efficiency, a relatively backward country. The competition it offers to the United States is not in terms of exports. The U.S.S.R. is hardly in a position, especially after the wartime destruction suffered by its industries, to export manufactured goods, except possibly to the less developed countries of the Near and Middle East, and Asia. Nor is there any immediate prospect that it will be able to compete seriously with the United States in the export of raw materials, which are urgently required for its own industrial reconstruction, or foodstuffs, in which it is experiencing grave shortages. Russia's challenge is that of a country which, because of its own boundless need for all kinds of products, offers a huge market for the exports of other nations. In this respect, Russia has and may continue to have a greater power of attraction for the raw material and food-producing countries of Eastern Europe and the Balkans than the United States, which hitherto has been more concerned in increasing its own exports than in encouraging imports from existing or potential customers.

1. RUSSIA'S POST-WAR TRADE PROBLEMS

Today Russia, having launched its fourth Five-Year Plan, which calls for an increased tempo of industrialization as well as for the reconstruction of devastated areas, is seeking to obtain raw materials and manufactured goods by all methods at its disposal. There is little doubt, as indicated by Stalin in his reply to a questionnaire submitted by Hugh Baillie of the United Press on October 21, 1946, that the U.S.S.R. would prefer to purchase the products it needs, especially machinery and tools, in the United States, whose technical "know-how" arouses the admiration and envy of the Russians. To make such purchases, however, the Russians would have to obtain a substantial loan in this country. At the end of the war it was reported that the United States might consider an application from Moscow for a loan or long-term credit similar to that extended to Britain in 1946. Russia, it was said, had wanted a credit of six billion dollars, and the counter-offer of the United States, reportedly delayed by the temporary misplacement of pertinent correspondence, had been approximately one billion dollars. The tide of public sentiment, however, has since then been running so much against Russia that it appears doubtful, at the present time, that Congress would approve any credits for reconstruction of Russia's economy, especially in view of the drastic cuts in governmental expenditures contemplated by the Republican party.

In the absence of a loan from the United States, Russia has resorted to a wide range of measures to fill its immediate needs. It has removed machinery and tools—in fact, entire factories, sometimes accompanied by workers and technicians —from occupied countries, especially the Russian zones of Germany and Austria, as well as Hungary and Romania, claiming part of this equipment under the head of reparation for the damage done to Russian industry by the Axis powers. It has channeled the production of factories in neighboring countries into its own economy by requiring the fulfillment of specific quotas, or by obtaining a controlling interest in factories and other enterprises through the seizure of shares formerly held by the German state or by German private owners, on occasion furnishing the raw materials needed for production. It has also concluded a series of bilateral trade treaties with all nations willing to enter into such agreements, under which Russia exchanges raw materials and certain foodstuffs for finished goods. Some of these bilateral agreements are linked in such a way as to create what is in effect triangular, or even broader, trade. For example, under the Russo-Polish trade treaty, the terms of which have not been made public, it is understood that Russia sends raw cotton from Central Asia to Poland, whose noted textile center of Lodz had served before 1914 as an important source of supply for the Czarist Empire until Polish exports, following World War I, were diverted to Western markets. Polish textile factories transform Russian cotton into cotton goods, part of which are retained by the Poles, part sent to Russia in payment for the raw cotton, and part to an industrial nation like Switzerland. The Swiss, in turn, send precision instruments, watches, and other manufactured goods, which Russia and Poland both lack, to Poland, and the Poles retain part of these manufactured goods, sending the balance to Russia. While such bilateral arrangements usually make no provision for financial transactions, this is not true of the Russo-Swedish treaty of October 6, 1946, which provides for a five-year Swedish credit to Russia.

2. STATE MONOPOLY OF TRADE

To understand the present conflict of economic interests between the United States and Russia, and to appraise the possibility of adjustment in the future, it is necessary to glance back at the character and course of Russia's foreign trade. Before 1914 Russia was primarily an exporter of grain (although it experienced severe periodic famines, it was known as "the granary of Europe") and certain raw materials, notably oil, manganese, timber, and precious stones and metals, particularly platinum, as well as furs. Its imports consisted primarily of manufactured goods, which the Russian economy, then still in the early stages of industrialization, was unable either to produce at all or to produce in adequate quantities, and raw materials for industry. The investment of foreign capital, chiefly British, French, German, and Belgian, financed the development of some industries and other enterprises, especially railways, tramways, and oil refineries. During World War I the Czarist government, to meet wartime emergencies, introduced a considerable measure of control over the country's foreign trade.

Following the establishment of the Soviet régime, and initial experimentation with a mixed economy under the New Economic Policy (NEP), the Soviet government assumed increasing control over all foreign trade operations, which were integrated into the program of internal economic development. At the present time the state has a complete monopoly of foreign trade. All foreign trade operations are handled by the Ministry (formerly Commissariat) of Foreign Trade, which directs, plans, and controls the country's foreign economic relations. The Ministry, headed for many years by Anastas I. Mikoyan, is represented in foreign countries by Trade Delegations (Torgpredstva), or by special corporations, such as the Amtorg Trading Corporation in the United States. The planning functions of the Ministry are performed by the Department of Planning and Economics. Export and import activities are carried out by the Export and Import Administration respectively. A special section, the Eastern Department, directs trade with the Eastern countries—Turkey, Iran, Afghanistan, Western China, the Tuva People's Republic,* and the Mongolian People's Republic. Shipping and railway transportation are handled by the Chief Transport Administration, and problems of foreign exchange and credit policy by the Foreign Exchange and Finance Administration.

The actual work of preparing goods for export is assigned to monopolistic state corporations the principal of which are Eksportles (lumber and timber production); Soyuznefteksport (oil and petroleum products); Eksportkhleb (grain, sugar, poultry, and other foodstuffs); Eksportlen (flax, cotton, and articles made of these fibers); Soyuzpromeksport (chemicals, minerals, and some finished products); Teknoeksport (machinery, equipment, rolling stock, metal goods); Soyuzeksport (coal, manganese, and iron ores); Raznoeksport (raw hides, bristles, down and feathers, tobacco and tobacco products); Mezhdunarodnaya Kniga (books and other publications). Similar corporations exist also for imports. An annual export and import plan is drawn up by the Ministry of Foreign Trade under the supervision of the State Planning Commission of the U.S.S.R. (*Gosplan*). Since the economic plans for the country as a whole are estimated on a long-term basis of five years at a time, export and import plans are drawn up on a similar basis.

The existence of a state monopoly of foreign trade enables the Soviet government not only to consider the purchase of

* Since the end of World War II the territory of Tannu Tuva has been incorporated into the U.S.S.R.

goods in terms of the country's economy as a whole, but to decide such questions as whether certain products formerly imported can henceforth be produced at home, thus releasing available foreign exchange for the purchase of products not previously imported or imported only in limited quantities. In other words, the program of exports and imports is directly geared into the economic development of the country at a given time. The foreign trade monopoly, moreover, makes it possible for the Soviet government to direct its trade into those channels which seem most desirable from the point of view of the U.S.S.R. not only economically but also politically. Such factors as political relations with a given country are considered along with the more technical problems of balance of trade, treaty obligations, currency restrictions, and so on. For example, Russia, although itself suffering from food shortages, shipped 500,000 tons of wheat to France on the eve of the May 1946 elections. In this respect, a comparison may be found in some recent aspects of United States foreign economic policy, notably Washington's decision to make loans or sell food primarily to countries which have been "friendly" to us, or have shown "gratitude" for previous gifts or credits.

The Soviet monopoly of foreign trade has been criticized abroad on the ground that it permits no free play for foreign private concerns, that it puts the private enterprise system at a disadvantage when matched with Russia's strictly controlled economy, and so on. The Russians, however, contend that their system assures greater stability to foreign trade over a period of years than do transactions between private concerns, and is thus an aid, not a hindrance, to private concerns abroad. This view is shared in increasing measure by many of Russia's suppliers, including Sweden and other Western industrial nations which have come to fear the instability of the United States economy. The Russians also point with pride to the record of the Soviet government in punctually meeting its financial obligations in connection with trade transactions. What the future may bring it is obviously difficult to predict. But in the past many private firms have found it possible to do business with the Russian state monopoly, and Russia's methods of sale and purchase have on the whole conformed to practices generally accepted abroad. At a time when the rest of the world was in the throes of the 1929 depression and its aftermath, Russia was widely accused of various malpractices, notably "dumping" and the sale of goods produced by "slave labor." It must be recalled, however, that at that time Russia, having just launched its first Five-Year Plan, was seeking to raise foreign exchange for the purchase of urgently needed machinery, tools, and other manufactured goods by the sale of raw materials and foodstuffs under highly unfavorable conditions, since prices of products it could export had declined on world markets far more sharply than prices of products it had to import. It was therefore ready to sell at any price, not for political reasons as was then suspected, but for reasons of economic stringency.

During the period 1921–1927, when Russia was recovering from the effects of World War I and civil war, it paid for a substantial part of its imports by exporting gold and by accumulating foreign short-term indebtedness. In those years Russia received no long-term loans, and was subjected to a wide range of discriminatory practices, such as sales of goods by "blocs" of suppliers who forced up prices on Russian purchases, refusal to accept commercial paper based on sales to Russia or to discount at accepted rates, and so on. The bulk of Russia's imports consisted of raw materials for the production of consumer goods, such as cotton, wool, hides, skins, and leather.

The first Five-Year Plan was inaugurated in 1928, just before the world was plunged into a great depression. Russia had to continue, and expand, imports to meet the needs of the Five-Year Plan—for example, tractors and agricultural machinery. Imports of consumer goods were cut to the bone, and imports of foodstuffs were limited to foods not produced in the U.S.S.R., mostly "colonial wares"—tea, coffee, cocoa, and rice. The principal exports continued to be grains (of which the Russian people had to deprive themselves), oil and oil products, timber and timber products, furs, cotton textiles, and sugar. The emphasis in imports was on means of production for the creation of heavy industries, rather than on mass consumption goods.

After 1931, when some progress had been made toward development of domestic industry, efforts were undertaken to reduce imports of means of production. For example, with the increase of domestic output, the import of agricultural machinery, mostly tractors, practically came to an end in 1934. The same was true of motor vehicles, notably trucks, and Russia even exported some vehicles to Eastern countries. By 1937 Russia was increasing imports of consumer goods and raw materials for industry, and decreasing imports of manufactured goods. As the country's economy was expanded under successive Five-Year Plans, it became less and less dependent on imports from abroad. Some observers believe that "the low level of the import of mass consumer goods was dictated entirely by considerations of foreign exchange," and that, had foreign exchange been available, the import of consumer goods would have been far larger.* In general, it can be said that, for Russia, foreign trade constitutes primarily a means of obtaining goods it cannot produce at home. It is entirely possible that, when the country's needs can be filled from domestic resources, imports will be drastically reduced.

In spite of the size of its population and the wealth of its

* Alexander M. Baykov, *Soviet Foreign Trade* (Princeton: Princeton University Press, 1946), to whose study the author is indebted for some of the material in this section.

natural resources, the U.S.S.R. has not hitherto played an important part in world trade. Russia's imports in 1913 accounted for 3.6 per cent of world imports, and this percentage had dropped to 0.9 per cent in 1937; while its exports in 1913 accounted for 4.2 per cent of world exports, and by 1937 had dropped to 1.3 per cent. Analyzing Soviet trade by countries, we find that Russia before 1939 exported to the industrial nations of the West mostly agricultural and timber products and industrial raw materials, while to the countries of the East it exported some manufactured goods. Because of concentration of the nation's efforts on development of its own as yet relatively backward economy, the content of Russian exports is far less varied than that of the advanced industrial countries of the West, and does not as yet differ markedly from the range of products exported by the Czarist Empire before 1914. It should be noted, however, in view of the post-war controversy concerning Russia's bilateral trade agreements, that before 1939 the foreign trade of the U.S.S.R. was "definitely multilateral in character, with a very stable distribution of exports between the major countries," and this was true also of imports.*

The Soviet government has used several methods to recoup the losses inflicted on its economy by the Axis countries, and to supply the Russian people with urgently needed consumer goods. Among these methods have been the collection of reparations in kind from former enemy nations, both out of existing assets and current production; requisitions of food and other products for the maintenance of armies of occupation, which at one time were estimated at over two million men; short-term bilateral arrangements with neighboring countries, both friends and former foes, for the barter exchange of goods; arrangements for "economic collaboration" with Hungary and Romania; and long-term agreements for the purchase of goods on credit, notably with Sweden.

* *Ibid.*

3. REPARATIONS FROM AXIS COUNTRIES

The Potsdam declaration of July 1945 gave Russia the right to remove capital goods and equipment from its zone of Germany as reparations, and to acquire shares in German enterprises; to receive 25 per cent of industrial capital equipment from the British and American zones, 10 per cent without payment or exchange of any kind in return, and 15 per cent in exchange for foodstuffs and certain raw materials from the Russian zone; and to acquire "German external assets" in Eastern Austria and the Axis satellites. Since "German external assets" has never been defined, the Russians have in a number of instances seized property once belonging to the citizens of Austria and the Axis satellites which was previously confiscated by the Germans during the Nazi occupation. No provision was made at Potsdam for joint Allied accounting or control of reparations. Nor had any agreement been reached by the Allies concerning the amount of reparations to be paid by Japan at the time that Russia stripped Manchuria of industrial equipment—for reasons of security rather than for economic considerations. It should be pointed out, however, that Russia's right to reparations from Germany was subject to two conditions —an agreed level-of-industry plan and an agreed import-export plan for Germany as a whole—conditions which Russia failed to fulfill.

While the Western powers have become increasingly concerned with the disruption that the removal of reparations in kind may inflict on the economy of Germany, Austria, and the Axis satellites, notably Hungary, Russia has taken the point of view that reparations serve a valuable twofold purpose. First, they contend, reparations are needed literally to repair the economic losses suffered by the United Nations, especially Russia, as a result of German devastation. Second, reparations perform the important task of reducing the industrial war potential of the defeated countries, especially Germany, which before 1939 was admittedly the most powerful industrial nation on the European continent.

While it is known that Russia removed large quantities of machinery, tools, and other equipment from its zones in Germany and Austria, in some instances taking along technicians and skilled workers connected with German enterprises, exact information as to the categories of goods and their estimated value is not available. In the case of reparations claimed and so far collected by Russia from the Axis satellites—Hungary, Romania, and Finland—the following information is substantially accurate as of May 1948.*

Under the armistice with Hungary that country was to pay Russia $200,000,000 originally over a period of six years, at $35,500,000 a year. When the full amount was not paid during the first year, January 1945 to January 1946, Russia extended the period of payment to eight years, with $21,800,-000 due the second year, and increased annually on a graduated scale until $30,000,000 would be due in the final years of the arrangement. By the end of July 1946 Hungary had paid a total of $20,000,000, mostly in industrial goods. In a note of July 23, 1946, the United States called the attention of the Soviet Union to "the grave economic plight of Hungary" due to "the over-burdening of that country with reparations, requisitions, and the costs of maintaining large occupation forces." It requested the Soviet government to instruct its representatives in Hungary to concert at an early date with the United States and British representatives there "in devising a program which would bring to an end the process of disintegration in Hungary, and at the same time provide a framework within which the rehabilitation of the country and its reintegration with the general European economy might be accomplished." Early in 1947 Hungary, an agra-

---

* All dollar amounts of reparations are expressed in 1938 prices and accordingly are considerably higher than would be the same amounts in current dollars.

rian country which had developed a number of industrial enterprises during the war and whose economy had been disorganized as a result of Russian levies, appeared to show signs of recovery. Russia has reduced requisitions on Hungary for maintenance of occupation forces, once estimated at 500,000, apparently because of reduction in their numbers.

The armistice with Romania obligated that country to pay $300,000,000 to Russia over a period of six years, the reparations year running from September to September. Romania, whose economy was only slightly affected by the war, is reported to have fulfilled its obligations so far. The payment of reparations, however, has wrought havoc with the resources of the country, which in the winter of 1947 reported conditions of starvation in certain areas. The reparations, originally to have been paid in foodstuffs, were modified so that payment could be made almost entirely in petroleum. Romanian oil owned by American and British concerns has been used to pay reparations to Russia, and negotiations are under way for Romanian compensation to Western owners of this oil at a "fair price." Romania also pays a sum for restitution of goods moved by that country from Russia during the war. Payments on this account amounted to $175,000,000 by 1946, and may come to another $200,000,000 before they are completed. Russian requisition of Romanian goods has so far amounted to $425,000,000.

The armistice with Finland obligated that country to pay $300,000,000 to Russia over a period of six years, subsequently prolonged to eight years. To date Finland, which has expanded industrial output for this purpose, has been fulfilling its reparations obligations punctually, and Russia has assessed little against the Finns in terms of restitution and requisition. Early in 1947 Finland was running about $4,-000,000 behind in its reparations payments to Russia. This arrearage came as a result of world shortage of raw and finished goods, not as a result of shortcomings in Finland's productive capacity. Finland has been unable to purchase abroad some of the materials needed for certain types of production, and lacking these materials has been unable to turn out all the machinery it had undertaken to furnish to Russia under its reparations agreement.

Russia has claimed no reparations from Bulgaria, and has sought to defend that country against reparations claims by other United Nations on the ground that the Bulgarian people voluntarily overthrew the government which had brought it into the war on the Axis side. Russia has also demanded no restitution from Bulgaria, although it has requisitioned some goods for the maintenance of occupation forces. During the autumn 1946 meeting of the Council of Foreign Ministers in New York Russia agreed to the demand of the Western powers that under the Bulgarian peace treaty Bulgaria should pay $25,000,000 to Yugoslavia and $45,000,-000 to Greece.

Russia has shown increasing interest in obtaining, as reparations, not only goods already available in Axis countries at the end of the war, but goods out of current production specially designed to meet its needs, and in some cases has been ready to furnish raw materials for the output of such goods. For example, under the Italian peace treaty, Russia is to receive $100,000,000 from Italy, chiefly in the form of goods out of current production, and is to provide Italy with some of the raw materials required for that purpose. At the Moscow conference Molotov demanded, without success, reparations out of the current industrial production of Germany's western zones which include the Ruhr valley and contain the bulk of German heavy industry, notably iron and steel, in contrast to the Russian zone, which produces chiefly foodstuffs and consumer goods.

4. RUSSIA'S TRADE AGREEMENTS WITH NEIGHBORING COUNTRIES

Another method used by Russia to obtain urgently needed goods is that of bilateral barter trade agreements. Since the end of the war Russia has concluded such agreements with eight neighboring countries of Northern and Eastern Europe —Finland, Poland, Czechoslovakia, Hungary, Romania, Bulgaria, Yugoslavia, and Norway. With slight variations, these agreements list goods to be exchanged by the two signatories, and set prices for those goods, usually in terms of U. S. dollars or Swiss francs, never in terms of the Russian ruble which is not quoted on foreign exchanges. These agreements do not differ materially from ordinary European bilateral agreements, whose number had grown in the interwar years, except for the important fact that they set the prices of goods to be exchanged. All agreements are shortterm, running in most instances for one year, never more than eighteen months. All provide for clearing arrangements, with the clearing balance to be kept in books by both parties.

Russia's bilateral trade agreements with its neighbors have been criticized by the United States on the ground that they are exclusive in character, violate Article VII of the American-Russian master lend-lease agreement of 1941,* and con-

---

* Report to the 78th Congress on Lend-Lease Operations, Article VII, p. 72.

"In the final determination of the benefits to be provided to the United States of America by the Government of the Union of Soviet Socialist Republics in return for aid furnished under the Act of Congress of March 11, 1941, the terms and conditions thereof shall be such as not to burden commerce between the two countries, but to promote mutually advantageous economic relations between them and the betterment of world-wide economic relations. To that end they shall include provision for agreed action by the United States of America and the Union of Soviet Socialist Republics, open to par-

stitute an obstacle to the development of freer multilateral trade, sponsored by the Washington administration. An examination of the actual terms of the treaties, however, does not indicate exclusive domination by Russia of the economies of the countries affected. True, for the duration of the trade agreements, these countries are to make deliveries of specified raw materials and manufactured goods to Russia, which are thus diverted from other markets, as well as from native consumers. In return, Russia supplies primarily some items of food and raw materials, but none of the manufactured goods required by the countries of Northern and Eastern Europe which, so far as can be determined, are free to negotiate for the purchase of such goods in Western countries and, in some cases, have already done so. It is true that the barter trade agreements may temporarily constitute a limitation on the economic relations of Russia's neighbors with other nations because of the current scarcity of the products they have for export, and which may have to be reserved, for the present, to fill Russia's requirements. Russia, however, has proved ready to make repeated adjustments in trade agreements when this appears to be necessary. For

---

ticipation by all other countries of like mind, directed to the expansion, by appropriate international and domestic measures, of production, employment, and the exchange and consumption of goods, which are the material foundations of the liberty and welfare of all peoples; to the elimination of all forms of discriminatory treatment in international commerce, and to the reduction of tariffs and other trade barriers; and in general, to the attainment of all the economic objectives set forth in the Joint Declaration made on August 14, 1941, by the President of the United States of America and the Prime Minister of the United Kingdom, the basic principles of which were adhered to by the Government of the Union of Soviet Socialist Republics on September 24, 1941.

"At an early convenient date, conversations shall be begun between the two Governments with a view to determining, in the light of governing economic conditions, the best means of attaining the above-stated objectives by their own agreed action and of seeking the agreed action of other like-minded Governments."

instance, the Russo-Finnish agreement has been modified several times during 1946–1947.

While the complete terms of Russia's trade agreements with countries of Northern and Eastern Europe have not been published, the following information concerning their principal terms has been collated from various authoritative sources:

Poland. Russia has a trade agreement with Poland providing for the exchange of $96,000,000 worth of goods each way. Poland is to deliver coal, steel, zinc, and other raw materials and manufactured goods, while Russia is to deliver cotton and certain other raw materials. The two countries also have a commercial treaty providing for the development and strengthening of economic relations, including most-favored-nation treatment.

Hungary. The Russo-Hungarian trade agreement provides for an exchange of $30,000,000 worth of goods each way. To date, Russia has delivered $7,000,000 worth of raw materials to Hungary, and the latter has delivered some cement to Russia.

Bulgaria. The Russo-Bulgarian trade agreement provides for an exchange of $36,000,000 worth of goods each way. Under a supplementary trade agreement Russia is to deliver a large quantity of wheat to Bulgaria.

Romania. The Russo-Romanian trade agreement provides for an exchange of $20,000,000 worth of goods each way. During 1946, the first year of operation, it is reported that Romania received $13,200,000 worth, and sent to Russia $7,500,000 worth of goods.

Yugoslavia. The Russo-Yugoslav trade agreement provides for mutual exchange of goods, but the value of the exchange is not known.

Czechoslovakia. The Russo-Czechoslovak trade agreement provides, not for a list of goods to be exchanged, as in the other agreements, but for the procedure under which the

Russians and Czechs will make trade contracts. It also differs from other trade agreements by fixing the values in terms of the Czech crown. Russia sends Czechoslovakia raw cotton, flax, pyrites, manganese, iron ore, nickel, zinc, petroleum products, asbestos, rubber, and chemicals. Czechoslovakia sends Russia rolling mill products, textiles, and boots.

Finland. The Russo-Finnish trade agreement of 1945 provided for delivery of Russian grain to Finland in exchange for Finnish nickel, cobalt, and sulphur ore, and repairs of Russian ships in Finland's shipyards. An agreement signed on April 20, 1946 provided for the exchange of goods between Russia and Finland during the latter half of the year to a global amount of $32,000,000, with possible additional trade provided for. Russia agreed to deliver to Finland 60,000 metric tons of rye, 40,000 metric tons of wheat, considerable quantities of fertilizers, and various amounts of sugar, coal, and raw materials. Finland was to supply to Russia 6,500 prefabricated houses, as well as barracks, lumber, chemical pulp, paper, paper products, and metals. In addition, private Finnish firms were authorized to make sales contracts directly with Soviet foreign trade organizations, to a total amount not exceeding $1,500,000 in both directions, subject to export and import regulations in both countries.

Norway. The Russo-Norwegian trade treaty of 1947 provides that Norway and Russia will exchange annually $8,000,000 to $12,000,000 worth of goods. The treaty runs for two years and is renewable indefinitely. Norway undertakes to deliver to Russia this year 10,000 tons of whale fats and 20,000 tons of fish, as well as other products. Russia, in turn, undertakes to deliver to Norway in the same period, 260,000 tons of coal and coke, 40,000 tons of grain, 110,000 tons of minerals, and other items, among them lumber, chemical products, precious metals, and fruits. Private Norwegian concerns are free to conclude cash deals with the Soviet Ministry of Foreign Trade apart from the treaty terms.

5. ECONOMIC COLLABORATION ARRANGEMENTS

In addition to these trade agreements, Russia has made arrangements with Hungary and Romania for a controlling share of some of these two countries' principal industrial and shipping enterprises by seizing, as German external assets under the Potsdam declaration, shares in these concerns previously confiscated by the German state or by German individuals. Under the economic collaboration agreement with Hungary, joint Russo-Hungarian organizations are set up, through which the Soviet government acquires a 50 per cent interest and control of bauxite production, oil and petroleum refining, coal production, power plants, electrical and agricultural machinery enterprises, the chemical industry, air and motor transport development, agricultural research, and a bank to finance these enterprises. To give a specific example of how such an arrangement works, Russia and Hungary have established a joint stock company for oil and petroleum production called *Sovmagnaft*. The assets Russia placed in this company included the German oil concession *Manat*, seized by the Russians as a German asset, and some other German holdings; while Hungary contributed to the joint enterprise the petroleum installation of Malj, the refinery of Szouy, which has a capacity of 250,000 tons, and the royalty of 15 per cent of the crude output of American wells owned by Maort, a Hungarian-American company connected with Standard Oil of New Jersey. *Sovmagnaft* is composed of three companies for marketing and transporting oil, and is exempted by Hungary from all import and export duties.

A similar economic collaboration arrangement has been concluded by Russia with Romania, providing for the "participation of Soviet capital and technical assistance in the intensification of Romanian economic activity." Russo-Romanian companies, also organized on a 50–50 basis, are to

control the following economic enterprises: petroleum production, navigation, shipbuilding, hydroelectric production
and development, air transport and civil aviation, timber,
glass, mining, and metallurgy. While Romanian oil fields
owned by American concerns are not directly affected by the
Russo-Romanian collaboration arrangement, oil from these
fields is bought by Romania for delivery to Russia as reparations. The United States and Romania have so far failed
to agree about the price to be paid by the Romanian government for this oil.

From the point of view of the United States, this series
of agreements constitutes unwarranted penetration by Russia into the economies of neighboring countries, to the detriment of other nations which either had trade and financial
interests in this area before 1939, or hoped to develop such
interests after the war. From the point of view of Moscow,
these arrangements represent an attempt to obtain access to
foodstuffs, raw materials, manufactured goods, and transportation facilities which Russia either lacks altogether or does
not possess in sufficient quantities for the fulfillment of its
economic program and the satisfaction of the growing needs
of its population. Unlike the United States and Britain, Russia has no capital for investment in the enterprises of relatively undeveloped countries, and has resorted to the device
of using German assets seized as reparations in lieu of capital. The 50–50 arrangements, as seen from Moscow, do not
differ materially from joint-stock companies previously
formed by citizens of Western countries for the development of resources in nations regarded as backward—for example, the Anglo-Iranian Oil Company, in which British
interests have a controlling share of 51 per cent and a part
of whose output, beginning in 1947, has been assigned to
Standard Oil of New Jersey and Socony Vacuum. To Westerners the fundamental difference is that the controlling share
in a wide range of enterprises in Eastern Europe and the

Balkans is now held not by private Russian investors, but by the Soviet state, with its control of Russia's economy and its monopoly of foreign trade.

6. RUSSO-SWEDISH TRADE AGREEMENT

Russia, however, is ready to make financially orthodox arrangements for foreign trade whenever credits for this purpose are made available by other countries, as indicated by the Russo-Swedish trade agreement. This agreement, signed by Russia and Sweden in Moscow on October 7, 1946 and approved by the Swedish *Riksdag* on November 13, consists of two treaties—one concerning credits to be extended to Russia by Sweden, and the other listing goods to be exchanged by the two countries. The Swedish government grants Russia a credit of one billion crowns ($278,500,000) to be used during a period of five years, although some Swedish deliveries, because of production difficulties, will not be made until the sixth year. In principle, a credit of 200 million crowns is to be advanced annually, but transfers from one year to the following may take place, with the understanding that the credit is not to exceed 300 million crowns in any one year. Total Swedish deliveries of goods on credit during the next five or six years will amount to about 850 million crowns. The remaining 150 million will be used to pay for freight and other charges. During the first year, primarily due to the inability of Swedish industry to assure immediate fulfillment of Russia's requirements, deliveries will be relatively small, and it is estimated that in 1947 Sweden's total shipments of industrial products to Russia will not amount to more than 45 million crowns—compared with Sweden's 1937 exports to Britain valued at 452 million crowns, to Germany valued at 314 million, and to the United States valued at 220 million. Russia is to repay the Swedish credits within fifteen years at an annual rate of 3 per cent. During the first three years, however, no interest will be charged, and due to this and certain other stipulations the actual rate will be only 2⅜ per cent.

The list of goods to be exchanged by the two countries offers an interesting forecast of Russia's export and import plans for the duration of the fourth Five-Year Plan. Swedish deliveries on credit will include equipment for electric power stations, steam power works, mechanized extraction and concentration of ores, mechanization of forestry and, possibly, of peat extraction, housing construction and production of housing materials, steam locomotives, trawlers, and other mechanical equipment. Sweden is also to supply various kinds of high quality steel and steel products, drilling pipes, steam boiler tubes, materials for the manufacture of ball bearings, ball and roller bearings, optical and measuring instruments, spare parts for turbo-generators, and other industrial products, as well as products of agriculture and fisheries —such as horses, breeding stock, herring, and so on. Russia, in return, will send to Sweden various industrial and other raw materials, such as chromium and manganese ore, asbestos, gypsum, nickel, silver, platinum, mineral oils, cotton and flax, as well as certain quantities of pig iron and rolling mill products which will be used for the manufacture of equipment that Sweden is to deliver to Russia on credit. The Soviet Union is also to supply Sweden with fertilizers, such as apatite and potash, which Sweden previously obtained from Germany.

While Russo-Swedish negotiations were in progress, the United States, in a note addressed to Sweden, "stated its concern regarding the effect of long-term, bilateral agreements of an exclusive nature for the exchange of goods on our objectives for the multilateral expansion of trade." It indicated its hope that Sweden "will have inserted in any bilateral agreement an appropriate clause permitting modification to conform to any general multilateral basis." It also communicated to both Sweden and Russia its desire to promote multilateral trade on a nondiscriminatory basis in accordance with its "Proposals for Expansion of World Trade and Employment," which were subsequently discussed at the London conference of November 1946 on the establishment of an International Trade Organization. In addition, in its note to the U.S.S.R., the United States expressed the hope that that country would not undertake commitments which would be contrary to the principles of Article VII of the master lend-lease agreement. To this point the Soviet government replied that the character of the trade negotiations with Sweden bore no relationship to the principles of Article VII.

In answer to American comments, Swedish spokesmen pointed out that, as a result of the war, Sweden had lost its principal market in Europe—Germany—and was merely seeking substitute outlets for its exports in the Russian market, which offered prospects of stability; and that, at most, Sweden's exports to Russia over the next five years would amount to only 10 to 15 per cent of its total exports, a percentage that could hardly be regarded as exclusive. After the Russo-Swedish agreement went into effect, several of the Swedish industries scheduled to fill the needs of the U.S.S.R. reported that their production facilities were not adequate for the task, and Sweden imposed restrictions on imports to avoid the danger of inflation. Since the conclusion of the Swedish-Russian trade agreement, Swedish industries have found it difficult to fill some of Russia's requirements, and as a result trade between the two countries has been smaller than anticipated.

7. OUTLOOK FOR THE FUTURE

Given existing conditions, both within the U.S.S.R. and in the rest of the world, what conclusions can be drawn as to the probable course of Russia's foreign economic relations with other countries over the next five or ten years? With international commerce in a state of flux, and political readjustments still in the making all over the globe, only the most tentative conclusions can be reached, among them the following:

a) Russia has suffered grave economic losses as a result of the war. At the present time it is confronted with serious shortages not only of consumer goods, foodstuffs, and certain raw materials, but also of labor. Lack of man power is directly responsible for accelerated demobilization, which demonstrates more convincingly than any pleas for disarmament or professions of peace that the U.S.S.R. does not anticipate war in the near future.

(b) The foreign trade monopoly is an integral feature of Soviet planned economy. Other countries which have adopted measures of national economic planning, for example Britain, have come to recognize that domestic planning involves planning also of foreign trade, and, in fact, logically calls for measures of international planning. While there is no doubt that Russia's economic policy, like that of other countries, is affected by political considerations, the economic aspects of the foreign trade monopoly must not be neglected. As previously noted, Russia uses foreign trade to obtain the goods it lacks or cannot produce at a given time. It is from this angle rather than that of political domination of neighboring countries, that Russia's post-war bilateral barter trade agreements must be viewed.

(c) The U.S.S.R. needs all kinds of machinery, tools, and equipment for various heavy and light industries and the transport system it proposes to rebuild, expand, or create anew under the fourth Five-Year Plan. During the period of reconstruction it will offer a stable market for a wide range of manufactured goods produced by the industrial nations. Once its own industrial production has achieved levels at which domestic needs can be adequately filled, imports of corresponding products will be curtailed or altogether abandoned. It is possible that, at such a time—still some distance in the future—available foreign exchange would be applied to the purchase of growing quantities of consumer goods, which have hitherto been at the bottom of the Soviet government's import list.

(d) The Soviet concept of the role of foreign trade in a controlled economy, and the urgent need to reconstruct the areas ravaged by war, determine Russia's attitude toward international finance and international trade. Not only does the Soviet government rigidly control the country's exports and imports, but the internal currency, the ruble, not quoted on foreign exchanges, is operated by the government as a managed money system, unconnected with price levels or monetary fluctuations abroad. Nor does the Russian state have any foreign investments. Russia consequently has far less interest in international financial arrangements than the majority of other countries, which must adjust their economies in greater or lesser degree to changes in world economy. From the point of view of the Soviet government, the Bretton Woods institutions—the International Monetary Fund and the International Bank for Reconstruction and Development—are of value to Russia primarily as possible sources of international credit for the expansion of Russian purchases abroad, not as agencies for world financial stabilization. The Soviet leaders, moreover, have no intention of permitting these international institutions to intervene in the internal economic arrangements of the U.S.S.R. In the opinion of Soviet spokesmen, many of the provisions of the Bretton Woods agreement are devised primarily to deal with the peculiar problems of capitalist economy, and are inapplicable to the conditions existing in the U.S.S.R. While Russia uses gold to balance its international accounts when it does not have adequate amounts of foreign exchange, and is therefore interested in stabilization of foreign currency in terms of gold, it has been reluctant since 1936 to publish statistics on its current gold reserves and actual or potential production of gold bullion. This reluctance to submit statistical data for international scrutiny is regarded by some observers as one of the reasons for Russia's failure to ratify the Bretton Woods agreements by December 31, 1945, as it would have had to do to become a charter member of the Fund and Bank.

(e) Russia, for its part, also has to face some hard facts in international economic affairs. Among them is the fact that, at its present stage of economic development, it is not in a position to furnish to the countries whose products it wants the machinery and tools they were formerly able to obtain from Germany, Britain, and the United States. This means that, after a given time, when existing machinery and tools have been worn out or have become obsolete, Russia, if it tried to bar neighboring countries from trade with the Western powers, would find that it had merely succeeded in killing the goose that laid the golden egg.

Available evidence indicates that, while Russia is seeking to obtain an important share of the output of neighboring countries on a short-term basis, it is not preventing them from establishing economic contacts with the rest of the world—provided these contacts do not result in attempts to oust Russian economic interests and, with them, Russian political influence. Russia's foreign economic policy is often compared to that of Nazi Germany. Germany, however, itself a highly industrialized country, had little to gain by the industrialization of Eastern Europe and the Balkans. On the contrary, it preferred to maintain the countries of that area at a level of development where they could serve as sources of food and raw materials for the German people and a market for German exports. Russia, by contrast, stands to gain, in the immediate future at least, by the expansion of industrial production in neighboring countries, since it can absorb, on a barter basis, practically all they can produce. Poland, Czechoslovakia, Finland, and Hungary, to name only a few examples, have all sought to obtain credits in the United States for the purchase of industrial equipment and other manufactured goods, and have displayed an active interest in renewing their pre-war ties with Western countries.

American and British businessmen, however, are not interested in developing a substantial volume of trade and investment with Russia's neighbors until they are certain that they will receive better treatment than that accorded, to cite one instance, to Allied oil companies in Romania, and that joint stock companies set up by the Russians in Romania and Hungary will not receive treatment so favorable as to constitute discrimination against private foreign concerns. The decision of the Soviet government to abstain, and force its neighbors to abstain, from participation in European discussions concerning the Marshall plan, was regarded as an attempt to roll down an economic, as well as political, "iron curtain" across Europe. This impression was strengthened by increased efforts on Russia's part to supply some of the most urgent needs of neighboring countries, which might otherwise have been filled by gifts or paid imports from the United States. To understand Russia's attitude toward the Marshall plan, it must be borne in mind that the Kremlin, however unjustifiable this may seem to us, regards American aid to Eastern Europe and the Balkans as an entering wedge for political intervention which, the Russians believe or claim to believe, could be only anti-Russian intervention. Yet Russia's capacity to develop what has been referred to in the American press as the "Molotov plan" by further extension of barter agreements, is obviously limited by the as yet low productivity of Russian industry and agriculture, and the growing demands of Russian consumers. The fate of the Marshall plan east of Berlin might have been far different if it had not been preceded by the outspokenly anti-Russian Truman Doctrine. Moreover, American emphasis on the need to rebuild German industry, which is resented by other victims of Nazism besides the Russians, and the prevalent fear in Europe of having to make a fateful choice between capitalism and communism, when most European countries want neither, operated in favor of Russia and against the United States.

To sum up, Russia, although still a backward country industrially, is playing an important part in international economic affairs, not because of the value or volume of its foreign trade, which remains small, but because it offers a vast market for all kinds of manufactured products, both capital equipment and consumer goods. This market, moreover, is determined for five-year periods in advance under successive Five-Year Plans and is strictly controlled by the state monopoly of foreign trade. The two factors of unlimited need for imports and stability of controlled import conditions attract to Russia all countries which are seeking outlets for their products, including some of the leading industrial nations of Western Europe like Britain, Sweden, and Switzerland who, in the past, have found the United States unreceptive to increased imports. Yet because of its industrial backwardness Russia cannot supply even to relatively undeveloped countries the manufactured products they need for their post-war reconstruction and can obtain in adequate quantities only from a nation with a high level of industrial production like the United States. Thus both in the political and in the economic spheres Russia and the United States, poles apart in historical development, ideas, and practices, ultimately challenge each other in the eyes of the rest of the world as sources of ideological influence and dispensers of material advantages.

PART IV

PROBLEMS OF RUSSO–AMERICAN RELATIONS

9. What Kind of Democracy?

Now that we have seen how the political and economic configuration of the post-war world appears to the Russians, what may be said to be the principal problems that create or threaten to create friction between Russia and the United States? Are these problems susceptible of adjustment, given willingness on both sides to arrive at an understanding, or are they of a character to make war inevitable? On what points is it possible to reach a compromise without giving the appearance of "appeasement"? On what points is it advisable to be "firm" or "tough" without giving the appearance of irremediable hostility?

1. MUTUAL PRECONCEPTIONS—TRUE OR FALSE?

In analyzing this country's relations with Russia it is more important than in the case of most other nations to weigh not only the effect of tangibles like military might or loans or strategic bases, but also such intangibles as the ideas the United States and Russia have developed about each other during the past quarter of a century. False as the preconceptions each of the two countries has about the other may seem to detached observers, these preconceptions have acquired just as much validity as if they were true, and exercise a powerful if sometimes unrecognized influence on the making of policy in Washington and Moscow. The Russians,

although in many ways more attuned to the United States
than to any other Western power, have built up for their
people the idea that this country is the bulwark of reactionary capitalism, opposed to the desire of backward nations
for independence and social progress, and an imperialistic
nation bent on acquiring all the resources and bases it can
get hold of with the ultimate objective of blocking, or even
subjugating the U.S.S.R. This Russian concept of the United
States, somewhat mellowed by wartime contacts between
the two countries, has been revived in full force since the
end of the war, and given a newly sinister emphasis following the victory of the Republicans, whom the Russians
regard as sworn enemies of Roosevelt's policy of Russo-
American coöperation. The United States, for its part, has
built up the idea that Russia is the inspiration of all movements for change, irrespective of historic antecedents or
geographic location, and that the consolidation of the Russian system spells the end of free private enterprise and democracy throughout the world. This concept, held in abey-
ance during the war in deference to "our Russian ally," has
also emerged since V–E Day with renewed vehemence, and
has been given a powerful impetus by Russia's prolonged
occupation of former Axis territories, its barter trade arrangements, and its policy of fostering "friendly" governments in neighboring countries. Were Russia's ideas of
America and America's ideas of Russia accepted as reality,
American reactionary imperialism would appear irreconcil-
ably counterposed to Russian aggressive revolution, with no
outcome possible except a world-shattering collision. In such
circumstances there would be little hope left for mankind
in a century described by the French writer Albert Camus
as "the century of fear," and the atomic bomb would be
merely a symbol of inevitable cosmic destruction.

2. CONFLICT OF UTOPIAS

The real conflict between the United States and Russia is both much deeper and more susceptible of adjustment than the already outworn concepts of imperialism and revolution would imply. It is only outwardly concerned with clashing claims to territories or natural resources—although such clashes have arisen and may arise, for example, about bases close to the Arctic region or the Dardanelles, or about the oil of the Near East. Fundamentally, however, it is, as has often been repeated but usually with little inner comprehension, a conflict of ideas or, perhaps, as Camus has put it, of utopias. The United States is convinced that it has found the secret of individual liberty and material prosperity. Russia is equally convinced that it has found the secret of "socialist democracy" and mass welfare. Yet to millions of people in the rest of the world who fear the industrial collectivism typified by Detroit almost as much as the political collectivism typified by Moscow there sometimes seems little to choose between two utopias, both magnificent in conception but, in the opinion of non-Americans and non-Russians, in each case as yet inadequately fulfilled.

This conflict of ideas, which permeates the world atmosphere like some penetrating emanation from which there can be no escape, must somehow or other be resolved before any of the concrete political and economic problems that have arisen between the United States and Russia can be given realistic consideration. It is idle to discuss the statute of Trieste, or free navigation of the Danube, or the character of elections in Poland, or the future of the Dardanelles, or the tug of war between Right and Left in Latin America, or relations between Chiang Kai-shek and the Chinese Communists, until we are clear in our own minds as to the general principles we are trying to apply in each specific

instance. To try to settle these questions by invoking old for-
mulas like the rights of minorities, the "open door," spheres
of influence, the sovereignty of small nations, "equality of
economic opportunity," is like trying to cure cancer with
old wives' potions. Compromise reached in these terms may
afford temporary relief to an ailing world, but the source of
the disease remains untouched. This disease is the profound
confusion into which the Western world has been thrown by
the disappearance of old established values without as yet the
substitution of new ones—a confusion made to appear all the
more threatening by the seemingly impregnable confidence
of Communist doctrinaires.

3. SYMPATHY FOR CHANGE THE GUIDING THREAD

What is the guiding thread that might help to lead us out
of the labyrinth of Russo-American controversies? This
thread is the realization that history does not stand still, that,
much as we wish, we cannot stop the clock at the point at
which we in this country had achieved what we rightly regarded as an unrivaled measure of personal liberty and economic prosperity, that our greatest danger lies not in being
destroyed by Russian atomic bombs but in becoming identified as supporters of the *status quo* all over the world. Once
we have reached this conclusion, we shall no longer be as
mentally distraught as we have been by such questions as
whether or not we should support reactionaries in Greece,
or Spain, or Argentina, or China, or Germany as a counter-
weight to Communism. We shall not like Communism any
better, because the political dictatorship of Russia, with its
suppression of civil liberties and its secret police will remain repugnant to Americans. But we shall begin to see that
reaction fosters Communism instead of halting it. And we
shall start searching for some alternative course which would

permit changes to be effected by peaceful means wherever
and whenever they appear necessary, in the hope thereby of
averting resort to force which is invariably the last recourse
of those who have despaired of orderly reform.

Once we have firmly grasped this guiding thread, we shall
come to the conclusion reached by Secretary of State George
C. Marshall after a year of grueling efforts to bring about
reconciliation between the reactionary elements in the Central government at Chungking and the violent revolutionary
elements among the Chinese Communists in Yenan. His conclusion was that the United States must find and follow a
middle course of supporting neither extremists of the Right
nor extremists of the Left but, in the case of China, the group
he described as "liberals." Had this conclusion been reached
and firmly adhered to by the United States after V–E Day,
much of the post-war friction with Russia could have been
avoided; for the ideological vacuum left in Europe by the
defeat of Germany and in Asia by the defeat of Japan, not
having been filled by forward-looking American ideas,
proved an understandable temptation for the expansion of
ideas advocated by Russia. Yet even under these favorable
circumstances Russia's ideas did not gain the ascendancy
widely prophesied for them during the war, when it was
thought that revolutionary movements would sweep the
globe in the wake of untold suffering and destruction. Democracy, it was then believed, had become as obsolete as
the dinosaur. In the grim world bequeathed to us by German
and Japanese depredations, it was said, there could be no
room for individual freedom.

4. THE MIDDLE WAY

These predictions were by no means widely fulfilled.
While political alignments, like geological formations, have
been shifted by the seismic convulsions of war, they have

for the most part been shifted not all the way to the extreme Left, but to varying points Left of Center. The moderate character of this shift has been due to two main causes: the victory of Labor in Britain, and disillusionment with Russia. The Labor victory of 1945, two months after V–E Day, brought to Britain a mixed political and economic system which is neither totalitarian nor unfettered laissez faire, neither Russian nor American, but combines the maintenance of personal liberty essential for the growth of the individual with the voluntary acceptance of social controls essential for the growth of the community in an industrial civilization. Britain's socialism, which alarmed many Americans who identify sócialism with communism and regard both as anathema, gave heart to groups in Europe and other continents who had rejected the men and institutions responsible for the rise of Nazism and Fascism, yet were unable to accept the political dictatorship of Communism. It gave heart, too, to dependent peoples in colonial areas who believed that the Labor government would show genuine concern to accelerate their advance toward independence—as was soon proved to be the case in India and Burma.

At the same time, the hope aroused a quarter of a century before that the Bolshevik revolution in Russia would provide solutions for the complex problems of our modern industrial era had begun to fade as the countries occupied by Russian troops learned at first hand about actual conditions in the U.S.S.R. While the political and economic system developed by the Soviet leaders is understandable in the light of Russia's own historical experience, it is being gradually recognized as inapplicable to the more advanced nations west of Russia, nurtured in traditions of liberty. Moscow's appeal for "socialist democracy" and the rights of the "toiling masses" remains potent in countries which today are at a level of development comparable to that of Russia in 1917 and which, finding little that is familiar to them in Western conditions, hope to benefit by Russia's experience. But, strange as it may seem to some of us who have come to think of Russia as in the vanguard of revolution, the Russians, when tested by the standards of Western civilization, appear reactionary in their adherence to political authoritarianism at home and in their insistence on strong-arm nationalist methods abroad.

Americans, who pride themselves on effective action, often seem paralyzed in world affairs by mental confusion. But meanwhile the Russians, after twenty-five years of intense effort and incredible deprivation climaxed by a devastating war, have lost something of their momentum. As a Russian intellectual said to the American journalist Richard Lauterbach in 1946: "There is a crisis in the Soviet Union. Not a crisis of economics, you will have that I think. Ours is chiefly a crisis of the spirit. There is a great evidence that the well springs of creative energy which every social earthquake releases are dangerously close to drying up. Perhaps we were drained too much by the war. Burned up, you say . . . We are so weary. The slogans are weary. The words seem to have lost their life. Even the new banners look old and tired. But the people want something new."

The growth of British socialism and disillusionment with the form of socialism established in Russia have combined to foster the spread of what may be described as the "middle way" in both politics and economics. Practically every postwar government in Europe has had Communists, often able technicians in key posts of responsibility such as Hilary Minc, Polish Minister of Commerce and Industry, or François Billoux, former French Minister of Health and Minister of Defense. The bulk of popular support, however, has been given with striking uniformity, from France to Hungary, from Norway to Italy, and in Germany as well, to parties which before 1939 might have been classified as Leftist—the Socialist or Social Democrats, and the Catholic parties favoring social reforms on the lines of Papal encyclicals, notably *Rerum Novarum,* among them the *Mouvement Républicain Populaire* of Georges Bidault in France and the Christian Democrats of Alcide de Gasperi in Italy. If the world becomes stabilized at the political point it had reached by 1947, we may see a period dominated by a new Center— a Center recruited primarily from the Left, and committed to economic and social transformations which a decade ago would have been regarded as revolutionary, especially in countries of Europe east of the Rhine which before 1939 were still dominated by remnants of feudalism.

The question, however, is understandably asked whether Communists like Minc and Billoux, no matter how technically qualified or genuinely determined to advance human welfare, will honestly coöperate with non-Communist political groups who share some of their ideas for reform, or will merely prove to be Trojan horses in the governments they have entered, using their offices to undermine democracy and implant Communism. This question cannot yet be answered with assurance. But two things seem clear. First, attempts to exclude Communists from participation in political life of this or that country by banning Communist parties, prohibiting the circulation of Communist literature, and barring Communists from office, will tend to drive the Communists underground, creating a greater threat to democracy than that constituted by their present activities. Second, a determined and sustained effort by the new Center —Socialists and Christian Socialists—to improve economic and social conditions, with continued aid from the United States, preferably through United Nations channels, offers the most convincing test available of whether socialism, practiced by democratic methods, can provide the combination of personal freedom and tolerable living standards which so far has been achieved only in a few areas of the world. Until this test has been squarely faced by the United States, Communist agitation is bound to continue with some degree of success, as it has in such diverse places as Italy, France, and the countries of Latin America. Even though the Communists oppose American aid to Socialists, the United States will then at least be in a far stronger position to challenge Communism effectively than during the period since V–E Day, when it gave the impression that it would support any group, no matter how reactionary, which was hostile to Communism and Russia. The need for re-orienting American policy in this respect was indicated with remarkable clarity by Secretary of State Marshall in his final statement on China, when he said that in that country the United States should aid neither the extreme re-actionaries nor the extreme Communists, but "liberal" ele-ments, among whom, by implication, he included moderate Communists.

5. WHO ARE THE LIBERALS?

The fundamental problem in the relations of the United States and Russia is whether this country, itself born of revo-lution against authoritarianism and colonial rule, will oppose or accept the new "liberals" emerging in Europe, in Asia, in Latin America. If we oppose them, we may find that the rest of the world, shocking as it may seem to us, will agree with Moscow in regarding this country as the last bulwark of conservatism, or even of reaction. If we accept them, and give them our technical assistance in rebuilding the economy of a shattered world, we may find that we can renew our pioneering spirit on as yet uncharted frontiers, and help others fulfill, in their own way and within the context of their own historical experience, what we have been proud to call the American dream.

In seeking to chart a middle course in international affairs, American officials have been faced with three major difficul-ties. First, and perhaps most important of all, the majority of the American people, in spite of a predilection for bold experimentation in industrial development unmatched in the world, are inclined to be fearful or suspicious of political and economic changes in other nations, especially changes that appear to challenge the concept of free private enterprise. This apprehensive attitude is due, in large part, to lack of knowledge concerning the historic development of people outside our borders which causes many of us to assume that conditions in Russia, or China, or, to take a country more akin in tradition, Britain, are comparable to our own. As a result, reforms in other nations which in terms of local experience are not only desirable but often long overdue are regarded here as dangerously revolutionary, and some Americans identify all reform movements, whatever their source, with Communism.

The second obstacle to clarification of our policy is that in many countries the groups we might regard as liberals are small in number and, while usually rich in gifts of intellect and integrity, are poor in material power and political experience, and often divided among themselves. In countries like Russia in 1917 or China, Hungary, or Argentina today, the middle class, seedbed of liberalism, is still too limited—due to the lag in industrialization, growth of urban communities, and general education or even literacy—to form a stable balance wheel between extremism of Right and Left. The United States is therefore confronted with the grave question whether, by supporting "liberals" in a given country, it may be romantically backing a lost cause, and thereby strengthening one or the other of the extremes.

The third difficulty is the mental confusion induced by the tendency to identify any trend "to the left" with Russia. This tendency causes many Americans to believe that the Russians are responsible for unrest wherever it occurs, without inquiring into the possibility that such unrest might be inspired by local conditions whose causes antedate Lenin, and even Karl Marx. It is true that Communists, both Russian and native, have frequently taken advantage of existing maladjustments in this or that country to further the interests of Russia or of the local Communist party. And the fact that Russian Communists originally achieved a position of influence by underground activities which fostered conspiratorial tactics — tactics that in our day were found of great value by resistance movements operating against Nazi rule—has caused many Westerners, sometimes with justification, to fear "infiltration" and "boring from within." It is certainly important to inquire into the methods of the Communists and to ascertain whether they do or do not menace democratic institutions, and, if they do, what measures should be taken to prevent the menace. Such probing, however, should be guided not by blind panic but by understanding of conditions which, even if Communism did not exist, would still stir up ferment in many parts of the world, and of our own possible responsibility for the existence of these conditions. If we are to protect the house of democracy against sapping "termites"—the phrase Arthur Koestler, a former Communist, once used about Nazism and more recently applied to Communism—we should concern ourselves, first of all, with seeing that it is built on sound foundations adequate, not to the circumstances of previous centuries, but of the century in which we live.

6. DEFINING OUR OBJECTIVES

If the guiding thread of sympathy for change were used by the United States, how would we deal with specific political situations that involve the possibility of conflict with Russia? In China, which under adverse circumstances could easily become a battlefield between Russia and the United States, Secretary of State Marshall proposed that, instead of favoring the reactionary and military elements in Chungking with material aid, as the United States had done while it attempted to act as impartial mediator between Chiang Kai-shek and the Communists, this country should support the liberals, who gave the best promise of establishing what we would regard as democracy. The most important question raised by Marshall's unusually candid and penetrating analysis was what kind of aid the United States should give the liberals to help them carry out their program. Should we give material aid—loans, credits, technical assistance? Should we go farther and undertake military intervention if it proves necessary to protect the liberals against pressure from the extreme Right or the extreme Left? In short, assuming that it is in our interest to assure the ultimate success of the liberals, should we make their cause our own, and intervene on their behalf to the full extent of our great political, economic, and military power?

The mere posing of these questions indicates how little thought we have given thus far to our policy with respect to Russia, beyond the almost reflex action of rejecting any proposal or development even remotely connected with the influence of Russia or of communism. We have hitherto acted on the assumption that mere lip-service to democracy abroad—insistence on "free and unfettered elections," displeasure when such elections were not held, verbal commendation of opposition parties and candidates with no attempt to give them practical aid of any kind—would be sufficient to force the retreat of communism and assure the triumph of democracy. At best we have, at the eleventh hour, extended financial assistance to liberal groups, as when we gave a loan to Léon Blum on the eve of the June 1946 elections or eased our restrictions on credits to Poland as the January 1947 elections drew near—thus furnishing Communist and associated parties the opportunity to claim that "reactionary capitalists" were trying to buy votes by "dollar diplomacy." At worst we limited ourselves to diplomatic protests on behalf of Mikolajczyk in Poland, and against Perón in Argentina, Groza in Romania, the Fatherland Front in Bulgaria, and so on. Then, when the groups we had favored failed to win, we quietly let them drop out of sight, and proceeded to recognize or at least maintain some form of relations with the governments established by procedures we had previously denounced and threatened not to accept. This method of advancing only to retreat has had the double-barreled effect of making the United States appear weak and ridiculous in the eyes of its critics, and impotent and unreliable in the eyes of its friends. It stands in sharp contrast to the method pursued by Russia which, whatever its other faults, has, by and large, made a practice of being harsh and intransigent with its enemies, but stanch in supporting its friends—with the result that even Europeans who would like to rely on this country have commented that Russia is "serious," while the United States is not. This is not altogether surprising, since Russia considers every move it makes in world affairs as a matter of life and death, while we have hitherto tended to look upon world affairs as a theater-goer looks at a play—hissing the villain, applauding the hero, but feeling no responsibility to jump on the stage and help the hero bring the villain to his knees.

If we are to meet Russia on equal terms we shall have to abandon the nonchalant attitude of the spectator and accept full responsibility for the ideas of democracy we profess and urge other nations to put into practice—or else stop denouncing Russia and the nations that follow Moscow's lead. Nothing is so derogatory to the prestige of the United States as to adopt the role Hitler once ascribed to Britain—of being "governess" to the world—and then fail to administer the threatened punishment. In each specific instance we should reach a decision not from fear of Russia or communism, but on the merits of the case as we see it. Otherwise, every decision we take will be warped by an attempt to make it fit some idea, true or false, that we may have of what Russia likes or does not like. And we shall then either be inclined to yield all along the line, without stopping to inquire into the long-run results of our concessions, as we were forced to do during the war when there was no other choice; or else we shall go to the other extreme, widely favored in this country since the war, of being indiscriminately "firm," also all along the line, without stopping to inquire into the long-run results of our rejections.

Once we begin to base our decisions not on mere reaction to Russia's initiative, but on our own objectives, much of the fog in which we have been floundering since V–E Day will begin to lift. We may not be able to provide all the answers, but we can at least begin by asking pertinent questions. What is our objective in Poland? To prevent it from falling under Russia's influence—or to help the Poles reconstruct their devastated country, make themselves secure against the renewal of German aggression, create the atmosphere of economic well-being and security from external attack that could ultimately be favorable to the growth of a Polish form of democracy? If the latter, then is it possible for us to find a common ground for coöperation with the government bloc of Communists, Socialists, and dissident Peasant party members which has been ruling Poland, irrespective of its attitude toward Russia? What is our objective on the Danube? To insist on rights for our trade —or also to see to it that the countries of the Danubian area have an opportunity to rid themselves of the ills of a backward economy, to benefit by the techniques of modern industrialization, to make effective use of the Danube for the fullest possible expansion of regional economic coöperation? What is our objective in Latin America—to stop the upsurge of communism, as Senator Vandenberg described it, or to show concern for the welfare of workers in the tin mines of Bolivia and on the rubber plantations of

Brazil, to aid in the spread of hygiene and education, to support projects for the development by modern methods of industry and agriculture, as Nelson Rockefeller has undertaken to do in Venezuela and Brazil? What is our objective in China—to oppose the influence of the Chinese Communists because they have the sympathy of Russia, or to use our own influence with the Central government to end civil strife, to speed agrarian reform, to assure civil liberties not only on paper in the new constitution but in actual practice? What is our objective in Germany and Japan—to bar Russia from participation in the affairs of the defeated Axis nations, or to make every effort in our power to eradicate Nazism and Fascism, to transform the economic and social fabric so as to give greater scope to groups of the population who had not been directly identified with the Axis political and military hierarchy, to demonstrate, by the behavior of our own armed forces and civilian administrators, not merely by textbooks, that democracy is superior to totalitarianism? James Reston of the *New York Times*, in the course of his 1947 tour of Europe, summed up our dilemma well when he asked: "How can the United States revive Europe economically without at the same time reviving or maintaining a privileged class that does not share United States ideals or objectives? . . . How can the United States, to put it another way, block the expansion of totalitarian communism without sustaining the very kind of privilege that contributes to the success of communism?"

If we try to define our own objectives in this way, instead of first wondering what Russia's objectives are, we shall not necessarily, or even frequently, be in agreement with the Soviet government, because there are fundamental differences in our views which no amount of wishful thinking can gloss over. But at least when we disagree we shall do so not in blind automatic refusal to accept any proposal made by Russia, but on the considered ground that this or that

Russian proposal does not accord with our objectives, while another does or may. The Russians are shrewd and alert negotiators. As long as they believe that we are unsure of our own ends, that we are merely groping our way around a dark room wondering where the exit is, they will continue to use any means they can to achieve their own well-defined ends, and will make no effort to point out the possible exit. Instead of leaving the initiative in the hands of the Russians, as we have done again and again, sometimes out of sheer lack of knowledge or imagination, sometimes out of what seemed paralysis of the will, let us point out the targets we think should be aimed at, and set the tone of the negotiations. There can still be ample room for the compromises that have to be made in all forms of relations between nations, but at least we shall make our position clear at the start, and not give vague intimations of far-reaching plans, only to recede from them as time goes on, with the result that those Russian negotiators who had warned their government of the need for concessions to the United States are then held up to ridicule in Moscow. We shall also then acquire a reputation for reliability among other nations which unfortunately we do not at present possess because of our sharp, and to non-Americans often inexplicable, swings from isolation and aloofness to intervention and involvement, with little or no consideration for the effect our acts or failures to act have on the very nations we want most to count among our friends.

7. SOME FORM OF INTERVENTION INEVITABLE

We shall have to realize, however, that any measures we take to support "liberals" abroad will constitute intervention, and will be so considered by Russia. In the past we have acted on the assumption that we can tell various countries what government they should have, yet deny any intention of intervening in their affairs, as the State Department, for example, did after the Polish elections of January 1947 when it declared that the United States "firmly intends to maintain its interest in the welfare of the Polish people," but does not wish to intervene in Polish internal affairs—a statement that is a complete *non sequitur*. Instead of pretending to ourselves—for we deceive no one else—that intervention by this country somehow or other does not constitute intervention as it would be understood if practiced by another country, we should be prepared to take the consequences of our political decisions. Conversely, if the United States decides to refrain from intervening in a given situation, that, too, constitutes a form of intervention, as we discovered from our experience in Spain when our decision not to intervene in the civil war redounded to the benefit of Franco and to the detriment of the Spanish Republicans. In short, we have to learn that anything a great power like the United States does or does not do in world affairs affects the actions of other nations. This simple fact, which the American people, long accustomed to an attitude of detachment in international relations, have found it extremely difficult to grasp, has been clearly understood by Russia, which intervenes wherever it considers its interests to be at stake, uses whatever methods appear required to achieve its ends, and makes no pretense of disinterestedness. The tendency of the United States—as well as Britain—to call intervention in other nations by more euphonious names only serves to confirm the traditional Russian thesis that Anglo-American policy is imbued with hypocrisy.

But whatever measures we decide to take for the purpose of aiding "liberals," we must also realize that no amount of aid on our part will of itself lead to the establishment of democracy on the western pattern in countries unprepared for democratic institutions by past history and present conditions. The best we can do is to help these countries create the economic and social conditions that might foster some form of political liberty—not necessarily the form familiar to the United States and Britain. In the last analysis it will be the desire of peoples for liberty that will shape free institutions. As Judge Learned Hand has so rightly said: "Liberty lies in the hearts of men and women; when it dies there no constitution or law, no court can save it; no constitution, no law, nor court can even do much to help it. While it lies there, it needs no constitution, no law, no court to save it." Distressing as it is to English-speaking peoples who in a small sector of the world have nurtured over centuries institutions of political liberty, there are other areas of the world whose peoples have so far shown little or no longing for political freedom—among them Germany and Japan. Will Russia be among these areas? If it should prove to be, that too is a fact we have to grapple with. But we have to learn that neither military victory nor economic inducements can force democracy to grow, and that there is an infinite variety of political institutions adapted to the traditions and stage of development of different peoples.

10. "Equality of Economic Opportunity"

On the economic plane the main controversy between the United States and Russia concerns the Russian state monopoly of foreign trade, which directly conflicts with the concept of freer multilateral trade advocated since the war by the United States. This country is now far more conscious than it was before 1939 of the value of foreign trade for American economy. It has become increasingly clear that our war-expanded industries cannot be kept in full production, and hence cannot assure "full employment," unless markets are found abroad for products that cannot be easily absorbed by domestic consumers. This country, traditionally, has favored the "open door" policy. Secretary of State John Hay, in his "open door" note of 1899, was concerned, among other things, with the efforts of the Czarist Empire to dominate the economy of Manchuria, an area rich in strategic raw materials, potentially capable of industrialization, and, consequently, of becoming a market for American exports. Today the "open door" is not merely a matter of general policy for this country, but an urgent necessity. The United States has therefore become the principal advocate of multilateral trade through the reduction and eventual abolition of existing trade restrictions, in contrast to Russia's policy of bilateral barter treaties and Britain's preferential arrangements with the Dominions.

Russia realizes that, in its present economic condition, it cannot compete with the United States as an exporter of capital or manufactured goods, or even food. It fears that this country, by offering loans to Russia's neighbors for the purchase of American goods, will not only make it difficult for the Russians to obtain the goods they need, but that the flag will follow trade, and that American political influence will penetrate in the wake of loans and goods. That is why the Russians denounce what they call America's "economic imperialism" and "dollar diplomacy." That is also why Russian Foreign Minister Molotov, at the Paris Peace Conference in 1946, questioned the "unlimited application" of the principle of "equality of economic opportunity" enunciated by former Secretary of State Byrnes, declaring that "it is convenient for those who are trying to use their capital to subjugate those who are weaker." The Russians realize that they will be unable in the foreseeable future to "catch up with," let alone "surpass," the standard of living achieved in the United States, and that this standard of living, if shared by the United States with other countries, is an ace Russia cannot match. They would like to convince themselves, and convince other countries now vacillating between the Russian and American systems, that the economy of the United States is inherently unstable, and that a new depression will bring about disastrous unemployment and general economic breakdown. The United States, for its part, fears that Russia, by its network of bilateral trade arrangements, will create for itself an exclusive sphere of economic control, supplemented by military force and ideological propaganda, and bar American trade from Eastern Europe and the Balkans, as well as from adjoining areas of the Near and Middle East and Asia. Yet the very people in this country who have most vigorously opposed Russia's state monopoly of trade and bilateral trade treaties—as well as similar agreements concluded by other countries, for example, Argentina—are also

in the ranks of those who oppose renewal of American reciprocal trade arrangements and other modest measures
designed to encourage freer international trade, favor higher
duties on wool, and would consider any proposal to reduce
American tariffs as positively revolutionary.

1. U. S.–RUSSIAN TRADE

What practical steps could be taken to alleviate economic
conflicts between the United States and Russia? In pre-war
years exports from the United States to the Soviet Union
consisted mostly of equipment and raw materials for heavy
industry, transportation machinery, cotton, small quantities
of wheat (for the Far Eastern region of the U.S.S.R. more
easily accessible by sea than by overland transport), hides,
and some chemicals, especially sodium compounds. Exports
of consumer goods consisted of a very few articles of domestic use, which in the peak year of 1938 were valued at
$1,000,000. American imports from the Soviet Union were
for the most part furs, lumber mill products, animal products
for further manufacturing, raw materials for textile and
paper industries, and a few industrial and unmanufactured
goods, notably manganese ore, anthracite, and asbestos. The
United States, however, offered no market for the principal
agricultural and raw material products exported by Russia
to other countries. In the early years after 1919, trade between the United States and Russia was hampered by nonrecognition of the Soviet government, and the consequent
reluctance of American concerns, with one notable excep-
tion, the International General Electric Company, to grant
long-term credits for Soviet purchases here. But even following recognition in 1933, which was spurred by the hope
of American businessmen to find a market in Russia for manufactured goods and did, in effect, stimulate trade between
the two countries, the total value of American exports to

Russia averaged $50 million a year, while the value of imports averaged about $25 million a year.

As has already been noted, with the growth of industrial production in Russia, purchases of certain products here by the Russians were curtailed, or completely terminated, notably agricultural machinery and motor vehicles, while purchases of other equipment, for example equipment for oil refineries, were increased.

World War II sharply altered both the volume and the content of American-Russian trade. The cash value of United States merchandise exports to Russia rose to $104 million in the peak year of 1941. From one-third to nearly one-half of this country's total exports to Russia during the war years consisted of military goods (including aircraft, tanks, explosives, firearms, and other strictly military items), which were supplied under lend-lease. The United States also sent, on a lend-lease basis, large quantities of machinery (including industrial and electrical machinery, and agricultural machinery and implements), raw materials needed for war production, as well as wearing apparel and foodstuffs, chiefly for the needs of the Russian Army. Such consumer goods as were imported by Russia during the war years consisted principally of goods exported from the United States in the form of relief and charity, especially in 1943 and 1944. From Russia the United States, during the war years, imported goods that had not previously figured on its import list, among them lumber and pulpwood, magnesite, lead, diamonds and emeralds, platinum metals, crude phosphates, and some other nonmetallic mineral products.

It should be noted that Russia's annual imports from the United States before 1939 always considerably exceeded its exports to this country. In spite of this persistently unfavorable balance of trade, the Soviet government, holding a high opinion of the quality of American technical production, continued to place orders here for machinery and tools, and during the period 1924–1933 the United States ranked second only to Germany as a source of Russian imports. After 1933 American exports to Russia rose steadily, while with the approach of war Russian imports from Germany declined, and by 1938 this country emerged as Russia's principal source of supply, a position it occupied throughout the war years.

During the four war years, 1941 to 1945, the United States furnished to Russia $11,141,000,000 in lend-lease or approximately one-fourth of the $45 billion total of lend-lease shipments (Britain being the principal recipient, with about $30 billion). Russia's reverse lend-lease contributions for the same period totaled $2,213,000,000. As in the case of most other lend-lease recipients, Russia received a credit enabling it to purchase stocks ordered but not delivered by the time the United States terminated lend-lease in September 1945. This credit amounted to between $300 million and $400 million. As pointed out above, the United States is at present trying to obtain from Russia settlement of a percentage of the cost of lend-lease articles having a peacetime use.

2. CAN WE SELL WHAT RUSSIA WANTS TO BUY?

What are the prospects for post-war Russo-American trade? In order to purchase abroad the machinery, tools, and equipment it needs, the U.S.S.R. must obtain long-term credits or a loan from the exporting country, or else ways and means must be found of expanding that country's imports of Russian goods. Few nations today are in the financial position to extend large-scale long-term credits, or grant a substantial loan, except the United States; and the United States also happens to be the country where the U.S.S.R., other things being equal, would prefer to purchase the industrial products it needs. Two American officials—Ernest C. Ropes, chief of the U.S.S.R. division of the Department of

Commerce, and Lewis L. Lorwin, staff economist of the Department—declared after a visit to Russia in 1946 that "there is almost no limit" to what the Russians would purchase in the United States "if a credit of $1,000,000,000 which has been discussed were advanced by the Export-Import Bank."

Among the items the U.S.S.R. would like to purchase in the United States, in order of importance to the Russian economy, are railroad transport equipment (locomotives, cars, signal equipment, axles, trucks, maintenance equipment); steel forging, pressing, and rolling machinery, including new machinery invented in the United States that would eliminate old machinery now in use; electric furnaces and electric generators; petroleum drilling and refining machinery to assist the expansion of the Soviet oil industry; coal and other mining machinery; air-conditioning and refrigeration machinery to assist in modernizing Soviet factories and homes; machine tools of the most intricate and complicated types for use in many kinds of industry; port and cargo handling machinery; and construction equipment.

It seems very unlikely, under present circumstances, that the United States Congress would authorize a substantial loan to Russia. Trade, however, would be considerably facilitated by the conclusion of a commercial agreement, which would encourage extension of credits to Russia by private concerns here, as was done before the war. At the present time, in spite of opposition in Congress to exports which might strengthen Russian economy, many American products are actually being imported by Russia—not directly, but through reëxport by other countries, notably Britain and some of the nations of Latin America. In the absence of a loan or credits, Russia would face two major difficulties in paying for imports from the United States. First, as has already been pointed out, this country does not need most of the foodstuffs and industrial raw materials which form the bulk of Russia's exports to other countries; and second, even such products as Russia used to sell to the United States may be in short supply for some time to come, owing to the stepped-up requirements of the Russian economy. A study of the list of products newly imported from Russia by the United States during the war years may reveal fresh possibilities of increasing Russian sales to this country, but the sober fact must be faced that, under the most favorable circumstances, Russia imports more from the United States than the United States imports from Russia. A continuing unbalance of trade to the disadvantage of the U.S.S.R. must therefore be anticipated.

If Russia cannot obtain credits here, and cannot substantially increase its exports to this country, it may be expected to follow the makeshift policy briefly described above of obtaining manufactured goods wherever it can by whatever methods seem best adapted to the specific situation. Leaving all political considerations aside, it is to Russia's advantage to place orders for goods in countries which are willing to absorb its products in return. Under these circumstances, barter trade, while repugnant to the American view of the future course of world commerce, offers the most promising immediate possibility for fulfillment of the fourth Five-Year Plan without an unbearable burden on the Russian people.

Hitherto Russia has displayed no interest in the International Trade Organization (ITO), but the principal industrial nation in the Russian orbit, Czechoslovakia, has participated in the ITO negotiations, and even after the Communist seizure of power in February 1948, Prague announced its intention to share in ITO activities. While Russia controls exports and imports directly through its foreign trade monopoly, and its own tariffs are therefore relatively meaningless, it presumably has a definite interest in reduction of tariff barriers by other nations against its own exports.

3. A LOAN PLUS DOMESTIC STABILITY

If, however, the United States wants to create conditions that would make it less urgent for Russia—as well as many other countries in the throes of post-war reconstruction—to resort to barter trade, it will have to do more than advocate freer multilateral trade and denounce bilateral trade agreements. In its economic policy toward Russia, as in its political policy, the United States should lead not from fear but from confidence in its own faith in the viability of the free enterprise system. Instead of rejecting the idea of a loan to Russia for the purchase of American manufactured goods, as suggested in 1946 by the report of the Colmer Committee which feared that American exports to Russia would merely strengthen a potential enemy, the United States should consider the possibility of granting a substantial loan subject to the usual commercial safeguards. Such a loan would be far more effective than any pledges of international coöperation in demonstrating to Russia that this country has no intention of blocking its economic development, and is sincerely ready to assure it "equality of economic opportunity." It will then be up to Russia to prove whether it has the administrative and technical skill to make good use of the opportunity. If Russia does not supply adequate labor to run its farms, factories, and mines because it insists on keeping large bodies of men under arms, that will be its economic loss, which it will then not be in a position to blame on the outside world. But this is a problem it must solve for itself; and attempts to attach military or political conditions to a Russian loan, as proposed by some American officials, would merely convince Moscow that it had been right in the past in assuming that foreign loans were instruments of political domination. No matter how great may be the impetus given to Russia's industrial development by an American loan, the United States will remain ahead, and can easily maintain in the future the lead it has won by a century or more of industrialization. Nor should we delude ourselves into thinking that, by withholding a loan, we shall prevent Russia from becoming industrialized. We shall then only encourage it to obtain industrial equipment elsewhere by methods that would defeat our plans for expanding our own export markets.

Whether American financial aid to Russia could be extended by the United States and accepted by Moscow within the framework of an overall plan of European reconstruction was the crucial question at the Paris conference of June 27, 1947 held to discuss Secretary Marshall's suggestions of June 5. At that conference Russian Foreign Minister Molotov made it clear that the Soviet Union was interested in obtaining financial aid from the United States, but only on condition that this aid should be applied to prosecution of its national Five-Year Plan, not as part of a coördinated continental program that might require adjustment of Russian plans to those of other countries. Mr. Molotov also insisted that first priority in any aid the United States might offer Europe should be given to nations devastated by Germany, thus relegating to the background such aid as Washington might want to extend to former enemy countries, notably Germany. Molotov's statements at the Paris conference revealed anew both the envy with which Russia views the war-expanded economy of the United States, and the fear that "capitalist" loans might merely be an entering wedge to force changes in Soviet economic concepts and practices.

In addition to a loan to Russia, we should, if we genuinely believe in freer multilateral trade, maintain and expand the program of reciprocal trade agreements, and consider the possibility of tariff reductions. Liberalization of our own trade methods would be the most convincing way of coun-

teracting what we denounce as illiberal trade methods on
the part of other countries. It is true that reciprocal trade
arrangements and tariff cuts may require certain readjustments in our domestic economy, to compensate enterprises
whose business may be unfavorably affected by such measures. But if we are not prepared to make some sacrifices for
the purpose of achieving our own objectives in international
trade, we are hardly in a position to demand sacrifices from
Russia or other nations.

Another policy the United States would have to follow
to promote multilateral trade is to grant loans or credits to
countries devastated by the war, and to colonial areas that
are seeking to become industrialized. No matter how attracted these countries may be by Russian ideas, their leaders
realize that Russia, at its present stage of economic development, is not in a position to furnish them with the machinery and tools they need for their own reconstruction. For
this equipment, as well as for technical assistance, they must
turn to the United States. But many of the countries which
most need American aid also happen to be within range of
Russia's military power. It is unrealistic for us to expect that
we can persuade them to accept loans on condition that they
dissociate themselves from Russia, or oppose Russia's objectives in Europe and Asia. If such a possibility was at any
time envisaged in the formulation of the Marshall Plan, it had
no prospect of realization under existing conditions in Eastern Europe and the Balkans.

Does this mean that financial and trade relations between
the United States and the area of Europe dominated by
Russia are excluded? There is no doubt that the countries
of this area, including Russia itself, need tools, machinery,
and raw materials which at present are available only in the
United States, and would welcome the possibility of obtaining them through loans or long-term credits. Moreover, the
successful operation of the European Recovery Program
assumes at least partial resumption of trade between East and

West—unless the United States is prepared to increase its financial aid to the nations of Western Europe, either for additional purchases here, or for development of alternative sources of supply in other continents, notably Africa. Economic experts who have studied conditions in Eastern Europe believe that a relatively small investment in countries like Poland and Czechoslovakia would produce valuable results —a conclusion supported by the European Economic Commission of the UN in a report published in April 1948. At the same time, it must be recognized that in countries where Communists are now in full control American economic aid, whether in the form of private credits or government loans, would redound in the first instance to the advantage of Communist regimes. Only over the long run, when social and economic conditions have been improved through reconstruction and development, can it be expected that less dictatorial political institutions may conceivably develop.

Above all, the United States must endeavor to set its own house in order, so that the Russians, who have gone on the assumption that recurring and ever more catastrophic crises are an inevitable result of capitalism, may be proved to have based their calculations on erroneous premises. Nothing would so strengthen belief in Russian ideas as a major depression creating widespread unemployment in this country and inflicting economic disaster on other nations which had linked their destiny to that of the American system. We have proved to our own satisfaction, and to that of other peoples, that our system can provide greater material advantages than any other yet in existence. The Russians are challenging us to prove that we can not only maintain the standards we have already achieved, but do even better in the future, not only to assure our own well-being but also to increase that of nations outside our borders.

11. The Big Two and the UN

Now that both the United States and Russia have emerged from semi-isolation and have decided to play an active part in the United Nations organization, their policies and actions are more than ever subject to scrutiny and comparison by other nations. As each of these two great powers—great in size of territory and population, in wealth of natural resources, in industrial output actual or potential, in military might, and in widespread influence of ideas—faces the test of public discussions in the General Assembly, the Security Council, and other organs of the UN, neither can any longer take refuge in professions of faith or merely taunt the other for past mistakes or failures. Each must prove over and over again, in open forum, that it is ready to practice what it preaches. Whatever each may privately feel about the practical possibility of the "peaceful coexistence" of two fundamentally different systems, within the UN both great powers publicly act on the assumption that they do and will coexist in peace. And at Lake Success, as also in the Allied Control Councils in Berlin and Vienna and in the Far Eastern Commission in Washington, Americans and Russians, much as they may suspect or dislike each other, must listen to the other's views on the main political, economic, and social issues that make up the fabric of day-to-day relations between nations. Tedious as negotiations with the Russians often seem to Westerners, owing to the Russian method of going over and over the same ground from committees to Council, from

Council to General Assembly, repeating *ad infinitum* the same arguments and voicing the same objections, a certain interplay of ideas does take place. It is only through such interplay of ideas, slow and unconstructive as the process often seems to those who participate in it, rather than through spectacular brief encounters in the full glare of publicity, that threads of mutual understanding can begin to be woven between the United States and Russia.

1. GREAT POWERS VERSUS SMALL

Not that the two great powers which, in case of aggression, would have to furnish the bulk of military force to the Security Council, see eye to eye as yet on some fundamental features of international organization. The United States, in accordance with its concept at home that all individuals, no matter whether strong or weak, rich or poor, are equal before the law, holds the view that all sovereign states, whether great or small, are equal in the UN, and must receive a hearing. Russia, in accordance with its concept that the rights and duties of individuals are determined by the state which, in effect, is the political dictatorship of a small group of self-appointed leaders, holds the view that the activities of the UN, especially with respect to security, should be directed by a limited inner group of great powers, not elected by the international community but self-appointed by reason of their military and industrial strength; and that the small nations must accept the decisions of the great, on the ground that these decisions are intended to assure the general welfare. Because of this divergence on the role of small states in the UN, some people have assumed that the United States is a champion of the rights of small states, as contrasted with Russia's aspirations to great-power dictatorship.

Actually, however, aside from the fact that Russia objects to majority voting in international conferences because it expects to be outvoted by the nations which follow the course set by the United States and Britain, the divergence between the Big Two is more apparent than real, as can be seen by their attitude toward the much disputed veto in the Security Council. Some commentators have given the impression that the veto was included in the San Francisco Charter solely at the insistence of Russia. The fact is that the United States was just as insistent as Russia on retention of the veto by the great powers, believing that otherwise the Charter did not stand a chance of being ratified by the Senate. Russia's concept of the veto is based on its conviction that unanimity among the Big Five—and especially among the Big Three—is as essential in time of peace as it was in war, and that the veto is necessary to assure such unanimity. The United States agrees that, without accord by the great powers, the work of the UN will come to a standstill, and has given no indication that it intends to abandon or curtail the veto in the Security Council, no matter what pressure is brought to bear on it by leading small nations like Australia and Cuba. To this extent the United States, like Russia, accepts limitations on the sovereignty of small states as compared with the great or, to put it in another way, accepts the attribution of special rights to the great powers.

Where Russia has differed from the United States is that, contrary to an understanding reached in San Francisco, it has made frequent, not sparing, use of the veto, and has taken the view that the veto could be used to prevent discussion of a question brought before the Security Council as well as action by the Council against an alleged aggressor. The United States, by contrast, has taken the view that the veto should be used sparingly, that it should not be invoked during discussion of a question, and could be used only when the time had come for the Council to reach a decision concerning application of military force. The controversy over the veto has clearly revealed some difference in ways of thinking between the United States and Russia. The Russians, who brook no political dissension or even discussion at home, want to be free, by virtue of the veto, to cut short any discussion in the Security Council that may appear to threaten their interests. The Americans, accustomed to untrammeled and often vituperative political discussion, find nothing objectionable in discussion of any given issue before the Security Council but, having historically preferred to play a lone hand in world affairs, want to make sure that this country retains the right not to become involved in any punitive action against an alleged aggressor that the Council may recommend. Both the United States and Russia, although committed to international action through the United Nations organization, still want to hold on to the attributes, vestigial as they may seem, of national sovereignty.

2. THE ATOM BOMB AND THE VETO

The problem of the veto was raised in a sharp form when Bernard M. Baruch, American member of the Atomic Energy Commission of the UN, declared on June 14, 1946 that punishment of violations of the proposed convention on international control of atomic energy lies at the very heart of the security system, and that "there must be no veto to protect those who violate their solemn agreement not to develop or use atomic energy for destructive purposes." Mr. Baruch presented a proposal for the creation of an international Atomic Development Authority which would be entrusted with wide powers of inspection over the development and use of atomic energy. The functions of the ADA would include collection of complete and accurate information on world supplies of fissionable raw materials, uranium and thorium, and control of these materials; managerial control or ownership of all atomic energy activities potentially dangerous to world security; power to control, inspect, and license all other atomic activities; the duty of fostering the beneficial uses of atomic energy; and research and development responsibilities "of an affirmative character" intended to put the Authority in the forefront of atomic knowledge and thus to enable it to comprehend, and therefore to detect, misuse of atomic energy. Following establishment of the ADA, severe and certain penalties should be devised for any nation committing violations of international atomic control, and individuals concerned with such violations should be held personally responsible for their actions, in accordance with the principles laid down for the trial of war criminals at Nuremberg. Mr. Baruch thus established a close link between the discovery of the atomic bomb and the simultaneous, equally far-reaching, formulation of the concept announced by Justice Robert H. Jackson, that individuals are responsible for acts that lead to war. Once an adequate system of international control has been established, the United States, according to the Baruch proposal, undertakes to stop manufacture of atomic bombs, to "dispose" of its stockpile, and to turn over to the ADA the secret of their manufacture—which at present this country shares in part only with Britain and Canada.

The primary objectives of Russia—which, so far as is known outside its borders, does not yet possess the secret of the manufacture of atomic bombs although its scientists and German scientists brought to Russia for this purpose have been hard at work on the problem—are to obtain information about manufacture of the bomb, and to insure outlawing of its production as well as destruction of existing stockpiles in this country. The Russian proposal in the Atomic Energy Commission, drafted before the Baruch proposal was made public and presented by the Russian delegate, Mr. Gromyko, stressed the need for outlawry of the bomb rather than for control of the new weapon, and national rather than international punishment of violations of the convention for control of atomic energy. The Russians promptly indicated that, in their opinion, Mr. Baruch's suggestion for waiver of the veto in case of violations of atomic energy control was a backdoor attempt to evade the veto, on which the U.S.S.R. has set such great store. The United States, in turn, made it plain that it would not give up manufacture of atomic bombs, or destroy existing stockpiles, or sign an international convention on the subject until the two principles of international inspection and waiver of the veto had been accepted by the United Nations.

With the same persistence that has marked all their activities in international gatherings the Russians, when they had failed to achieve their objective in the Atomic Energy Commission, returned to the assault in the Political and Security Committee of the General Assembly in November 1946 by trying to have information about atomic weapons included in the reports on armed forces which member nations, at Molotov's original suggestion, were to submit to the UN. When this proposal was defeated, Molotov, who at the opening of the General Assembly had urged general disarmament, announced that Russia would be ready to accept international inspection for disarmament in general and for atomic weapons in particular, and would agree to waive the veto for day-to-day operations of the atomic control commission. At the same time he pressed for progressive reduction of armaments, by which he meant, as Foreign Vice-Minister Vishinsky soon made clear, abolition first of all of the atomic bomb which, he said, hangs over the world like "a sword of Damocles." The core of Molotov's proposal was the creation of two new commissions "within the framework of the Security Council" to control fulfillment of UN measures about general disarmament and about war use of atomic energy respectively. This proposal, in the opinion of Australia and Canada, as well as the United

States and Britain, would make decisions of the UN not only on atomic energy, but also on disarmament in general, subject to the veto in the Security Council. It would thus undo the work so far accomplished by the Atomic Commission, whose establishment as an independent organ responsible to the Security Council had been approved by Russia during the first session of the General Assembly in January 1946.

When the Atomic Energy Commission, following conclusion of the General Assembly's session, resumed its work in December 1946, the United States insisted that first priority should be given by the Security Council to the commission's proposals for atomic energy control, while Russia insisted that first priority should be given to the Assembly's resolution on general disarmament, contending that control of the atomic bomb was only one of the aspects of a disarmament program. Mr. Baruch himself had intimated in June 1946 that control of the atomic bomb is but one step, important as it is in the context of present-day events, toward the objective that for centuries has been eluding mankind —abolition of war itself. The U.S.S.R., as insistent on national sovereignty as the United States had been until recently, steadfastly resisted all proposals for international inspection and punishment of violations by individual citizens.

The fundamental issue, as revealed in the debate on disarmament in the Political and Security Committee of the General Assembly, is not whether the veto power in the Security Council should be abandoned (as we have already seen, the United States has no intention of giving up the veto over measures for enforcing the Council's decisions), but whether certain questions can be excluded from the area covered by the veto, notably the use of atomic energy for war purposes. Warren R. Austin, permanent delegate of the United States to the UN, who in January 1947 succeeded Mr. Baruch as American member of the Atomic

Energy Commission, indicated that this country favored the establishment of another body in the United Nations organization in which the veto would not apply, thus by-passing the Security Council, which is just what the Russians had feared when they first learned the contents of Mr. Baruch's proposal. Commenting on this new proposal Henry P. Fletcher, former Under-Secretary of State and member of the United States delegation at Dumbarton Oaks, who had had an opportunity to learn at firsthand Russia's views on the veto, stated in a letter to the *New York Times* on January 27 that there was very slight chance "of acceptance by Russia of this expedient." He then went on to say: "Assuming, however, that this scheme could be adopted, it seems clear that it never could be effective without the support of Russia. And if Russian support were forthcoming, why divest the Security Council of its functions by an attempt to circumvent its powers and responsibilities? If, on the other hand, Russia or any of the other great powers should object to measures adopted by the proposed Atomic Control Commission, it is idle to suppose any action, individually or collectively, by members of the United Nations could be effective over such objection, and any attempt to enforce the decrees of this proposed commission would—unless there was unanimity among the three powers—almost certainly result in the destruction of the United Nations and lead very possibly to war."

Other countries besides Russia have questioned the wisdom of the American attempt to circumvent the veto reserved to the great powers in the Security Council under the UN Charter by creating a special atomic energy control body outside the Council, which would not be subject to the veto rule. It would, of course, be possible to consider amendment of the Charter to excise the veto power from its provisions, as has been suggested by Australia and Cuba. But the United States is opposed to such an amendment, since it wants to retain the veto over decisions of the Council to use military force against an alleged aggressor. Another and more practicable proposal which has received increasing attention is that, instead of by-passing the Charter or amending it, the United Nations should invoke the two articles in the document which would be applicable to violations of an international convention for control of atomic energy. These articles are Article 1, which states that the purposes of the United Nations are, among others, "to take effective collective measures for the prevention and removal of threats to the peace, and for the suppression of acts of aggression or other breaches of the peace"; and Article 51, which states that "nothing in the present Charter shall impair the inherent right of individual or collective self-defense if an armed attack occurs against a Member of the United Nations, until the Security Council has taken the measures necessary to maintain international peace and security." In other words, even if one of the great powers should veto a decision of the Security Council to punish violations of the atomic control convention, the other members of the United Nations have the "inherent right" to resort to "individual or collective self-defense" against such violations, assuming that these violations take the form of an armed attack, that is, actual use of the atomic bomb. Other violations, such as the manufacture of bombs contrary to the provisions of the convention, might not call for such drastic action, and might conceivably be included among the "day-to-day operations" of the Atomic Control Commission which, according to Mr. Molotov's statement in the Political and Security Committee of the General Assembly, would not be subject to the veto. If Russia should decide to veto punitive action by the Security Council, the other members could not force it to participate in collective action, and their best—and promptest—recourse would then be to act under the provisions of Article 51 of the Charter.

From the point of view of other countries, both the United States and Russia have displayed some intransigence in the discussions of atomic energy control. While Russia has been criticized for demanding outlawry of the atomic bomb without making clear what it was prepared to do to reduce its own military strength, notably its land army, now the largest in the world, the United States has also been criticized for failure to take the initiative in linking the use of atomic energy for war purposes with the problem of disarmament in general. On the question of atomic energy control, as on other international issues, the United States and Russia are both confronted with the question of how much longer great powers, while officially expressing faith in world organization, will insist on maintenance of unlimited national sovereignty on matters in which they are particularly concerned.

3. TAKING SIDES IN THE UN

On other major problems so far considered by the United Nations organization, the Western powers have again and again allowed the initiative for moral leadership to slip out of their hands into those of Russia. At the San Francisco Conference Molotov spoke to the world press as a champion of the rights of colonial peoples, although no one familiar with conditions in the U.S.S.R. would pretend that its citizens enjoy all the rights Moscow demands for Indonesia or Palestine. At Lake Success the Russians questioned the sincerity of American proposals for international trusteeship over former Japanese mandates in the Pacific, supported India's plea for improvement in the treatment of Indians in South Africa, opposed Marshal Smuts's demand for incorporation of the mandate of Southwest Africa into the Union of South Africa, and remained in the vanguard of nations urging intervention in Spain against Franco. Russia's attitude toward all these questions can be easily attacked by skeptics on the ground that the Soviet government is merely using Indonesia or South Africa, Spain or the Japanese mandates, as a convenient propaganda weapon against the United States, Britain, and other Western nations. The fact remains that the United States, too, has an opportunity to make propaganda for its ideas, and has at its command for this purpose technical means far superior to those of Russia. Not only that, but until recently the United States would have been the first to support the rights of colonial peoples and to oppose dictatorship—and in fact still vigorously opposes dictatorship in Poland or Romania, although less so in Spain or Argentina. Yet again and again it is Russia which appears to be on "the side of the angels." And once Russia has taken a stand on a given international issue, the United States, because of its tendency, already noted, of reacting unfavorably to any policy proposed by Moscow, then places itself in a position where it appears to be supporting the side of reaction or, at best, passive resistance to change.

Under these circumstances Russia does not even need to resort to the method, of which it has been suspected, of trying to create within the UN a new Popular Front of socialist and communist nations, as it has sought to create combinations of socialists and communists within neighboring countries. Merely by enunciating policies that express the desires of colonial peoples and advanced nations which have adopted socialist programs, or by supporting the proposals of these nations, Russia aligns itself on their side, or aligns them on its side, whatever view one may take of its procedure. It would be a mistake to assume that what holds Leftist groups together, or associates them with Russia, is solely Russian propaganda, or even propaganda backed by Russian bayonets. More important as a cement between them is a community of views which cannot be destroyed either by Western counter-propaganda or by the threat of use of atomic bombs on the part of the Western powers. The United States can meet this community of views only by sympathetic understanding of the problems of colonial peoples and war-impoverished industrial nations, and by imaginative and constructive efforts, through the agency of the United Nations organization, to relieve these problems by collective action. If the United States can take the leadership in that direction without merely waiting as it now does to react to Russia's initiatives, the United Nations organization will have an opportunity of demonstrating that it can forge links between peoples more lasting and less subject to violent disruption by arbitrary force than the class loyalties fostered by international communism.

The fundamental problem today in the UN is that this organization was founded on the assumption, perhaps held more firmly by Russia than by the United States, that the "unanimity" or coöperation for common ends achieved by the great powers during the war could be maintained for peacetime purposes. The growing rivalry between Russia and the United States has played havoc with this assumption, and has consequently interfered with the work of the UN. It is only fair to point out that other nations besides Russia, when confronted with comparable issues in the UN, have displayed similar reluctance to accept international decisions—for example The Netherlands on Indonesia, and South Africa on the treatment of Indians and the proposed annexation of the mandate of Southwest Africa. What is needed is not merely reform of Russia—or the United States —but gradual subordination of all nationalisms to the aims of international organization.

The question is often asked how the rivalry between Russia and the United States could be resolved. Is there any possibility of some new division of spheres of influence, such as that effected by France and Britain in 1904, by Britain and Russia in 1907—settlements which together resulted in the formation of the Triple Entente? It is as yet premature to indulge in detailed speculation on this point. But what can be said is that today the balance of power must be sought not in this or that geographic area, but over the entire globe; and that it must be struck not merely in strategic or political terms, but also in terms of some adjustment, if not reconciliation, between two rival economic systems.

12. Is War Inevitable?

War is never inevitable if by that phrase we mean that war is a natural phenomenon like a tornado or a tidal wave that no amount of human knowledge and advance preparation can possibly avert. It becomes, or at least comes to appear, inevitable only when opportunities to avert it by various forms of action have been allowed to pass through lack of information, heedlessness of warning signals, apathy, aggressiveness arousing counter-aggressiveness, or conscious desire to have the catastrophe occur. All of these phenomena characteristic of periods preceding the actual outbreak of war have become tragically familiar to a generation which has witnessed two world wars in a quarter of a century, and are again observable in what we had optimistically anticipated would be a "post-war" period. The United States and Russia, the two protagonists in any major conflict that may occur, both know little about each other, and such information as each possesses is often distorted by mutual prejudice and fear. Meager information, in turn, has caused both countries to place sinister interpretations on each other's actions. Each, in its own way, following the traditional course of its interests, has reached out for greater power as a result of World War II—Russia by seeking to expand its influence over neighboring countries through military force and Communist propaganda, and the United States by trying to acquire new strategic bases on grounds of security and larger markets for its exports on grounds of "equality of economic opportunity." What has seemed like security to Russia has looked like aggressiveness to the United States. What has seemed like security to the United States has looked like aggressiveness to Russia. In this country some people have been heard to say, "Since we shall have to fight Russia sooner or later, we might as well fight now," while we still possess the secret of the atomic bomb. The *Politbureau*, fully aware of Russia's terrible war losses, can hardly take so lighthearted a view of another war. Its leaders, however, have probably also viewed 1948 as the year of decision—not through war, but through a drive to achieve Communism wherever possible before the European Recovery Program got under way.

It is true that, in this country, such statements are made for the most part by private individuals (although some of them occupy positions of prominence and influence), while in Russia they are inspired by policy-making officials. But the distinction, which seems crystal-clear to Americans, is not always as obvious to Russians, who find it difficult to believe that there is no close interaction between the press and the government, and between former officials of the American government like George Earle and William C. Bullitt and present policy-makers in Washington.

Aggressive talk in both countries is welcomed by all those individuals and groups throughout the world who, for a variety of reasons, feel they have something to gain by war if it should result in the military defeat of Russia and the destruction of the Soviet system. Combustible materials that might easily flare up into another war are everywhere visible.

If, however, responsible counsels prevail in Washington and Moscow, what course should we follow to avert war between the United States and Russia? There are at least four main points to consider in setting a course away from war:

1. GREATER KNOWLEDGE OF RUSSIA

Many of the assumptions about the strength and weakness of Russia are based on sheer ignorance of readily ascertainable facts, or on wishful thinking, whether malevolent or benevolent. It is true that the Russians, by a wide range of restrictions, make it extremely difficult for foreigners to obtain accurate information inside the U.S.S.R. Responsible observers, however, have pointed out that most foreign correspondents in Russia do not make full use of such information facilities as are available to them. The main reason for this is that most of them have little or no knowledge of either the Russian language or Russian history, and therefore write like men who see through a glass darkly. Knowledge of both language and history are just as important in covering Russia as they are in covering Britain, and should be required qualifications of all foreign correspondents sent to Moscow. Then, at least, their likes or dislikes will be based on reasoned and informed conclusions, not on emotional reactions to situations which, being unfamiliar, are apt to seem sinister or, at best, peculiar. To achieve this purpose, American institutions of learning should introduce intensive courses in the Russian language patterned on those organized by the Army during the war, and should offer courses in Russian history, with special stress on contemporary developments, in which students should make use of Russian as well as American and other Western publications.

It would be well, of course, if similar efforts could be made in Russia to obtain accurate information about the United States, which is all too often portrayed in Russian newspapers as a land of unemployment, strikes, bread lines, lynchings, and other unpleasant features regarded as an integral part of "bourgeois capitalism." The State Department has already contributed to such efforts by the publication of a magazine in Russian for distribution in the U.S.S.R. entitled *Amerika*, containing excellent articles on various aspects of American life of which we can be justly proud, and with which Russians have been hitherto relatively unfamiliar. In 1947, moreover, the State Department inaugurated a series of daily Russian-language broadcasts beamed to Russia. These give objective accounts of this country's activities in foreign and domestic affairs, as well as discussions on topics of interest to both countries, such as housing, health, education, and so on, offering in addition programs of classical and popular music. The British Broadcasting Corporation estimates that there are 500,000 short wave sets in use in the Soviet Union, and the State Department broadcasts from Munich go over medium wave length, making them more widely accessible.

Of lasting value are the special opportunities for integrated study of various aspects of the U.S.S.R. offered to graduate students at the Russian Institute in Columbia University headed by Professor Geroid T. Robinson, well-known authority on Russian affairs, and similar programs established at other universities, notably at Harvard. Useful, too, are the translations into English of selected articles in the Russian press inaugurated by the University of Washington. Other projects for informing the Russians about life in the United States, such as the exchange of students which has been frequently urged in this country, will apparently have to wait for a more propitious moment, when the Soviet government will be less fearful than at present that its young generation may become contaminated with Western ideas inimical to the Soviet system. All possible contacts between Americans and Russians in nonpolitical fields, however, should be encouraged, in the hope that through coöperation in technical activities such as the protection of health under the World Health Organization, or recreational activities such as chess, the two peoples will come to see that, much as they differ in their political and economic concepts, they have many human interests in common. Such contacts should not be allowed to be stopped by fear on our side that we might become "infected" with Communist ideas. No barrier has yet been invented to prevent the circulation of ideas, and not even dictatorships have succeeded in creating hermetically sealed societies. If our own ideas are not strong enough to withstand contact with those of the Russians, then it is high time that we should overhaul our ideas and make them stronger.

2. GREATER KNOWLEDGE OF OUR OWN POSITION IN WORLD AFFAIRS

Not only is it important for us to acquire greater knowledge of Russia before we can formulate an intelligible policy toward that country, but it is also important for us to have a better understanding of the position of the United States in world affairs in this atomic bomb era. Too often our foreign policy appears to be based, on the one hand, on a generous desire to help the rest of the world and to share with all peoples, at least by way of adjuration and advice, the benefits of our way of life; and, on the other, a narrow and selfish desire to fold in upon ourselves, and to deny to all but the citizens of this country the advantages of free migration and free trade, which in the past contributed so richly to the growth of our own society. Our understandable determination to preserve what we have achieved here from encroachments by new doctrines and new institutions could all too easily, unless we are vigilant, develop into a determination to prevent any attempt at change elsewhere that may threaten the pleasant existence we would all like to enjoy. This fear of change can readily be rationalized into a conviction that if there were no Communists, and if Russia did not exist, all would be well, and we would somehow resume where war forced us to leave off in 1939. Such an assumption causes us to see the world in false focus, and to blame the Russians for any attempt at reform, both inside and outside our borders.

More adequate knowledge of world history would aid us

to appraise the course of contemporary events. It would also help us to understand that the phenomenal rise of the United States in less than two centuries from the status of scattered British colonies in a continental wilderness to the position of the greatest power in the world calls for abandonment of provincial or, shall we say, colonial attitudes toward world affairs, and the exercise of responsibilities commensurate with the authority the United States is potentially capable of exercising among other nations. Above all, we may learn that we cannot preach acceptance of the free enterprise system by other nations unless we ourselves practice it by desisting from nationalistic restrictions on foreign trade; or expect peoples living under substandard economic and social conditions to develop traditions of political liberty comparable to our own. Once we have clearly ascertained our own position in the modern world, we shall be better placed to compare our actual and potential power with that of Russia and to know, again on the basis of information and not of emotion, where we can afford to yield, and where, for the sake of the world community, it is incumbent for us to stand firm. We may then come to the conclusion that a great power like the United States must not be motivated in its foreign policy solely by fear of Russia, but must instead present both to Russia and to other nations constructive ideas based on our capacity for giving constructive aid. We may also discover that a great power can afford to yield on small things, while standing firm on fundamental principles.

3. RECOGNITION OF BASIC ISSUES

The basic struggle between the United States and Russia, as we have already noted, is a struggle of ideas. We should recognize that our main difference with Russia concerns not the necessity for economic and social progress, on which we generally agree, but the need for establishing and fostering civil liberties. On this basic issue it is impossible for us to compromise in the sense of pretending that civil liberties as we know them exist in Russia today. At the same time, we must understand the historical conditions which, in Russia, have produced lack of the concept of civil liberties familiar to the Western world, and ask ourselves what conditions are necessary for the future emergence of this concept, not only in Russia, but in other countries where it does not yet exist or has barely begun to develop. If it is true, as Westerners are inclined to believe, that improved material conditions and eradication of illiteracy facilitate—although they do not necessarily create—conditions propitious to the growth of individual liberty, then it should be our endeavor to encourage as rapid development of such conditions as possible in Russia, instead of trying to prevent or slow down the industrialization of that country as has been suggested by some Americans fearful of Russia's potential industrial competition.

At the same time, we must be prepared to see the emergence in Russia, and in neighboring countries, of political institutions of a character different from those of the English-speaking nations, and must not reject them merely because they are unfamiliar to us. As Joseph Barnes, foreign editor of the *New York Herald Tribune* has pointed out, there is constant danger that, because of our fear of Communism and of Russia, we may oppose, in other countries, ideas and practices, such as wider land distribution, which we would have been the first to favor had we had the enterprise and imagination to take the initiative in spreading them instead of leaving it to Russia. We should have the sportsmanship to admit that the Russians, and Communists in other countries, may have some good ideas, and examine proposals originating from Russian or Communist sources on their merits, instead of automatically rejecting them. As has been pointed out above, most peoples are not prepared to accept either the American or the Russian system in undiluted form. Sooner or later we and the Russians will have to learn to bring about a synthesis that may be acceptable to the rest of the world.

4. IT TAKES ALL KINDS TO MAKE A WORLD LIKE OURS

Above all, if we hope to avert war, we must accept the fact that at no stage in history has the entire world achieved exactly the same level of political, economic, and social development. Some peoples have forged far ahead, only to suffer devastation at the hands of newcomers usually described as "barbarians" or "revolutionaries" who, in turn, eventually became settled and conservative. Others have lagged way behind, then have suddenly emerged on the world stage to play unexpectedly important parts, only to yield their place in the spotlight to nations of ancient lineage which, after being temporarily submerged in the shadows, have reappeared again with new splendor. If we were to wait until all the world had become democratic, or if the Russians were to wait until all the world had become Communist, before any of us undertook measures of international organization, we would be postponing this task to the Greek calends. Every generation has to work with such materials as are at hand, and for those objectives which at the time appear to be attainable even though they may not correspond to our ideals. Today many people disappointed with the League of Nations and distrustful of the UN fervently preach the immediate establishment of world government. There is no doubt that world government should be our ultimate goal. But human institutions are not born full-grown. They must be carefully nurtured, and pruned, and provided with the proper climatic conditions if they are to flower and bear fruit. Western plans for world government which assume that, if Russia does not want to coöperate on our terms, then the rest of the world must band together without Russia, are as unrealistic as any plans the Russians may be evolving for a world government on their own terms which, unless accepted by this country, they would then proceed to develop without the United States.

Whether we like it or not, the United States and Russia are in the same world. When the Russians say that between their system and ours war is "inevitable," they base their calculations on the belief that what we call free private enterprise is shot through with contradictions which will eventually bring about its resort to war and its eventual downfall. We ourselves are aware of contradictions that exist in our society, of the gap that remains between the American dream and the fulfillment of that dream. Yet the majority of Americans are convinced that our system, in spite of its acknowledged faults, has provided the greatest personal freedom, the widest opportunities for achievement, and the highest living standards so far known in the world. Nothing is gained by glossing over the profound differences between the United States and Russia in historical development, and consequently in political, economic, and social concepts and practices. But, as Sidney Hook has well put it, "a world of common values is not a necessary condition of peace. Required are not common values, but a set of common rules or procedures which will enable us to negotiate our very genuine—and sometimes desirable—differences in values with a minimum of coercion." Both countries share an optimistic faith in progress which, as André Malraux has pointed out, is not a European (or Asiatic) value, but a value peculiarly characteristic of American and Russian civilization. This faith, which the United States, in far greater measure than contemporary Russia, is in a position to implement with technical means, may ultimately provide a meeting-ground for the United States and the U.S.S.R.

But material progress alone, as we have discovered in this grim century, is not enough. In the final analysis the two systems which now compete for the attention and support of the rest of the world will be judged not only by their material achievements, but by their capacity to satisfy the insatiable aspiration of man for a comprehensible explanation of the reason for his existence—a reason once provided by religious faith but which, in an age of scientific inquiry, must be found not through faith alone, but through the conviction that one's existence contributes in some way to the welfare of the human community. The war that should be made inevitable is not the war on the field of battle, but the war against hunger, disease, illiteracy, poverty, and fear. In this war there are no frontiers, and there should be no ideological differences. In this war the United States and Russia can fight side by side as peacetime allies.

13. The Opening of a New Chapter

The adoption by an impressive bipartisan majority in the United States Congress of the European Recovery Program substantially in the form proposed by the Truman Administration opened a new chapter in American foreign policy—and thereby made it possible to open a new chapter in relations between the United States and Russia. The Marshall Plan, the seed which flowered into the ERP, was the first important constructive step taken by this country since the end of World War II. It represented an acknowledgment that the United States had emerged from that war as a great power which could no longer merely intervene in conflicts that appeared to threaten this nation's survival, only to withdraw, after victory, from all responsibility for their outcome. The American people, through harsh experience, have learned that foreign policy is not a "one-time thing," to be applied only when it suits our interests or convenience, but must be a channel for the continuous and, if possible, consistent expression and application of national objectives in world affairs. We have also learned that peace, no less than war, imposes obligations on all peoples, and requires great efforts and expenditures—but efforts and expenditures which can never be as costly as those of war, and contribute to the creation, not the destruction, of moral and material values.

By making it clear beyond the shadow of a doubt that the United States is in the world "for keeps," this country has acquired the weapon it had hitherto lacked for reaching a possible settlement with Russia. Until now, as a nation, we had been divided between the urge to preserve peace by making concessions to Moscow, and the urge to "crack down" on the Russians even if this involved another world war. Both approaches were tried, and the result was that, in the eyes of other nations, American foreign policy weaved, sometimes almost crazily, between two extremes. Some of our spokesmen denounced the late President Roosevelt for his alleged "appeasement" of Russia. But they often forgot to mention that the concessions they particularly criticized—notably the Yalta conference—had been agreed to at a time when the outcome of the war in Europe was not yet certain, war in Asia still promised to be long and bloody, and the atomic bomb was not yet in the armory of the United States. Others attacked the "get-tough-with-the-Russians" course attributed solely to the Truman Administration, but which Roosevelt might also have had to adopt had he lived, and contended that it would be easy to settle matters with the Kremlin. But they often forgot to mention the various actions of the U.S.S.R. which have caused anxiety, fear, and hostility in the United States. The rapid shifts in public opinion about American relations with Russia, and the growing controversy which in some quarters assumed a tone of frenzy, threatened to create a sort of national schizophrenia hardly conducive to the cool consideration of decisions that would spell life or death not only for the United States and Russia, but for the entire world.

1. POINT AND COUNTER-POINT

What, in final count, have been the practical results of the mounting struggle between the two great superpowers who shared military triumphs but have found it impossible to agree on the peacetime uses of their joint victory? As the curtain is gradually lifted from some of the diplomatic secrets of the war, it becomes clear that, at least six months before Yalta, Britain had proposed to Russia wartime division of spheres of influence in Eastern Europe without first consulting the United States—and, according to the memoirs of Cordell Hull, had notified Washington only after this procedure had been suggested by the Kremlin. Mr. Hull says that he strongly opposed such an arrangement, on the ground that the concept of spheres of influence was contrary to American foreign policy—only to bring from Winston Churchill the retort that the United States itself had such a sphere in South America. Under pressure from Churchill, and during a temporary absence of Mr. Hull, President Roosevelt acquiesced in the British proposal, with the result that Hungary, Romania, and Bulgaria were recognized by Britain and the United States to be in Russia's sphere, and Russia, in return, recognized that Greece was in the British sphere—with Yugoslavia divided between Britain and Russia on a fifty-fifty basis.

This arrangement, which at the time was understood to be for military purposes, sheds new light on the Yalta conference held while war was still raging in Europe, at which Roosevelt and Churchill obtained from Stalin a pledge that "free, unfettered elections" would be held in the liberated countries of Eastern Europe—most of which, apparently, had been acknowledged to lie in Russia's sphere. Stalin's failure to fulfill this pledge in a form acceptable to the Western powers was perhaps the most important single cause for the sharp change in American sentiment toward Russia. Discussions of this problem, however, usually gave little heed to the prewar political development of the countries of Eastern Europe, or the feasibility of elections on the Western pattern in the wake of prolonged and destructive war and civil strife.

When Russia made it clear that it would hold the positions it had gained during the war in Eastern Europe, and sought to advance its influence into other areas, the United States, which had rapidly demobilized after the war, turned to the policy of "containment." This policy, first indicated by President Truman for Greece and Turkey but later thought of in broader terms, was based on the general assumption that economic aid to key countries along the periphery of Russia would serve as a dike against further spread or infiltration of Russian and Communist influence. Whatever may have been the original expectations of those who formulated the "containment" policy, it soon became apparent that economic aid would prove insufficient unless accompanied by military aid, at least in the form of advice and supplies if not yet of American armed forces. More and more, however, was heard about the necessity of taking a "calculated risk," and units of the American fleet were sent into the Mediterranean, where not only Greece and Turkey, but also Italy and Trieste, had become important nerve-centers of the "cold war."

But close on the heels of the Truman Doctrine came the Marshall Plan which, without outright repudiation of the "containment" policy, marked the first step toward adoption of a positive, instead of merely negative, policy with respect to Russia. Whether it was seriously believed at the time that Russia would accept the invitation to take part in the Marshall Plan is not yet clear, but some sources in Washington have suggested that it would have proved very difficult to obtain Congressional approval for an economic aid program that would have included the U.S.S.R. However that may be, Russia not only rejected the Marshall Plan for itself, but insisted on similar action by the countries of Eastern Europe, of whom at least two—Czechoslovakia and Poland—had indicated definite interest in the American proposal. Accusing the United States of "economic imperialism" and of encroaching on the sovereignty of the nations to whom aid was offered, Russia countered the Marshall Plan with establishment in Belgrade of the Cominform, which signalized the revival in militant form of the Communist International, officially disbanded during the war. The Soviet government also offered its neighbors counterattractions for what they had lost by nonparticipation in the Marshall Plan in the form of credits, grain, and some industrial equipment under five-year barter trade arrangements. In addition, the countries of Eastern Europe and the Balkans concluded with each other and with the U.S.S.R. agreements for military assistance—although talk of an Eastern European federation initiated by Georgi Dimitrov of Bulgaria was scotched by *Pravda* as premature.

Most discussions in this country concerning Russia's attitude toward the Marshall Plan have been based on the assumption that the Soviet government opposes the recovery of Europe, and hopes to perpetuate conditions of misery, ferment, and strife which would be favorable to Communism. A distinction must be drawn here between Russia's attitude toward countries which have Communist regimes, and those where the Communists are at present excluded from governments, as in France and Italy. In countries ruled by Communists, notably Poland and Czechoslovakia, there is no evidence that the Soviet government has sought to prevent economic recovery. On the contrary—though it must be pointed out that this recovery was due in considerable measure to the aid of UNRRA, over 70 per cent of whose funds were supplied by the United States—Russia has itself rendered some assistance to these countries in spite of its own wartime devastation. It is true, of course, that Russia has sought to gear the economies of neighboring countries to its own economy, now in process of reconstruction, by encouraging industrialization, especially the development of heavy industries—but this development may in the long run prove to the advantage of the countries of Eastern Europe, which before 1939 had been peculiarly dependent on Germany as a source of manufactured goods, and consequently vulnerable to German pressure.

So far as can be judged, what the Soviet government has opposed is not the recovery of Europe as such, but recovery on a pattern outlined by the United States, and under circumstances which give this country, because of its superior industrial potential, a decisive role in the shaping of the continent's economy. Even if the *Politbureau* were convinced that the United States was animated solely by the most selfless motives, it would still be disturbed by the prospect that this country, which until now has played no important part in European affairs except in time of war, would assume a dominant, if not controlling, position among European nations. The Soviet government's attitude, however, is reinforced not only by its traditional suspicion of "capitalist" powers, but also by its belief that the United States is not averse to the rebuilding of Germany, both as a "workshop" of Europe and as a bulwark against Russia and Communism. It also believes that the United States plans to rally Western Europe including the Germans in that anti-Russian coalition which the Kremlin has so long forecast—and which its repeated forecasts, and its own measures of opposition, are bringing into being, like a genie out of a bottle.

Whether the Soviet leaders had planned all along to proceed rapidly with the consolidation of their sphere of influence, or whether their plans were crystallized and hastened by the impending passage of the European Recovery Program, remains for the moment a matter for hypothesis. Many reasons have been adduced for Communist seizure of power in Czechoslovakia. Some observers believe that the Communists, fearing the 1948 Czechoslovak national elections would reveal that they were losing ground, or at least not gaining, decided to take no chances. Others contend that the decision of the National Socialists to withdraw from the cabinet upset the delicately poised coalition, and provided the Communists with an opportunity to effect a coup they might have otherwise hesitated to launch. It is generally believed that the Soviet government, without whose acquiescence if not outright assistance the Czech Communists would probably not have acted, had begun to fear that some Czech leaders might attempt to orient Czechoslovakia economically toward the Western powers in the hope of benefiting at least indirectly from the ERP. Such a development, in Moscow's opinion, might have deprived Russia of the industrial equipment it was counting on obtaining from Czechoslovakia, the principal industrial nation in Eastern Europe. At the same time, it is thought that the Czechs, because of their geographic proximity to Russia and their long-time affinity with Slav interests, had little choice but to follow the course set by Moscow, and were not prepared to resist Russian pressure.

Whatever may have been the reasons for the Communist seizure of power in Prague, what we do know is that it immediately solidified the determination of the Western nations to erect a dam against further advances by Russia and Communism through a wide range of internal and external measures. Steps were taken, even in countries like Britain and Holland which had been notably free of hysteria, to prevent Communists from holding important posts in government service and in the labor unions. In Brussels, on March 17, Britain, France, and the Low Countries concluded a fifty-year military alliance. In Paris the sixteen Marshall Plan nations set up machinery for the most effective joint utilization of American aid under the ERP. France and Italy, on March 20, signed a customs union providing for closer integration of their economies, following the example already set by the Benelux group—Belgium, the Netherlands, and Luxembourg. Plans for a Western European federation, hitherto nebulous, began to be discussed in terms of practical possibilities, with the blessing of Winston Churchill.

While the United States still refrained from abandoning its traditional policy of "no entangling alliances," President Truman, in his address of March 17 to a joint session of Congress, expressed sympathy for the formation of the Western European Union of five nations at Brussels. The Europeans pointed out that military aid from the United States would be needed to implement any federation, and talk was heard of standardizing the armaments of all Western nations, including the United States. Meanwhile, as the "cold war" between the United States and Russia approached its climax with the Italian national elections of April 18, in which both great powers openly intervened by all the political, economic and military methods at their disposal, President Truman proposed that this country adopt universal military training and restore the draft so as to be ready to oppose aggression. The United States, together with Britain and France, called on Russia to return Trieste, coveted by Yugoslavia, to Italy, and gave up its previous support of Palestine partition, for fear that Russia might use partition as an opportunity to send troops into the Near East, with its valuable resources of oil needed for the success of the ERP as well as for American security. The two great powers accused each other of planning to use Norway for strategic purposes. At the International Conference of American States in Bogotá, Secretary Marshall called on the Latin American countries to align themselves against Communism. And at the end of March Washington asked the UN Atomic Energy Commission to abandon further efforts to reach agreement as to a world atomic control agency.

2. NO PEACE—NO WAR?

Thus, on the eve of the third anniversary of V–E Day, the two great powers which had succeeded in defeating

Germany appeared arrayed for a new war, which in the opinion of even the most bellicose spokesmen would spell unbelievable, perhaps final, disaster for the continents where it would have to be waged—Europe and Asia. Yet in spite of the somber portents which the course of events might well justify, there still remained the possibility that wiser counsel might prevail, and that while there would be no immediate peace, there would also be no immediate war. This possibility was enhanced by the very fact that the United States had turned from a negative to a positive policy. For now this country holds certain bargaining points which it has not held since the war—and is therefore able to talk to Russia not merely in terms of empty threats, as before, but of concrete realities.

The most important of these bargaining points is unquestionably the European Recovery Program. It was because the Soviet government clearly recognized from the outset that, in formulating the Marshall Plan, the United States had chosen a battlefield on which it is superior to Russia, and a weapon Russia cannot match, that it opposed the Plan with such vigor and bitterness. Once the program is under way, once its beneficial results have become apparent, it will be increasingly difficult for Russia to prevent European nations from joining in continental reconstruction. Already fissures have appeared even in supposedly monolithic Communist blocs, notably in Italy. As was pointed out in Chapter 6, Communists, when they come to power in any given country, tend to assume some national coloration, even if purely for propaganda purposes. It is difficult, and may well prove impossible, for Communism to maintain at one and the same time national and international dynamics. The United States now has an unrivaled opportunity to aid the recovery of individual nations but, at the same time, to foster that future international coöperation through the coordination of national efforts which is already recognized by the sixteen Marshall Plan nations as a prerequisite to the success of the ERP.

At the same time, it is becoming increasingly evident that fulfillment of the ERP will require at least partial resumption of East-West trade, if the countries of Western Europe are not to become permanently dependent on the Western Hemisphere for certain essential foods and raw materials. For the time being, Eastern Europe is not furnishing the Western nations with products in amounts comparable to prewar figures. This is due, in part, to political retaliation for the refusal of the United States to grant credits to satellites of Russia; but in large part, too, to the wartime devastation suffered by these countries, and to their own postwar efforts at industrialization and agricultural modernization. These countries, for their part, urgently need tools, machinery, and raw materials which Russia, itself in process of reconstruction, is not in a position to supply. Both sides would benefit by expansion of trade. Sooner or later negotiations must be opened to increase exchanges between the West and the East—and this includes Russia. When that time comes, the question of an American loan to Russia may again come into the foreground.

3. PROSPECTS FOR NEGOTIATIONS

Diplomatic feelers were put out by both the United States and the U.S.S.R. shortly after adoption of the European Recovery Program by the American Congress. The revelation by the Moscow radio on May 10 that American Ambassador Walter Bedell Smith and Russian Foreign Minister Molotov had exchanged statements about the respective policies of the two countries had widely varying repercussions. On the whole, the State Department was praised for having taken the initiative to inform the Kremlin, first, of the reasons why this country views Russian actions with suspicion; and, second, of Washington's intention, while maintaining the policy developed during the past year, to hold the door open to future negotiations. Considerable criticism was expressed, however, both here and in the capitals of Western European nations, about the method chosen by the United States for conveying this message to the Soviet government—especially Washington's failure to inform our potential allies concerning what has been interpreted as a unilateral approach to Russia, no matter how limited in its objective. The subsequent declarations by President Truman and Secretary of State Marshall that the American statement communicated by Ambassador Bedell Smith on May 4 represented no change in policy were discounted in some quarters, and Secretary Marshall's insistence that, if negotiations were to take place, they must proceed through the UN and other existing international agencies, was regarded as in contradiction to the initial démarche in Moscow, which had been undertaken outside the UN framework.

The Soviet government, for its part, was criticized by many, both here and in Europe, for having taken advantage of what, according to accepted diplomatic practice, would normally be regarded as confidential exchanges, to launch a public campaign for new negotiations with the United States. Critics pointed out that Mr. Molotov, in his reply of May 9 to Ambassador Smith's communication, had completely passed over the blunt American criticisms of Russia's postwar foreign policy, and instead had seized this occasion to list actions of the United States which the Soviet government considers to be inimical to its interests. Other observers, however, took the view that it was unrealistic to expect the government of the U.S.S.R.—or, for that matter, of any great power—merely to acquiesce in the criticisms made by another great power, and that the United States, if adequately informed about the processes of diplomacy in gen-

eral and Russian practices in particular, should not have
been as surprised as it appeared to be at the use Mr. Molotov
made of this incident. What, asked some observers, did the
United States hope to achieve by its statement? Would it
have preferred to have Russia reject it outright, or pass it
over in silence? If not, then was not Russia's reply, propagandistic as it might be in tone and shrewdly calculated
in intent, the kind of reply Washington had sought to
elicit?

The real issue, however, appeared to be not the real or
alleged mistakes in diplomatic handling of the Washington–
Moscow exchange, but the character of the settlement that
might conceivably be arrived at as a result of renewed
Russo-American negotiations. The most notable points of
the Molotov statement of May 10, in the opinion of many,
were the emphasis on the need for some form of commercial understanding that would not encroach on national
sovereignty—a criticism the Russians keep on making about
the ERP; and the prospect of defining the respective spheres
of influence of the two postwar superpowers. The possibility of a commercial understanding which would cover
not only the interests of the United States and Russia but,
far more important, the development of economic relations
of East and West in Europe, has become a matter of paramount importance since the official launching of the ERP.
This was made clear by Russia's neighbors, Poland and
Czechoslovakia, during the meeting in Geneva, April 26-
May 8, of the UN Economic Commission for Europe, on
which these two countries, as well as the United States and
Russia, are represented.

As to the possibility of delimiting respective spheres of
influence, it is increasingly recognized that the balance of
power gradually developed since the nineteenth century
was irrevocably broken up by two world wars. If a new
balance is to be established, it will have to be established
not with reference to this continent or that, as was true in

the days when Britain and France, or Britain and Russia, succeeded in agreeing on spheres of influence in Africa or the Middle East, but on a world scale. This means, as some American spokesmen have pointed out, that a definition of interests affects the destiny not merely of a few countries, but of the entire globe. But what procedure will prove most productive of results under the circumstances? Should the United States insist that future negotiations be carried on solely through the UN, which hitherto Washington has considered too weak to deal with the Truman Doctrine, the Marshall Plan, and the partition of Palestine recommended by the General Assembly—or should the United States and the U.S.S.R. negotiate simultaneously both in the UN and through bilateral discussions in Washington and Moscow?

A partial answer to this question was given by Premier Stalin on May 17 in a radio broadcast in which he accepted the sweeping program outlined by Henry A. Wallace in an open letter to Stalin of May 11 "as a good and fruitful basis" for discussion and settlement of the differences between the two great powers. Mr. Wallace's letter ranged over all matters in controversy, from general reduction of armaments to evacuation of troops from Korea, from world development of nondiscriminatory world trade to defense of democracy and civil rights in all countries. Critics of this new exchange were quick to point out that Mr. Wallace's program might turn out, in practice, to favor Russia and not the United States; and that Stalin's answer to Wallace constituted intervention in the preëlection campaigns of American political parties. In spite of these criticisms, however, Washington indicated that it considered Moscow's feelers as "encouraging." The American government, however, while reiterating that the door remains open to negotiations, stressed that the Soviet government must first demonstrate the sincerity of its intentions not by mere words but by acts—through adjustments in the many international agencies where the United States and the U.S.S.R. are at present deadlocked.

Repeated disillusionments and setbacks since the war have made everyone cautious about venturing optimistic forecasts. Yet, judging by reports of public opinion reactions here and in Europe to the Washington–Moscow exchanges, it would seem that the future is no longer wholly "impenetrable," as a Rome correspondent had written in the *Commonweal* on the eve of the Italian elections. Meanwhile, the United States, deeply as it affects Russia by the ERP, is itself being affected by Russia's actions in Europe and Asia. The struggle against Communism has had the result of causing its opponents to recognize the need for political, economic, and social changes which had been either deprecated or thought to be premature. When the Pope, in the midst of preëlection controversies in Italy, declared that there could be no return to "rugged individualism," and that some form of socialism would have to be accepted, he was expressing the thoughts of many leaders of varied political backgrounds all over the world. It was recognized, more and more, that neither economic aid alone, nor economic aid backed by military force, would check Communism; that the most effective weapon against the Communist police state is voluntary and constant adaptation of human relations, both within nations and among nations, to the rapidly changing conditions imposed on us all by industrialization, by the development of new weapons, by the altered concepts of sovereignty and security. From these changes no nation can remain completely immune—not even Russia. We cannot, by our own volition, change the situation in Russia, or bend the Soviet leaders to our objectives. But given the exercise of wise and magnanimous statesmanship on our side, we now have in our hands brand new, peacetime, weapons with which we can open a new chapter in American-Russian relations—and thus clear the way to gradual stabilization of the world.

Appendix I. Tables on Russo-American Trade

I. United States Merchandise Trade with the U.S.S.R.—Annual Average 1911–1938 and Annual 1929–1944 [*]

[Value in thousands of dollars]

Yearly average or year	Exports, including reexports to U.S.S.R.		General imports from U.S.S.R.	
	Value	Per cent of total U. S. exports	Value	Per cent of total U. S. imports
1911–15 . .	44,853	1.8	15,613	0.9
1916–20 . .	135,933	2.0	5,678	.2
1921–25 . .	32,049	.7	4,651	.1
1926–30 . .	77,665	1.6	17,592	.4
1931–35 . .	33,122	1.6	13,180	.8
1936–38 . .	48,670	1.6	25,106	1.0
1929 . . .	85,011	1.6	22,551	.5
1930 . . .	114,399	3.0	24,386	.8
1931 . . .	103,717	4.3	13,206	.6
1932 . . .	12,641	.8	9,736	.7
1933 . . .	8,997	.5	12,114	.8
1934 . . .	15,011	.7	12,337	.7
1935 . . .	24,743	1.1	17,809	.9
1936 . . .	33,427	1.4	20,517	.8
1937 . . .	42,892	1.3	30,768	1.0
1938 . . .	69,691	2.3	24,034	1.2
1939 . . .	56,638	1.8	25,023	1.1
1940 . . .	86,943	2.2	20,773	.8
1941 . . .	107,524	2.1	30,095	.9
1942 . . .	1,425,442	17.6	24,656	.9
1943 . . .	2,994,828	23.1	29,850	.9
1944 . . .	3,458,982	24.3	49,698	1.3

[*] "United States Trade with Russia (U.S.S.R.) during the War Years," *International Reference Service* (U. S. Department of Commerce), II (41), December 1945.

II. PRINCIPAL COMMODITIES IN UNITED STATES TOTAL EXPORTS, CASH AND LEND-LEASE, TO THE U.S.S.R., ANNUAL 1941–1944 *

Commodity	Value (in millions of dollars)				Percentage distribution				Exports to U.S.S.R. as percentage of total U. S. exports			
	1941	1942	1943	1944	1941	1942	1943	1944	1941	1942	1943	1944
Exports of United States merchandise, total.	105.3	1,422.9	2,990.0	3,457.0	100.0	100.0	100.0	100.0	2.1	17.8	23.3	24.4
Military exports [1]	29.5	733.7	1,291.1	1,060.4	28.1	50.9	43.2	30.7	2.9	24.3	23.2	19.4
Machinery [2]	27.5	100.8	401.4	636.1	26.1	7.1	13.4	18.4	3.9	13.5	34.1	43.5
Electrical, and apparatus	6.2	24.0	98.1	181.6	5.9	1.7	3.3	5.3	4.2	15.9	36.6	41.7
Industrial, total	21.3	70.6	290.3	433.5	20.2	5.0	9.7	12.5	4.5	13.5	36.0	50.3
Metalworking	6.4	49.5	157.4	187.8	6.1	3.5	5.3	5.4	2.7	20.8	36.0	69.1
Agricultural, and implements	(³)	6.1	13.0	21.0	(⁴)	.4	.4	.6	(⁴)	8.7	12.6	12.6
Meats, dairy products, eggs, and other foodstuffs	.6	165.3	523.5	504.7	.6	11.6	17.5	14.6	.1	16.7	31.6	28.6
Automobiles, parts, and accessories	13.0	114.1	65.1	315.5	12.4	8.0	2.2	9.1	3.8	26.4	23.8	49.4
Motortrucks, busses, and chassis, new	11.9	104.2	54.8	246.2	11.3	7.3	1.8	7.1	8.0	38.5	36.0	60.9
Iron and steel-mill products	2.1	91.1	111.9	131.5	2.0	6.4	3.7	3.8	.4	15.4	18.2	23.9
Chemicals and products, excluding explosives	1.7	22.8	59.1	108.0	1.6	1.6	2.0	3.1	.7	8.5	17.4	26.6
Wool cloth and dress goods	.2	8.8	49.9	94.1	.2	.6	1.7	2.7	13.1	90.7	98.2	97.5
Aluminum and manufactures	1.0	18.1	36.4	60.5	.9	1.3	1.2	1.7	9.9	56.5	50.0	65.2
Copper and manufactures	2.1	30.8	39.6	57.4	2.0	2.2	1.3	1.7	4.4	37.4	36.4	55.9
Rubber and manufactures	.6	13.8	57.5	54.9	.6	1.0	1.9	1.6	1.1	21.3	42.9	29.7
Brass and bronze manufactures	.8	29.1	39.4	51.5	.7	2.0	1.3	1.5	2.9	72.3	76.4	83.8
Vegetable oils, inedible	.9	7.3	34.1	49.3	.8	.5	1.1	1.4	7.8	42.0	68.6	80.5
Leather and leather manufactures	4.1	22.0	15.2	46.3	3.9	1.5	.5	1.3	14.0	55.7	38.3	69.1
Cotton manufactures	.1	5.3	23.9	42.8	.1	.4	.8	1.2	.1	4.5	13.3	19.5
Petroleum and products	11.1	8.8	24.4	40.5	10.6	.6	.8	1.2	3.9	2.5	4.7	4.2
Merchant vessels	....	14.9	92.4	31.8	....	1.0	3.1	.9	...	13.9	23.5	13.1
Freight cars over 10-ton capacity	1.9	(³)	2.4	29.0	1.8	(⁴)	.1	.8	34.4	.2	7.9	58.3
Commodities exported for relief or charity	.4	10.5	19.1	25.5	.3	.7	.6	.7	.9	32.8	32.5	21.3
Scientific and professional instruments, etc.	1.7	2.5	6.5	16.6	1.6	.2	.2	.5	5.5	10.3	18.2	9.8
Iron and steel advanced manufactures	1.3	6.5	16.2	15.6	1.3	.5	.5	.5	1.3	5.5	13.0	13.3
All other commodities	4.8	26.8	80.9	84.8	4.5	1.9	2.7	2.5	.5	2.8	6.0	6.5

*"United States Trade with Russia (U.S.S.R.) during the War Years," *International Reference Service* (U. S. Department of Commerce), II (41), December 1945.

[1] Represents aircraft, military tanks, explosives, firearms, and other strictly military items.

[2] Includes industrial machinery, electrical apparatus, and agricultural machinery and implements.

[3] Less than $50,000.

[4] Less than one-tenth of 1 per cent.

Appendix II. Suggested Reading

The number of English-language books published on Russia since 1917 is literally legion. Expert and layman, diplomat and journalist, historian and run-of-the-mill tourist, Communist and anti-Communist, have vied with each other to get at the heart of the so-called Russian enigma—often with about as much luck as those who preceded Oedipus in the endeavor to discover the secret of the Sphinx. Most Westerners have come to the task of understanding Russia and interpreting it to others ill-prepared because of ignorance of the country's history and its language. Many have been misled, consciously or unconsciously, into uncritical praise or indiscriminate denunciation by personal predilection for or personal disillusionment with the myth they had built about Russia. Because of the intensity of feeling, pro and con, aroused by the Bolshevik revolution, by the Soviet system, and by the post-war foreign policy of the U.S.S.R., every book and article on Russia must be read with some knowledge of the author's background, and of the preconceptions that may have affected his impressions and inspired his judgments.

From the vast mass of material published on Russia, the following works have been selected for the light they shed on contemporary developments. The reader who has no time for extended study of Russian affairs will find on page 304 a brief bibliography which includes basic works covering the most important aspects of the history and present conditions of Russia and of that country's relations with the United States, and representing a wide range of views on the most controversial topic of our times.

Historical Background. The best brief, well-rounded account is *Russia* by Sir Bernard Pares, veteran British authority on Russian affairs who has known the country well both in pre- and post-revolutionary times (New York: Penguin Books, 1943). In connection with this small volume, crystallizing the conclusions of decades of study and travel, should be read Pares' *A History of Russia* (fifth revised edition, New York: Knopf, 1947), a survey of Russia's development from earliest times to 1946. *A History of Russia*, by George Vernadsky, Russian-born professor of history at Yale University (New Haven: Yale University Press, fourth printing, 1946) remains useful, especially when supplemented by the same author's detailed *Political and Diplomatic History of Russia* (Boston: Little, Brown, 1936). For a Western reader by far the most thought-provoking survey of Russia's development is *A Short History of Russia* (New York: Reynal and Hitchcock, 1943) by B. H. Sumner, a British historian who, instead of giving the conventional chronological account usually confusing to those who are unfamiliar with Russia, analyzes the main forces which, in his opinion, have shaped the development of the country from earliest times through World War II. An illuminating summary of the effects of World War I on the Russian state, essential for an understanding of the Bolshevik revolution, is *The End of the Russian Empire* by Michael T. Florinsky, Russian-born lecturer in economics at Columbia University (New Haven: Yale University Press, 1931). The most outstanding Russian work is *A History of Russia* by V. O. Klyuchevsky (5 volumes, London: J. M. Dent, 1911–1931), a translation unfortunately inadequate. Of general interest is *The Urge to the Sea* by Robert J. Kerner (Berkeley: University of California Press, 1942).

Revolution and Communism. Conflicting views on the objectives, methods, and history of Communism are too numerous to list at length in this selective bibliographical survey. A serious student of Russia will want to make an extensive study of the works of Hegel, Marx and Engels, Lenin, Trotsky, and Stalin, as well as of the many commentaries published by Communist disciples and dissenters. William H. Chamberlin, Moscow correspondent of *The Christian Science Monitor* for a decade, 1922–1933, gives a painstakingly detailed history of the Bolshevik revolution in *The Russian Revolution, 1917–1921* (New York: Macmillan, 1935, two volumes). Joseph V. Stalin's *Leninism* (New York: International Publishers, Vol. I, 1928, Vól. II, 1933) and *Marxism and the National and Colonial Question* (New York: International Publishers, 1936), as well as Leon Trotsky's *History of the Russian Revolution,* a very personal and brilliant account (New York: Simon and Schuster, 1932, 3 volumes) and his *The Real Situation in Russia* (New York: Harcourt, 1928) and *The Revolution Betrayed* (New York: Doubleday, 1928) are essential for an understanding of the Stalin-Trotsky controversy. Alexander Kerenski has given his view of the Bolshevik revolution in *The Crucifixion of Liberty* (New York: John Day, 1934). *Soviet Communism: A New Civilization?* (New York: Scribner, 1936, two volumes) by the British Fabian leaders Beatrice and Sidney Webb, although uncritical and sometimes downright naïve, contains a good deal of interesting and useful material. Louis Fischer, American correspondent in Moscow during the twenties and early thirties, long known for his admiration of Soviet ideas and practices, explains why he became increasingly critical of the Soviet system after 1936, and urges "double rejection" of Fascism and Communism and strengthening of democracy in *The Great Challenge* (New York: Duell, Sloan and Pearce, 1946). Leland Stowe, another well-known American correspondent, while reaffirming his faith in Jeffersonian democracy, points out the reasons why Communist ideas have influenced some of the peoples of Europe in *While Time Remains* (New York: Macmillan, 1947). William Henry Chamberlin, who was bitterly disillusioned with the Soviet system, records his impressions in *The Confessions of an Individualist* (New York: Macmillan, 1940), which should be read along with his *The European Cockpit* (New York: Macmillan, 1947).

A penetrating although somewhat exaggerated analysis of the influence of Soviet ideas and practices, friendly to Russia, is *The Soviet Impact on the Western World* (New York: Macmillan, 1947) by Edward H. Carr, former member of the British Foreign Office, now Wilson Professor of International Politics at University College of Wales and editorial writer on the London *Times*. Arthur Koestler, a former member of the Communist party, has expressed his revulsion for Communist methods in a brilliant novel dealing with the purges of the middle thirties, *Darkness at Noon* (New York: Macmillan, 1941) and in *The Yogi and the Commissar* (New York: Macmillan, 1945), but has shown little real comprehension of the intrinsic concepts of democracy, as indicated by his violent novel about Jewish terrorists in Palestine, *Thieves in the Night* (New York: Macmillan, 1946).

Impressions of Foreign Correspondents. To the long shelf of earlier books on Russia by foreign correspondents, notably Walter Duranty's *I Write as I Please*, Eugene Lyons' *Assignment in Utopia*, and William H. Chamberlin's *Russia's Iron Age* and *Soviet Russia*, reflecting widely divergent views on developments in Russia during the first decade or two of Soviet rule, should be added the new crop of the war and post-war years. Of these the two that give the most vivid close-up of the Russian people are *Round Trip to Russia* by Walter Graebner, who visited Russia in 1942 (New York: Lippincott, 1943); and *These Are the Russians* by Richard

Lauterbach, an excellent reporter, who spent 1943 and 1944
in Russia (New York: Harper, 1945), returning there after
the war for a trip from Vladivostok to Moscow which he
recorded in *Through Russia's Back Door* (New York; Harper, 1947). Wallace Carroll of the United Press, in *We're In
This With Russia* (Boston: Houghton Mifflin, 1942); Alexander Werth, Russian-born correspondent for the London
News Chronicle, in *Moscow Diary* (New York: Knopf,
1942); Henry G. Cassidy, in *Moscow Dateline, 1941–1943*
(Boston, Houghton Mifflin, 1943); Larry Lesueur, in
Twelve Months That Changed the World (New York:
Knopf, 1943); James E. Brown, in *Russia Fights* (New York:
Scribner, 1943); and Harrison Salisbury of the United Press
in *Russia on the Way* (New York, Macmillan, 1946) all cover
something of the same ground, but each contributes some
valuable personal comments in his interpretation of Soviet
policy at home and abroad. The most thoughtful and probably the most enthusiastic of recent correspondents' books is
Russia Is No Riddle (New York: Greenberg, 1945) by Ed-
mund Stevens of the *Christian Science Monitor;* the most
critical is W. L. White's *Report on the Russians* (New York:
Harcourt, Brace, 1945), which received wide publicity because of its condensation in the *Reader's Digest*—a condensation that did not give an altogether fair impression of the
views of the author, who on his first trip to Russia was not
unnaturally struck by the shabbiness of a country in the grip
of war, and did not have the time, or perhaps the desire, to
look behind the outward façade.

The most interesting accounts of Russia at war, however,
were contributed by two nonprofessionals in journalism—
Eve Curie in *Journey Among Warriors* (New York: Doubleday, Doran, 1943), and Wendell Willkie, in *One World*
(New York: Simon and Schuster, 1943). Margaret Bourke-
White, in *Shooting the Russian War* (New York: Simon
and Schuster, 1942), illustrated with striking photographs

some of the points made by her writing colleagues. John Scott, who worked in a Russian factory in Magnitogorsk, and is now representing *Time, Life* and *Fortune* in Europe, gives a firsthand view of Soviet industrialization in *Behind the Urals* (Boston: Houghton Mifflin, 1942). In *Why They Behave Like Russians* (New York: Harper, 1947) John Fischer, a former American government official and now editor-in-chief of Harper's General (Trade) Book Department, who went to Russia with an UNRRA mission in 1946, offers a lively account, which stirred considerable controversy, of his impressions of Russia's war-devastated areas and the motives that animate the Soviet leaders. For a Polish account of Russia's wartime treatment of the Poles, the reader should look at *The Dark Side of the Moon* (New York: Scribner, 1947).

For a glimpse of what Russians think about the Soviet system and the effects of war it is helpful to read *I Saw the Russian People* (Boston: Little, Brown, 1945) by Ella Winter, and *Talks About Russia* (New York: John Day, 1945), Pearl Buck's report of her conversations with Masha Scott, Russian wife of John Scott. A vivid and moving picture of Russia at war as seen by Russian writers is found in *The Last Days of Sevastopol* by Boris Voyetekhov (New York: Knopf, 1943) and *Days and Nights* by Konstantin Simonov (New York: Simon and Schuster, 1945).

The People. Valuable scientific material on all major aspects of the population of the U.S.S.R. is contained in *The Population of the Soviet Union: History and Prospects* by an American authority in this field, Frank Lorimer (League of Nations, Economic, Financial and Transit Department, Geneva, 1946). Corliss Lamont, well known for his sympathy for Russia, gives a useful summary of information on the national composition of the Soviet population in *The Peoples of the Soviet Union* (New York: Harcourt, Brace, 1946). Hans Kohn, professor of history at Smith College offers a sympathetic account of Soviet policy toward national minorities in *Nationalism in the Soviet Union* (New York: Columbia University Press, 1933).

The Russian people are described enthusiastically but uncritically by Albert Rhys Williams in *The Russians, the Land, the People, and Why They Fight* (New York: Harcourt, Brace, 1943). Maurice Hindus, in his earlier books *Broken Earth* and *Red Bread*, and most recently in *Mother Russia* (New York: Doubleday, 1943), writes with understanding and affection of the men, women, and children of Russia with whom most diplomats and tourists hardly ever come in contact. An analysis of the Russian character as seen by a distinguished Slav leader is contained in *The Spirit of Russia* (New York: Macmillan, 1919) by Thomas G. Masaryk, first president of the Czechoslovak Republic. Edward Crankshaw, an English authority on Joseph Conrad, who was attached to the British military mission in Moscow during the war, has contributed a penetrating and well-written study of the Russian character in *Russia and the Russians* (New York: Viking, 1948). An invaluable source of information on the principal aspects of Russia's development during the past quarter of a century, viewed in historical perspective, is *Russia in Flux* (New York: Macmillan, 1948), a volume in which S. Haden Guest has presented in edited and abridged form two works by the distinguished British expert on Russia, Sir John Maynard, published originally under the titles *Russia in Flux* and *The Russian Peasant and Other Studies*. Nicolas Berdyaev, noted Russian philosopher, gives a remarkable picture of the Russian mind in *The Russian Idea* (New York: Macmillan, 1948). The reader who wants to become familiar with Russian thought and feeling must read the novels of Turgenev, Dostoevski, Gogol, Gorki, and Leo Tolstoi, the poetry of Pushkin and Lermontov, Alexander Block and Anna Akhmatova, and contemporary novels, among them Michael

Sholokhov's *And Quiet Flows the Don* (New York: Knopf, 1934) and Alexei Tolstoi's *Road to Calvary* (Toronto: Ryerson Press, 1946).

The Land. A useful compendium of information on many aspects of the U.S.S.R., friendly to the Soviet system, is *A Guide to the Soviet Union* by William Mandel, former Russian expert for the United Press, at present Hoover Institute Fellow in Slavic Studies at Stanford University (New York: Dial Press, 1946). For a succinct and up-to-date survey of Russia's natural resources and industrial potential, the best available source is *The Basis of Soviet Strength* by George B. Cressey, chairman of the Department of Geology and Geography at Syracuse University (New York: Whittlesey, 1945). Two British geographers, James S. Gregory and D. W. Shave, present a detailed geographical survey in *The U.S.S.R.* (New York: Wiley, 1946). A useful survey by a Russian geographer is Nicholas Mikhailov's *Soviet Russia: The Land and Its People* (New York: Sheridan House, 1948). Developments in Soviet Asia, and prospects for the future of that area are discussed by R. A. Davies and A. J. Steiger in *Soviet Asia* (New York: Dial Press, 1942).

The Political System. The political structure of the U.S.S.R. is well analyzed by Frederick L. Schuman, Woodrow Wilson, Professor of Government at Williams College in *Soviet Politics at Home and Abroad* (New York: Knopf, 1946). The best single volume on this subject, although published before the war, is *The Government of the Soviet Union* (New York: Van Nostrand, 1938) by the late Samuel N. Harper of Chicago University, pioneer in the field of Russian affairs, who was also the author of an excellent volume on *Civic Training in Soviet Russia* (Chicago: University of Chicago Press, 1929), and a more popular short book on the same subject, *Making Bolsheviks* (Chicago: University of Chicago Press, 1931). A useful summary of Soviet political theory is contained in *Soviet Philosophy* (New York: Philosophical Library, 1946) by John Somerville. An excellent summary of the Soviet government's policy toward religion, including wartime and post-war developments, is *Religion in Russia*, by Robert P. Casey (New York: Harper, 1946).

For the views of Russians who have criticized the ideas and practices of Soviet leaders, the most useful sources are *The Real Soviet Russia* (New Haven: Yale University Press, 1946) by David J. Dallin, Russian Socialist in exile since 1922, and *Forced Labor in Soviet Russia* by Dallin and Boris I. Nicolayevsky (New Haven: Yale University Press, 1947), and *The Great Retreat* by Nicholas S. Timasheff, Russian-born member of the sociology department of Fordham University (New York: Dutton, 1946). The Soviet government has been bitterly denounced by some of its former officials, notably Krivitzky and Barmine and, most recently, Victor Kravchenko in *I Chose Freedom* (New York: Scribner, 1946).

The Economic System. In view of the widespread controversy concerning the character and objectives of Soviet economy, good books on that subject are surprisingly few. The best are still two of the earlier works, *The Economic Life of Soviet Russia* (New York: Macmillan, 1931), by Calvin B. Hoover, then professor of economics, now Dean, at Duke University; and *Russian Economic Development Since the Revolution* (New York: Dutton, 1928), by a British economist, Maurice Dobb, who has since contributed two brief but excellent analyses favorable to Communism: *Soviet Planning and Labour in Peace and War* (New York: International Publishers, 1943) and *Soviet Economy and the War* (London: Routledge, 1941). *The Development of the Soviet Economic System* (New York: Macmillan, 1947) by Alexander Baykov contains much useful information. *Russia's Economic Front for War and Peace* (New York: Harper, 1942) by Aaron Yugow, a Russian émigré of left-wing sympathies who is critical of the Soviet system should be mentioned. The two most valuable volumes on the Russian monopoly of foreign trade are *Soviet Foreign Trade* by Alexander Baykov (Princeton: Princeton University Press, 1946) and *Russian-American Trade* by Mikhail V. Condoide (Columbus: Ohio University Press, 1946), both sympathetic to Russia's trade problems. An excellent brief summary is given by Harry Schwartz in *Russia's Postwar Economy* (Syracuse, New York: Syracuse University Press, 1947).

Main Threads of Foreign Policy. The most comprehensive, although in many respects uncritical, work on Soviet foreign policy remains *The Soviets in World Affairs* covering the period 1917 to 1929 (New York: Cape and Smith, 1930, two volumes) by Louis Fischer, who had access to Russian archives. T. A. Taracouzio, Russian-born former international law scholar at Harvard University, gives a critical analysis of Soviet foreign policy from 1917 to 1939 in *War and Peace in Soviet Diplomacy* (New York: Macmillan, 1946). David J. Dallin similarly analyzes recent developments in three books—*Soviet Russia's Foreign Policy, 1939–1942, Russia and Postwar Europe*, and *The Big Three: United States, Britain, Russia*, all published by the Yale University Press. A sympathetic account of Russia's policy in Asia is given by Harriet L. Moore of the American-Russian Institute in *Soviet Far Eastern Policy, 1931–1945* (Princeton: Princeton University Press, 1945). A highly critical view of Russia's objectives and methods in Europe is presented by Jan Ciechanowski, wartime Polish Ambassador to the United States in *Defeat in Victory* (New York: Doubleday, 1947). A Russian view on the post-war situation in the Balkans is presented with sympathy for the peoples of that area and for Soviet methods by the well-known journalist Ilya Ehrenburg in *European Crossroad* (New York: Knopf, 1947). Russia's policy toward Iran and the possibilities for Big Three coöperation in the development of that disputed country are considered by Arthur C. Millspaugh, former American administrator of the finances of Persia, in *Americans in Persia* (Washington: Brookings, 1946). Strikingly similar conclusions are reached and similar proposals are advanced for joint development of Eastern Europe by the Big Three in *Economic Development in S. E. Europe* edited by David Mitrany, Romanian-born economist now living in England (London: PEP, 1945). A useful survey of Russia's relations with the League of Nations which sheds a good deal of light on some of the problems that have developed concerning Russia's relations with the UN is given by Kathryn W. Davis in *The Soviets at Geneva* (Geneva: Kundig, 1934). Material on what President Roosevelt is said to have thought about Russia during the war years is offered in a very personal book by his son Elliott Roosevelt in *As He Saw It* (New York: Duell, Sloan and Pearce, 1946).

Russo-American Relations. The best brief summary of the history of Russo-American relations is *The Road to Teheran* by Foster Rhea Dulles, professor of political science at Ohio State University (Princeton: Princeton University Press, 1944). All students of relations between the two countries will want to read the much-discussed *Mission to Moscow* by Joseph E. Davies, American Ambassador to Moscow from 1936 to 1938 (New York: Simon and Schuster, 1941), as well as *The Strange Alliance* (New York: Viking, 1946) by John R. Deane, head of the United States military mission to Moscow during the crucial years 1943–1945, who gives a valuable account of the trials and achievements of wartime coöperation with Russia. Penetrating suggestions for the future conduct of relations with Russia are contained in *Where Are We Heading?* by Sumner Welles (New York: Harper, 1946). Hopeful answers to the question whether the United States and Russia can coexist in the same world are given by Pitirim A. Sorokin, world-renowned sociologist at Harvard University, in *Russia and the United States*

(New York: Dutton, 1944) and Harold H. Fisher, chairman of the Hoover Institute and Library on War, Revolution and Peace at Stanford University, in *America and Russia in the World Community* (Claremont: California, 1946).

Current Developments. On current developments in Russia, the reader will find useful material in the columns of the *New York Times*, the *New York Herald Tribune* and the *Christian Science Monitor*. Among the periodicals, *Life*, *Fortune* and *Foreign Affairs* frequently publish interesting articles on Russian affairs, and *The Nation* carries as a regular feature reports from its Moscow correspondent, Alexander Werth. The Foreign Policy Association publishes considerable material on Russia in its three publications—the weekly *Foreign Policy Bulletin*, the fortnightly *Foreign Policy Reports*, and *Headline Books*. Valuable information gathered and analyzed by E. C. Ropes, chief of the Russian unit in the Department of Commerce, now retired, has been issued in *Foreign Commerce Weekly*, which frequently carries analyses of economic developments in Russia and Eastern Europe. *The New Leader*, representing the Max Eastman-Chamberlin-Dallin point of view, is consistently critical of Russia. In Britain *The Economist*, the *Manchester Guardian* and the *London Times*, especially the first of these, publish excellent material, notably on the objectives and problems of Russia's post-war industrialization under the fourth Five-Year Plan. In France the leading Catholic monthly *L'Esprit*, edited by Emmanuel Mounier, carries thoughtful and stimulating discussions of the philosophy, aims, and methods of Communism. The reader familiar with the Russian language will want to read regularly the two leading Russian newspapers, *Pravda* (Truth), organ of the Communist party, and *Izvestia* (News), as well as the monthly magazine *Mirovoye Khozyastvo i Mirovaya Politika* (World Economy and World Politics), a Russian combination of *The Economist* and *Foreign Affairs*, in which many Western books on international affairs are reviewed at length. *Kultura i Zhizn* (Culture and Life), unfortunately not obtainable outside Russia, and the satirical magazine *Krokodil* (Crocodile) offer many interesting sidelights on Russian life. The Russian point of view is also available in English in the fortnightly magazine *The New Times*, published in Moscow as successor to *War and the Working Class.*

For the reader who has only limited time at his or her disposal, the following books selected from the above list are suggested for a bird's-eye view of present-day Russia and its relations with the United States: Pearl Buck and Masha Scott, *Talks About Russia;* Edward H. Carr, *The Soviet Impact on the Western World;* William H. Chamberlin, *Russia's Iron Age;* George B. Cressey, *The Basis of Soviet Strength;* Foster Rhea Dulles, *The Road to Teheran;* Samuel N. Harper, *The Government of the Soviet Union;* Victor Kravchenko, *I Chose Freedom;* Corliss Lamont, *The Peoples of the Soviet Union;* Richard Lauterbach, *These Are the Russians;* Sir Bernard Pares, *Russia* (Penguin); Frederick L. Schuman, *Soviet Politics at Home and Abroad;* Konstantin Simonov, *Days and Nights;* B. H. Sumner, *A Short History of Russia;* Nicholas S. Timasheff, *The Great Retreat;* and, for good measure, Joseph E. Davies, *Mission to Moscow;* John R. Deane, *The Strange Alliance;* Edward Crankshaw, *Russia and the Russians,* and Sir John Maynard, *Russia in Flux.*

INDEX